CONSERVATION/ECOLOGY
Resources for Environmental Education

by

David F. Harrah

and

Barbara K. Harrah

The Scarecrow Press, Inc.
Metuchen, N.J.   1975

Z
5322
.E2
H37
REF

Library of Congress Cataloging in Publication Data

Harrah, David F   1949-
    Conservation/ecology, environmental education sources.

    Includes indexes.
    1. Ecology--Bibliography. 2. Nature conservation--
Bibliography. 3. Environmental protection--Bibliogra-
phy. I. Harrah, Barbara K., joint author. II. Title.
Z5322.E2H37   016.30131   74-23055
ISBN 0-8108-0780-7

to

TAWNY

TABLE OF CONTENTS

ACKNOWLEDGMENTS

We wish to acknowledge the assistance we have received from the staffs of the Ferguson Library of Stamford, Connecticut and the Greenwich Public Library, Greenwich, Connecticut.

We would also like to note the special help and indulgence of James Godfrey, Director of Libraries, and his staff at the Rye Country Day School, Rye, New York.

INTRODUCTION

The groundswell of interest in and almost desperate concern for our environment transcends the limits of race, religion, nationality, social and financial status, profession, and even generation. No one is immune from the effects of pollution or the ominous consequence of wasteful exploitation of resources. Conservation is no longer a crusade for bleeding hearts and nature lovers; good earthkeeping is no longer the eco-freaks' domain. Both are necessities for all people's survival. So as the climaxing pressures of ecology and conservation capture the public's interest and cry out for national and even international attention, there is increasing need for educating the source of the environmental crisis: Man. Because, strictly speaking, man, and not the environment, is the problem.

The environment is by definition the aggregate of surrounding things, all of which did quite well before man began rearranging the natural order. And while a diligent review of ecological history points to greed as the propelling motivation behind man's harmful intervention (at least among those powerful and clever enough to make a sizable impact), ignorance on the part of the many of the consequences of human intervention is as great or possibly an even greater factor. If we have any hope of reversing our headlong rush towards extinction, enlightenment will have to replace our no longer so blissful state of not knowing the consequences of our acts. The burden of displacing this ignorance with knowledge falls, unavoidably, on education.

All education is environmental. Education is the imparting or acquisition of knowledge about the world of ideas, of earth, of the firmament, of the sea, the creatures of the skies, the oceans, the land, its vegetation, its composition, of man's endeavors, his failures, his success, his hopes, his skills, his legacies, his monuments to his past and his dreams for the future--in a word, about his environment, or,

more accurately, about the environment.   To single out "environmental education" as a discipline to be taught apart from
all others is therefore unrealistic and counterproductive.

There is an old joke that continues to circulate around the
San Francisco area:

> The garbage they throw in the Bay today,
> They drink with lunch in San Jose.

On the face of it, the couplet epitomizes an "ecological"
problem that can be easily rectified by implementing applicable pollution abatement technology.   But while the murky
waters that drift out of San Francisco to San Jose are undoubtedly "polluted, " the problem of cleaning San Jose's
water supply is not readily surmounted by a technological
device.   Nor is whatever prompts the San Franciscans to
dispose of their waste in the Bay an "ecological" problem.
It is, for starters, sociological, economic, and technological.
What makes up the specific contents of their garbage is the
consequence of our industrialized society.   What motivates
men to covet disposable products that may facilitate their
everyday existence but which despoil their living environment
is probably as much a psychological phenomenon as sociological.   Drinking the contaminated waters from the Bay of
course constitutes a medical problem for the person who
consumes it and the doctor who attempts to cure any ill effects.   The fish and wildlife sickened or killed by it will
concern biologists, botanists, oceanographers, chemists, the
food industry, tourism, and the general public.   Political
action on the part of outraged voters will eventually affect
government.   Should the pollutants touch the shores of alien
nations, international repercussions will ensue.

The factors which make up the environment problem
stem from and affect all areas of man's existence and the
whole question of "environment" comprises the multi-faceted
concerns and subjects of all the disciplines.   Solving our current crisis, therefore, necessitates broad understanding on
the part of all people of all the areas of our existence that
either cause, contribute to, or are effected by the "problem. "
The deus ex machina theory simply doesn't work.   Remedial
technologies generally pose problems as great as or even
greater than they were intended to solve.   Ultimately, this
is because everything within the biosphere and quite probably
beyond is linked together, or as one of our early environ-

mental heroes quaintly postulated, "Everything is hitched to everything else."

Since environment concerns all disciplines, and all education is environmental, environmental education is relevant to all academic disciplines and must be applied to every discipline in the classroom. Unfortunately this is rarely done. Modern education has divided the disciplines, and for lack of a more imaginative solution, has relegated the study of environment to the sciences or, worse still, to so-called environmental education classes that often as not degenerate into nature studies or sewage disposal analysis. The dangers of shunting the environment off to a specialized discipline or dealing with it purely as a science are manifold. One example is that science alone cannot solve the proliferating problems of pollution or deal with the intricate political, ecological, social, and administrative problems of conservation. It can only measure the manifestations or make projections for the future of each and offer relief for the isolated, non-causal symptoms of the overall problem. The cause is left unattended, festering under the technological placebo; sooner or later, somewhere else or in another form, it will reappear.

A second example is the emerging recognition that the study of the environment is the study of man's interaction with his surroundings--man-made, mental, abstract, as well as natural. The study of the environment as a purely natural science inhibits the student's understanding of it. The study of the environment is just as much a social as a natural science.

Thirdly, by slipping the pesky problem of the environment to the sciences, the rest of the disciplines tend to forget it. People, correspondingly, come to see the crisis as the scientists' responsibility: they invented the offending technology; they should correct it. Most people are perfectly amenable to the idea of driving the pollution-free automobile when the scientist comes up with one. And this, parenthetically, raises yet another danger: the sticky question of arbitrary measurement (the technique that the sciences are so adept at): what is a "safe" level of pollution? When a tenth or a hundredth of a point differentiates "healthy" from "acceptable" from "unacceptable" from "unhealthy" air quality, the whole thing bunches up on the brink of the absurd.

A last example is, given peoples' differing innate

proclivities and levels of understanding, by relegating a problem like environment to so narrow a discipline as science,
its relevancy becomes lost to the great majority of people.
Even the measurements are obscured in the highly cryptic
jargon of the discipline, and those not initiated into the cult
of scientese cannot understand the words and consequently
lose heart as well as interest.

By reintegrating the disciplines, however, students
will get a broad picture and a clearer understanding of the
problem. Interdisciplinary education, after all, is what liberal arts is all about--a corollary to the belief that the way
towards a better world is through the education of our children. We teach them what we have learned so they can
learn from the experience of their forebears and not perpetuate their mistakes. But if any one factor can be held ac-
countable for the mess we have made of our environment, it
is the fragmentation of our educational curricula that prevents
dissemination of the knowledge of man's mistakes to our children and obscures the whole of knowledge by magnifying its
parts. And in a world of ever-increasing population and diminishing resources, we can ill afford the luxury of more
and more specialization of the disciplines and the accelerating
drift away from the classical liberal arts education. We
must resurrect the methods whereby man learned enough
about everything to appreciate the interdependence of the web
of life.

How educators will integrate the environment into their special fields will obviously be up to the individual teacher, the
schools' general policies, and the curriculum and talent at
each professional's disposal. But as integration of environmental concepts into all disciplines has only recently emerged
as an effective teaching method, teachers, oftentimes, have
no idea of how and where to begin. The following paragraphs
exemplify a few of the infinite possibilities of integrating environmental considerations into conventional disciplines and
indicate the value to certain of these disciplines.

(1) Science, Technology, and Mathematics.
In resurrecting the pre-Aristotelian liberal arts (an
integrated educational system), science and technology will
assume their proper roles within the society and that society's
educational system. Today, in the United States, at the peak
of the country's technological success, there is growing skep-
ticism, even outright distrust, of the benefits of science and

its technologies, and while the danger of an anti-technological backlash does not forecast the immediate and total doom of science, the study and understanding of the natural and applied sciences as they relate to our total environment will assure their relevance in the future. They will, when tempered to fit the exigencies of a finite, fragile environment, remain invaluable as a measure and tool towards regaining and then maintaining the proper balance between man's instincts for survival, his quest for fulfillment, and nature's needs for its own development.

(2) Philosophy, Ethics, Social and Cultural History, Religion, and Political Science.
In reintegrating the disciplines and applying environmental concepts to each, no single element in the vast compendium of knowledge will be omitted in the search for the best possible life. And all disciplines will be brought to bear on the age-old and consuming preoccupation of man: how does he fit into nature, or what is his clout in what Stewart Udall calls the man-nature equation. This tantalizing notion has perplexed and intrigued the most talented of our intellects for as far back as recorded history reveals. From Copernicus to Galileo to Descartes to Samuel Clemens, scientists, philosophers, and homespun students of the condition humane have struggled to put their finger on man's proper place in the grand scheme of things and thereby justify his life's agonies as well as his joys. The entire structure of the American governmental system grew out of the political philosopher's quest for the optimum body politic and the great breakthroughs in science, from Archimedes' displacement to Edison's light bulb, happened out of man's search for his proper niche in the universe.

Man's assessment of his own rank on the great universal ladder, beginning with the Greeks, soared off the lower rungs into the dizzy realm of the gods. Before the humanizing of the deities by the plucky Hellenic mythmakers, the great gods of the Assyrians, the Egyptians, and the American Indians loomed majestically and often imperiously in the eyes of the beholden humans who worshipped out of love or dread. The environment fared relatively well. Man respected natural phenomenon and had a healthy regard for trees and birds and other wonders of nature that might harbor, belong to, or be the incarnation of a deity, benign or vengeful. The Greeks, however, refurbished their gods in man's own image; the Jews modestly inverted the ratio, believing God made man in His. But the combined influence of both

and the ascent of Judeo-Christian theology stirred up an ill
wind for nature, and man's own well-being took on a decided
vulnerability when he assumed dominion over his environment.
Neither the scientifically inspired warnings of Marsh, nor the
poetic entreaties of Muir and Thoreau have done enough to
effectively dampen the quest of the ambitious for power and
profit.   And now, in the final quarter of the twentieth century,
after hundreds of years of ignoring the laws of nature and
abusing the natural environment, man is faced with the reality
of Commoner's postulation that there is no free lunch.   Nature is calling in its loans.

(3) History, Economics, and Political Science.
The rise and fall of empires and the scars of war and
famine owe directly or indirectly to man's general misman-
aged use and abuse of nature, or more specifically to his use
and abuse of the land.   Contrary to early twentieth-century
education, economics, not politics or culture, dictates history.
Politics are merely the symptoms of economic constraints,
beneath which, invariably, lies the land.   One of many examples is the American Civil War, the generally reputed origins
of which are cultural and sociological: slavery and the southern agrarian plantation society versus the individualism and
the diversified economy of the North--decadent cotton colonels
and tobacco tyrants versus hard-working, upright, uptight,
God-fearing Yankee farmers.   Indisputably, cultural and sociological rivalries existed, along with the fermenting politics
that festered around the northern abolitionists and the southern
secessionists.   But beneath it all, the basic cause, was the
southern plantation owners' need for land.   Their need was
neither cultural nor political; it was economic.   At stake
was not their society but their existence.   The one-crop
economy depended on land and lots of it, because within a
generation, the fertile fields of Virginia and the Carolinas
wasted and acidified.   And to keep king cotton on the throne,
his apparatchiks rolled out the white carpet to the western
limits of Virginia, the Carolinas and Georgia, through Alabama, Tennessee, further and further west to the far reaches
of Texas until they were stopped dead in Spanish territory
that, without irrigation, was unsuited for growing either cotton or tobacco.   The only route left was north, and the quick-
ening pressures between slave and free states, the Compro-
mises, the Kansas-Nebraska Act, the border wars between
northern and southern ruffians, and the final conflagration of
war capped what can justifiably be called America's first environmental crisis: the collapse of southern land.

Innovative means of inserting awareness of environment into education curricula are as limitless as the teachers' powers of imagination. One good way is through the use of case studies; for example, of species exploitation, or of the depletion of non-renewable resources such as oil, or of the mismanagement of renewable resources (clearcutting), or, conversely, of enlightened forestry (Pinchot). The whole gamut of scholarly disciplines become applicable. In studying whaling, for instance, the economics of killing off the several species can be explored along with the specific repercussions to, for example, the nineteenth-century Nantucket economy when whaling· ceased to be profitable. What the effect was on family life when local whaling died and whalers went out, sometimes for years, on the open seas is a sociological problem. The confrontation of nations over who can hunt the few remaining whales today falls within the sphere of political science. Legal issues arise: what are the legalities of boycotts? and ethics: has man the right to extirpate a species? Art and literature, too, have all been touched by the broad subject of whaling.

No one teacher can teach all subjects with equal proficiency. This is one reason knowledge has been broken into disciplines. But through interjecting an awareness of the vast area of environment into a part of each class or curriculum, teachers of different academic bent can synthesize the fragments of education, which students often find irrelevant, and reweave the frazzled ends of knowledge. All too often environmental disaster strikes because when we alter one aspect of the life-web we do so in ignorance of the possible consequences to another. If the environmentally-aware educator can impart this revelation in his classes, his students of today--tomorrow's scientists, laborers, politicians, writers, teachers, mathematicians, planners, and doctors--will be able to bring this knowledge to their own professions and their own decision-making processes. And the teacher will have helped to bring the discordant branches of educational pursuits into harmony and thereby made a giant step toward making man, life, and knowledge whole again.

GUIDE TO THE USE OF THIS BOOK

To assist students and teachers in finding sources that will help them understand the broad picture of the environment, we have listed those most applicable in a variety of disciplines. We have not compiled or codified the purely scientific sources.

The annotated Section I contains books of general interest that are available at most public libraries. We have attempted to include at least one title for every reading level (for levels, see Grade Level Index at back of book) in each subject in addition to books for teachers' use. Samples of specialized or highly technical titles are also included for their value as references for both teacher and student.

Section II is an adjunct listing, comprising technical or narrowly defined references, books which are out of print but well worth digging up, and the not so readily obtainable books. If we were unable to obtain a title that looked interesting, rather than risk depriving the student or teacher of the knowledge of its existence, we included it with whatever information we could find. Late additions to Section II comprise Appendix 3; all index entries with asterisks refer to this appendix.

Books that are not included in either section above are those of such narrow scope or comprising such highly technical material that only professional water pollution engineers, for example, or electrostatic precipitator designers could find them useful. We also avoided the voluminous numbers of books dealing with the ethics and techniques of controlling population, including only those population books that deal with the overall environmental problem. Very few books on urban planning (or the lack of it) are mentioned, although urban design and large-scale planning undoubtedly are the key to future environmental quality. But the myriad books that touch tangentially are inadequate. The solid, practical, definitive works are only beginning to be written, and the best of these are not yet translated into English. A few interesting seminal

treatises on the subject, however, along with Lewis Mumford's classic, <u>The City in History</u>, are listed.

    We have also included a glossary (see Appendix 2) so
that the non-ecologist/environmentalist or budding ones will
never find themselves at a loss for words; a listing of current relevant periodical articles (Section III) about environmental education; a chronology of pertinent U.S. Government
legislation, and directories and listings of international, federal, state, and private groups and agencies from which
further information can be solicited.

    The word "ecology" within this text refers to that
science "which studies the interaction between organisms
and their environment." "Environment" refers to the broad
range of subjects dealing with pollution, technology, economics, and ecology. "Environmental" refers to the general
movement of concern for the environment that has become a
public preoccupation within the last ten years as a result of
the publication of <u>Silent Spring</u> (see book entry 57), the debate on the nuclear test ban treaty, and the increasingly visible effects of air and water pollution. It is distinct from
"conservation," which refers to the older Pinchot-inspired
concept of preservation and protection of natural resources,
the purpose of which was to save them for use by subsequent
generations.

Section I

ANNOTATED LIST OF BOOKS

GUIDE TO THE ARRANGEMENT

All books are arranged in numerical order and alphabetically by author or company, the editors of a magazine, or a group, whichever applies. Each book is entered under a separate number except where complementary works of the same author are annotated together. Subsequent references to any particular book (in the appendices) are indicated by its specified number.

Bibliographic Citation

Each title contains the following bibliographic information: author(s) and/or editor(s) and translator; title and subtitle; place, publisher, year of publication; reprint information; price for hardcover editions (PLB refers to publishers library binding) and text edition; price of paperback (pap); and whether or not it contains index, illustrations, and graphs. If the book is available in paperback from a publisher other than the original, a separate notation is made for the paperback edition.

Level and Subject Keys

Each title is rated according to reading level and subject after the letters L and S, respectively. The level indicates the assessment of the publisher or that in Books in Print. Where such a rating is not indicated by either the publisher or Books in Print, we have rated it according to our own assessment of the reading and content level. All levels cited are grade, not age, levels. All elementary levels are listed under the appropriate number, K (kindergarten) or PS (pre-school) -3, 4-6, or 5-7. Junior high school books are either referred to as "JHS & up" or by grade numbers 6-8 or 7-9. A book listed as JHS & up is deemed appropriate for reading or reference use by the average student from grades 7 through 12. HS & up can be

read and understood by any high school student; Adv HS &
up (advanced high school students and up) is reserved for
the better students in grades 11 and 12 as either texts, reference, or as a research source.   College level books are
included (College) for use by teachers and interested students
for reference purposes.   The words "All" or "Adult" refer
generally to directories and indexes (subject category DBI),
primarily picture books that all age and grade-level groups
will enjoy, or works recommended for teachers.

     The subject is indicated according to the key below.
Generally, only the principle topic or topics are cited, but
where the book examines fully a number of subjects, all are
listed.   Only when the whole spectrum of environmental topics
is covered are the individual disciplines amalgamated into
the general category of "O" (Overview).   In one or two instances it was impossible to categorize a book and rather
than attaching a symbol that might prove misleading, we have
omitted the subject indicator.

Book Annotations

     Bibliographic citations are followed by annotations, the
purpose of which is to summarize the basic usefulness of the
book, any special characteristics such as suggestions within
the text for pupil action, the relative ease or difficulty of the
book, and whether its orientation is scientific, social, historical, etc.   When helpful, biographic information about the
author or subject (in the case of bibliographies) is also included.

KEY TO SUBJECT ABBREVIATIONS

A   Anthology.   Any compilation of essays, speeches, or
         writings from other books.
Ag   Agriculture.   Books dealing with the production of food.
At   Art.   Books having application to the field of art and
         art classes.
B   Biography.
C   Criticism.   Any basic analysis of environmentalism
         whether friendly or hostile.
Cn   Conservation.   Books dealing with the broad topic of
         conservation.
Cr   Careers.   Books describing and explaining environ-
         mentally oriented employment.
Cs   Case Studies.   Books which either zero in on one

	particular case or which contain a number of different individual studies.
DBI	Dictionaries, Bibliographies, Indexes. All reference works.
E	Economics. Books dealing with the economic aspects of the environment.
Ec	Ecology. Books concerned with the science of ecology, including texts.
Ed	Education. Books for teachers, textbooks, and books with teacher's manual available.
Eg	Energy. Books dealing with the ramifications of energy production.
En	English. Books relevant to the English class.
Es	Endangered Species. Books dealing with animal species which are either extinct or nearing extinction.
Et	Ethics. Books dealing with environmental value judgments, ethical analysis, or religious aspects.
F	Forests. Books dealing with forests and forestry.
Fp	Food Pollution. Books dealing with harmful substances in food.
H	History. Books dealing with the past and the origins of contemporary problems.
Ha	Home Action. Books dealing with personal actions which when applied to daily living aid the environment.
I	International. Books dealing with global concerns or with nations other than the United States.
L	Law. Books dealing with the legal aspects of the environment.
Lu	Land Use. Books dealing with both the use and abuse of land and remedies for the latter.
N	Nuclear Power. Books dealing with atomic energy.
Np	Noise Pollution.
O	Overview. Books which deal with a wide range of topics or the environment as a whole.
Ol	Oil. Books dealing with all aspects of petroleum use.
P	Population.
Pc	Pesticides. Books dealing with chemical insect killers and possible alternatives.
Pn	Personal Narrative. Books written about the author's own experiences and feelings.
Ps	Political Science. Books dealing with governments and their interactions with people and the environment.
R	Reader. Books for the early grades which promote good reading as well as environmental awareness.
S	Strip Mining.

T   Technology. Books which analyze the effects of man's
        use of tools and machines.
U   Urban Planning.
W   Wilderness.
Wp   Water Pollution.
Wt   Waste. Books dealing with garbage.

ANNOTATED LIST OF BOOKS

1   ADAMS, Alexander B.   Eleventh Hour: A Hard Look at
        Conservation and the Future.   New York: Putnam,
        1970, $7.95, 378p, index
        L: Adv HS & up   S: O/Cn
        Former head of the Nature Conservancy ponders the
future and alternate courses of action for the 70's.   Details
successes and failures of many past cases and points out the
urgent need for popular support.

2   ADAMS, Ansel and Newhall, Nancy.   This Is the Ameri-
        can Earth.   San Francisco: Sierra, 1972, $15; also
        avail in pap, New York: Ballantine, 1970, $3.95
        L: All   S: At
        Graphic portrait of America by Adams, illustrious
pioneer in artist nature photography, and others.   Includes
some of Adams's best works.

3   ADAMS, Ruth.   Say No! The New Pioneers Guide to
        Action to Save Our Environment.   Emmaus, PA: Ro-
        dale, 1971, $6.95, 339p, index
        L: HS & up   S: Cs/Ps
        Case studies on fighting the good fight against en-
vironmental despoilers.   Includes run-down on past battles
over air, water, garbage, atomic energy, thermal pollution,
noise, and pesticides and effective courses of actions citizen
groups can adopt to curtail pollution and the pollution-makers.

4   ADLER, Cy A.   Ecological Fantasies.   New York: Green
        Eagle, 1973, $9.95, 337p, index, illus
        L: HS & up   S: C
        Exposes fraudulent emotional claims of some environ-
mentalists, but agrees, nonetheless, there are some real
problems that the Cassandras have helped to point out.
Worthwhile.   Cf. Maddox's Doomsday Syndrome (250), which
is better.

5   ALLEN, Shirley Walter and Leonard, Justin Wilkinson.

Conserving Natural Resources: Principles and Practices in a Democracy. 3d ed. New York: McGraw-
Hill, 1966, $11.95, index, bibliog
L: College   S: Cn
One of the leading textbooks on conservation and resource management. Includes historical developments also,
but basically is concerned with current problems and policies.

6 ALLSOP, Bruce. The Garden Earth: The Case for Ecological Morality. New York: Morrow, 1972, $5
($1.95 pap), 117p, index
L: Adv HS & up   S: Et
Using the garden as a model, Allsop gives solutions
for our present problems. Advises we live with nature, not
dominate it.

7 ANDERSON, Walt, ed. Politics and Environment: A
Reader in Ecological Crisis. Ref. ed. Englewood
Cliffs, NJ: Prentice-Hall, 1970, $7.95 ($5.90 pap),
362p
L: HS & up   S: A/Ps/O
Two-part anthology. First, good general overview of
the ecological problem. Second, weaker section on political
responses. Articles cover the Urban Environment, The Rur-
al Environment, Environmental Policy, Nature and Human
Nature, Population, Politics, and Pollution.

8 ARMSTRONG, Terry R., ed. Why Do We Still Have an
Ecological Crisis? Englewood Cliffs, NJ: Prentice-
Hall, 1972, $5.95 ($2.45 pap), 160p, illus
L: HS & up   S: A
Good introduction to the subject, but more relevant to
1970/71 than to 1974. It would have been fine, if it had
come out two years earlier. Armstrong's anthology of essays, therefore, is dated; today, most people have moved
beyond the level he is dealing on. The book is best used,
therefore, by the student or layman concerned with getting
a grounding on the subject.

9 ARNY, Mary T. and Reaske, Christopher R. Ecology:
A Writer's Handbook. New York: Random, 1972,
$2.50 (pap), 112p
L: HS & up   S: En/Ed
How-to-write book which concentrates on environmen-
tal subjects (e.g. students should keep an "ecology notebook").
Divided into sections: how-to-write, glossary of ecological
terms, and mechanics/usage. Good for English teachers try-
ing to make writing relevant.

10   ASIMOV, Isaac.   ABC's of Ecology.   New York: Walker,
      1972, $4.50 ($4.41 PLB), 48p, illus
      L: 3-5   S: R/Ec
      Asimov has a whole series of ABC's books for chil-
dren.   He details simply and succinctly various problems and
aspects of everyday life that are of concern or interest to
children.   This one on ecology, as are the others, is excellent, defining two ecological terms for each letter of the alpha-
bet.   Good pictures illustrate each term.   Examples: additive, algae, zoology, and zonation.

11   ATKINSON, Brooks.   This Bright Land: A Personal View.
      Garden City, NY: Doubleday (Natural History), 1972,
      $5.95, 201p
      L: HS & up   S: Pn/Cs
      The critic's personal view of the Everglades, Grand
Canyon, Mississippi River, California Condor, Redwoods, and
South Biscayne Bay, Florida.   All are seen as environmental
confrontation points.   "Required," says Library Journal,
which picked it as one of the 100 Best Sci-Tech Books of 1972.

12   AYLESWORTH, Thomas G.   This Vital Air, This Vital
      Water: Man's Environmental Crisis.   Rev. ed.
      New York: Rand McNally, 1973, $5.79 (PLB),
      192p, index, illus
      L: 6 up   S: Ap/Wp
      Scientifically oriented study of world air and water
pollution problem.   Revision encompasses recent developments
since its original publication in 1968.   Just as timely today as
then, covering all aspects of both subjects.   Chapter on careers open in environmental fields will be of interest to young
readers.

13   BARBOUR, Ian.   Earth Might Be Fair: Reflections on
      Ethics, Religion, and Ecology.   Englewood Cliffs,
      NJ: Prentice-Hall, 1972, $6.95 ($3.95 pap)
      L: HS & up   S: Et/A
      An anthology of essays on the ethical questions raised
by the environmental crisis.   Good discussion stimulator.

14   BARKLEY, Paul W. and Seckler, David.   Economic
      Growth and Environmental Decay: The Solution Be-
      comes the Problem.   New York: Harcourt Brace,
      1972, $3.25 (pap)
      L: Adv HS & up   S: E
      Excellent introduction to problem of the economics of
environmental decay and protection.

15 BARLOW, Elizabeth. The Forests and Wetlands of New
        York City. Boston: Little, Brown, 1971, $8.95,
        192p, index, illus
        L: HS & up   S: W/H
        Describes New York City's natural beauty in the pre-
development era and traces the few remaining pockets from
then up through modern times. Fully illustrated with prints,
maps, and photographs.

16 _____ and Alex, William. Frederick Law Olmsted's
        New York. New York: Praeger, 1972, $12.50,
        174p, index, illus
        Review of America's first and most influential land-
scape architect's studies for NYC. Contains even split of
narrative and documented original plans, photos, and maps
for Central, Prospect, and Morningside Parks, among others.
See also: Albert Fein's Frederick Law Olmsted ... (130).

17 BARON, Robert Alex. The Tyranny of Noise. New
        York: St. Martin's, 1970, $8.50, 294p, index;
        also avail in pap, New York: Harper & Row, 1971,
        $2.75, 352p, index
        L: HS & up   S: Np
        Anecdotal account of the noise problem by the head
of Citizens for a Quiet City. The facts are all there: what
noise is, price of noise, acoustic anarchy, and a design for
quiet. Well presented and a good, easy read.

18 BATES, Marston. Forest and the Sea. New York:
        Random, 1960, $6.95 ($1.95 pap), 277p, index
        L: HS & up   S: Ec
        Examination of all ecological regions with particular
focus on man's place in nature. Includes examples of the
historic results of man's tampering with the natural order
and discussion of possible future problems. Scientifically
oriented, but not overly technical.

19 BEATTY, Rita G. DDT Myth. New York: John Day,
        1973, $6.95 ($3.95 pap), 188p, index
        L: HS & up   S: Pc/C
        One of the "backlash" books, arguing for "a realistic,
not emotional policy for DDT." Rita Beatty does not advocate
wholesale use of the pesticide but thinks it should not be
banned completely. Good source for the other side of the
argument.

20 BECKMAN, Petr. Eco-Hysterics & the Technophobes.

Boulder, CO: Golem, 1973, $6.95, 216p, index
L: HS & up   S: C
Another "backlash" book attacking "eco-nuts" and
"technophobes." Fanatics, or so Beckman maintains, are
giving the environmental movement "the kiss of death" by
over-reacting.   Beckman describes himself as a supporter
of the general goals of the environmental movement.   Library
Journal: "highly recommended" 2/15/73.

21   BENARDE, Melvin A.   Our Precarious Habitat.   Rev.
        ed.   New York: Norton, 1973, $7.95 ($3.95 pap),
        362, index
        L: Adv HS & up   S: Fp/Wt/Wp/Pc/Ap
        A very technical treatment of environmental health
hazards including food additives, waste disposal, insecticides,
air and water pollution, and home hazards.

22   BENDICK, Jeanne.   Adaptation.   New York: Watts,
        1971, $4.50 (PBL), illus
        L: 4-6   S: Ec
        Bendick gives facts explaining how plants and animals
adapt to various environmental changes, then asks whether
they will be able to adapt to adverse environmental conditions
quickly enough to survive.   A persuasive argument for making
people use their own adapted characteristics and talents to
curtail pollution.

23   BENTHALL, Jonathan, ed.   Ecology in Theory and Prac-
        tice.   New York: Viking, 1973, $8.95, 384p
        L: Adv HS & up   S: A/I
        A collection of essays presented by 21 specialists at
the Institute for Contemporary Arts, London.   The first half
deals with theoretical and scientific aspects of environmental
problems; the second with current social issues.   Good
source for the British point of view.   "Popular, informative,
urbane; some stunning and novel insights" --Choice 11/73.

24   BILLINGTON, Elizabeth T.   Understanding Ecology: How
        All Living Things Affect Each Other and the World
        They Live in.   Rev. ed.   New York: Warne, 1971,
        $3.95, 87p, index, illus
        L: 7 up   S: Ec
        Billington explains the science of ecology (the study
of the relationship of living things to each other and their environment) and discusses--with text, graphs, and illustrations
--the environment, ecosystems, balance of nature, the biosphere, the world biomes (biome: a large geographic area

with somewhat uniform climate), the communities within the
biomes, habitats, energy, food chains, biogeochemical cycles,
and what the student can do to improve his environment. A
good, thorough, well-presented discussion. Fine photographs
and charts.

25 BIXBY, William. World You Can Live in. New York:
    McKay, 1971, $4.25, 130p, index
    L: 6-8   S: O/Ps
    A book for early adolescents detailing choice between
a clean and a dirty environment. Presents choice as one of
many that the child must make while on the way to becoming
an adult. Focuses on what the student can do and how he
can aid the efforts of citizen groups and the government.

26 BLACK, John. Dominion of Man: The Search for
    Ecological Responsibility. Chicago: Aldine, 1970,
    $7.50, 169p
    L: Adv HS & up   S: C/O
    Historical dissertation of man's attitudes towards his
environment by the professor of natural resources at the University of Edinburgh. Black argues that there is no "crisis"
per se, but that the question of ecological responsibility "cuts
to the very heart of economic and social philosophies. "

27 BLAU, Sheridan and Rodenbeck, John von B. , eds. The
    House We Live in: An Environmental Reader. New
    York: Macmillan, 1971, ($5.75 pap)
    L: Adv HS & up   S: A/En
    A well-organized anthology of essays chosen for good
composition as well as environmental applicability. Sections
on Causes, Solutions, and Dangers. Includes usual heavy-
weights such as Carson, Ehrlich, Hardin, Commoner, and
Fuller and imaginative selections from Walden, Malthus,
Fortune magazine, and other sources. A favorite: "Fumi-
fugium; or, the Inconveniency of the Smoake of London"
(ca. 1700). Written as a college text, but highest recom-
mendation also for above average high school students.

28 BLOOME, Enid. The Air We Breathe! Garden City,
    NY: Doubleday, 1971, $4.95 (PLB), unpag, illus
    L: 1-5   S: Ap
    Bloome, with clear text and excellent supportive
photographs (often full-page), begins by making the reader
aware that there is air all around us. She then points out
the crowded highways, trucks and cars, smokestacks, burning leaves, garbage dumps, and other sources of pollution

and their effects: soot on the window sill, furniture, odors
in the air, peeling paint on houses, etc.   At the end of the
book, Bloome describes what even very young children can
do about air pollution, how to look for signs of it in their
own towns, how to join clubs or start them, or even work
individually to make many people aware of pollution and the
need to stop it--by talking, acting, voting, and spending necessary monies to make the air clean.

29 _____.   The Water We Drink!   Garden City, NY:
          Doubleday, 1971, $4.95 (PLB), unpag, illus
          L: 1-5   S: Wp
          Companion book to her The Air We Breathe! (28) and
similarly the product of a long teaching (kindergarten) and
writing career coupled with her efforts to introduce children
to ecological problems and to show them how they can work
to improve their own environments.   In this book, she tells
what all is done daily with water and then asks what we'd do
if there were none for drinking, washing, cooking, swimming,
for animals, plants, etc.   With forceful questions sprinkled
throughout the text and excellent photographs, she builds her
case for stopping water pollution, because the rivers, streams,
and oceans belong to everyone, and everyone must work,
therefore, to stop polluting them.   She advises children to
look for wildlife in nearby streams and lakes, and if they
find none, to ask why, to write congressmen, talk about it
with friends, parents.   A good book.

30 BOCK, Alan.   Ecology Action Guide.   Los Angeles:
          Nash, 1971, ($2.45 pap); also avail, New York:
          Pyramid Publications, ($1.25 pap), 159p
          L: HS & up   S: O/Ha/Ps
          A guide to individual action that shows how to im-
prove your environment and your health without radically dis-
rupting your present life style: what vitamins protect your
lungs against smog;   how to purify your own drinking water;
what chemicals to avoid;   how to wash without detergents;
how to kill pests safely;   what kind of new car to buy;   how
to get rid of household and garden poisons, how to report
water pollution and get money for it;   where and how to use
economic pressure tactics;   how to recycle at home.   Includes hints on organizing and generating public interest.

31 BORGSTROM, Georg.   Harvesting the Earth.   Scranton,
          PA: Intext, 1973, $8.95, 237p, index
          L: HS & up   S: Ag/E
          Easy reading, timely exposure of man's careless

husbandry of scarce resources and resultant danger to the
ecosystem. Numerous and informative tables and diagrams,
plus discussion on food growing and harvesting, processing,
marketing, results of consumption--even dietetic value of
foods.

32 _____. Too Many: A Study of Earth's Biological
      Limitations. New York: Macmillan, 1969, $7.95,
      368p, index
      L: Adv HS & up   S: O
      Borgstrom, international food science authority, sites
and then dispels dreams of unrealistic potential sources for
beating the inevitable biological limits of our forest, soil,
and water resources. These include making fresh water out
of sea water, squeezing drinking water out of the polar ice
caps, dew, and air, getting food by cultivating the sea, chemical synthesis, using insects for livestock, etc. He argues
they are impractical, as they defy the basic biological laws
of life (not to mention common sense). They are expensive;
they would cause severe environmental problems such as what
to do with enormous salt residues from treatment plants.
The book is excellent and includes useful charts, graphs, and
tables which support his text.

33 BOY SCOUTS of America. Ecology Workshop Instructor's
      Guide. North Brunswick, NJ: B.S.A., 1972,
      ($3.60 pap), illus
      L: Adult   S: Ec/Ed
      A manual for organizing ecology fieldtrips and work-
shops. Shows the adult how to put together a workshop for
children and how to go about planning ecology fieldtrips and
how to look and what to look for during them. Detailed and
very useful.

34 BRADFORD, Peter. Giant Oil: The Machiasport Oil
      Fight. New York: Harper, 1973, 256p
      L: Adv HS & up   S: OL, Ps/Eg
      Discussion of issues of ecology, energy, self-govern-
ment, tax leveraging, congressional infighting, and foreign
trade considerations.

35 BRAGDON, Clifford. Noise Pollution: The Unquiet
      Crisis. Philadelphia: University of Pennsylvania
      Press, 1972, $15, 280p, index, illus
      L: HS & up   S: Np/Ps
      Examines the social basis for the techniques of con-
trol, the health hazards of noise pollution, government and

industry's response, and current public attitudes.

36 BRAND, Stewart, ed. The Last Whole Earth Catalogue.
       New York: Random, 1971 ($5 pap), 447p, index, illus
       L: JHS & up   S: DBI
       Last of the series devoted to bettering the environment
through access to tools and knowledge. Lists everything from
books to windmills. The Updated Last Whole Earth Catalogue is
scheduled for publication August 1974.

37 BRANDHORST, Carl T. and Sylvester, Robert. Tale of
       Whitefoot. New York: Simon & Schuster, 1968,
       $3.50 ($3.39 PLB), 78p, illus
       The life of a mouse, followed by beautifully executed
description of what happens to her after she dies and recycles
into the ecological system. Realistic, educational, and very
well done.

38 BRENNAN, Matthew J., ed. People and Their Environment.
       Garden City, NY: Doubleday, 1971 ($4.25 pap) each
       L: (1-12, as below)   S: Ed
       Titles are: General (1-3), General (4-6), Home Eco-
nomics (9-12), Outdoor Laboratory (1-12), Science (7-9), Social
Studies (7-9), Social Studies (10-11), Biology (1-12). A series
of booklets that gives the teacher suggestions on how to work environmental considerations into mainline curriculum.

39 BRONSON, Wilfred S. Freedom and Plenty: Ours to Save.
       New York: Harcourt Brace, 1953, $4.95, illus
       L: 1-5   S: R/Cn/H
       Now entering its second decade in print, this popular
book details for young children the history of conservation.

40 BRONSON, William. How to Kill a Golden State. Garden
       City, NY: Doubleday, 1968, $6.95, illus
       L: HS & up   S: Cs
       Horrifying account of what's been happening in Cali-
fornia recently. The pictures help tell the story which is
as absorbing as it is appalling.

41 BROOKS, Paul. The Pursuit of Wilderness. Boston:
       Houghton Mifflin, 1971, $6.95, 220p
       L: HS & up   S: Cs/W
       Documents what Brooks describes as eight examples of
recent battles in defense of the earth. He describes the enormous efforts to preserve what remains of the world's wilderness
areas such as the Florida Everglades, Alaska, and the African
Bush.

42 BROWER, David, ed. The Meaning of Wilderness to
    Science. San Francisco: Sierra Club, 1972, $5.75,
    144p, 48 illus, endpaper map
    L: JHS & up   S: W
    Includes all speeches from the sixth Biennial Wilderness
Conference, including those by Daniel B. Beard, Stanly A.
Cain, Ian McTaggert Cowan, Raymond B. Cowles, Frank
Fraser Darling, Luna B. Leopold, Robert Rausch, and G. M.
Trevelyan. Excellent photographs supplement text.

43 _____. Wilderness: America's Living Heritage. San
    Francisco: Sierra, 1972, $5.75, 204p, illus
    L: Adv HS & up   S: A/W
    Sierra Club Wilderness Conference speeches by (among
others), Douglas, Olson, Ansel Adams, and Udall. All speeches
are directed toward preserving our wilderness areas, and while
there is more emphasis placed on wilderness conservation than
on the environmental considerations, the latter are implied.
The wilderness qualifies as one of the more important elements
in the fight for a decent, livable overall environment, and the
book, therefore, in the environmental context, is solidly relevant. (From Seventh Biennial Conference).

44 _____, ed. Wildlands in Our Civilization. San Fran-
    cisco: Sierra Club, 1970, $5.75, 172p, 32 illus
    L: JHS & up   S: W
    Includes the principal papers and summary of the fifth
Biennial Wilderness Conference as well as summaries and high-
lights of the first four previous conferences. The history of the
Sierra Club's contribution to wilderness preservation is also
summarized. Contributory writings: those of Brower, Bridge
Cook, A. Starker Leopold, George Marshall, Charlotte E. Mauk,
Wallace Stegner, Lowell Sumner, Lee Merriam Talbot, and
Howard Zahniser, among others. As is customary with the
Wilderness Conference summaries, a wide scattering of fine
photographs.

45 BROWN, Lester, and Finsterbush, Gail. Man and His
    Environment: Food. New York: Harper & Row, 1972,
    $5.95, ($3.25 pap), index, illus
    L: Adv HS & up   S: Ag
    An extremely well presented, thorough, concise, and
non-technical treatment. Also in the series: Marx's Waste
(261), Murphy's Law (279), Gates's Climate (137). Also planned:
Robert Cook's Population, Lynton Caldwell's Policy and Administration.

46 BROWN, Tom. Oil on Ice. San Francisco: Sierra,

1971, $1.95, 160p, illus
L: HS & up   S: Ol
The controversial Alaskan North Slope discovery. Some-
what out of date, but an excellent political/scientific case study.

47 BRUBAKER, Sterling. To Live on Earth: Man and His
        Environment in Perspective. Baltimore: Johns Hopkins
        University Press, 1972, $6.95, 208p, index; also
        avail in pap, New York: New American Library, $1.50
        L: HS & up   S: E
        Prepared by the staff of Resources for the Future
for young adult readers. Discusses in detail the conflict between economic growth and environmental quality.

48 BUCHSBAUM, Ralph and Buchsbaum, Mildred. Basic
        Ecology. Pittsburgh: Boxwood, 1957, $3.50 ($2.35
        pap), 195p, index, illus
        L: 9-12   S: Ec
        A straightforward, strictly scientific book on the
science of ecology. Stresses the basic ecological principles.
Written for high school use.

49 BURTON, Virginia Lee. The Little House. Boston:
        Houghton Mifflin, 1942, $4.95 ($4.20 PLB), illus
        L: K-3   S: R
        The classic story of the country house closed in on
by ever-increasing urban sprawl. Happy ending, however;
house is lovingly retrieved by former resident and taken out
to a new rural site. But, of course, that was 1942, when
there was still ample wide open spaces to move out to.

50 BUSCH, Phyllis S. City Lots: Living Things in Vacant
        Lots. (Discovering Nature Series.) New York:
        World, 1970, $4.95, unpag, illus
        L: 4-6   S: Ec
        A volume of an excellent series which is entitled
Discovering Nature. Busch acquaints children with the ecology of living things in city habitats. Good supportive photographs by Arline Strong.

51 CALDWELL, Lynton Keith. Environment: A Challenge
        to Modern Society. Garden City, NY: Doubleday (Nat-
        ural History), 1970, $7.95 ($1.95 pap), 292p, index
        L: Adv HS & up   S: O/I/Ps
        A social scientist's survey of the relationship of man
to his environment. Three sections: Policy, Tasks, and
Management. Caldwell (an associate of the International
Union for the Conservation of Nature and Natural Resources--

IUCN), discusses past and present difficulties and recommendations for future policy. An excellent book, directed toward helping the general reader to understand that the relationship of individual behavior and social action to the environment is important to human welfare.

52 _____. In Defense of Earth: International Protection of the Biosphere. Bloomington: Indiana University Press, 1972, $8.50, 304p, index
    L: Adv HS & up   S: I/Ps/O
    Analysis and summary of the present condition of the environment from a social point of view. Prepared by Caldwell for the Stockholm UN conference. Interesting analysis of the potential for environmental administration.

53 CALLAHAN, Daniel, ed. The American Population Debate. New York: Doubleday, 1971, $8.95 ($2.50 pap), illus, 380p
    L: HS & up   S: A/P
    An anthology on population. Concentrates on U.S. problems, analysis, and possible solutions. Callahan, who writes a great deal on religious matters, brings to this account the moral and ethical considerations of the population debate.

54 CALLISON, Charles H. , ed. America's Natural Resources. Rev. ed. New York: Ronald Press, 1967, $6
    L: Adv HS & up   S: Cn
    Like Henry E. Clepper's Origins of American Conservation (68) an important study of American's general management of natural resources. Callison, however, focuses on present needs for adequate, effective resource management.

55 CARR, Donald E. Death of the Sweet Waters. New York: Norton, 1966, $6.95, 257p, index, illus; also avail in pap, New York: Berkley, 1971, $1.25
    L: HS & up   S: Wp
    Detailed, well-written, inclusive account of water pollution in the United States. Only mercury is omitted, the book having been published before this poison, too, found its way into our waters.

56 CARRICK, Carol. Beach Bird. New York: Dial, 1973, $4.95 ($4.58 PLB), unpag
    L: K-3   S: R/Ec
    Portrays the daily life of a seagull who inhabits a tidal wilderness untouched by man. The other inhabitants interact to maintain the balance of nature, as they struggle over food and territory. Simple enough for independent

reading and provides excellent supplementary material for nature study units.

57   CARSON, Rachel.   Silent Spring.   Boston: Houghton
         Mifflin, 1962, $6.95, 368p, index, illus; also
         avail in pap, New York: Fawcett World, 1970,
         $1.25; rev. ed. , Fawcett World, $0.95 (pap)
         L: HS & up   S: Pc
         The book that blew the lid off of the pesticide con-
troversy.   Details how DDT and other pesticides accumulate
as they pass through food chains.   An historic work which
sparked the contemporary ecology movement by jolting the
public with the prediction that a spring was not far off when
no birds would be alive to herald it.   Voted one of the best
environmental books by Friends of the Earth.

58   CARVAJAL, Joan and Munzer, Martha.   Education: A
         Selected Bibliography.   Danville, IL: Interstate,
         1971
         L: Adult   S: DBI/Ed
         Bibliography for teachers that includes books on nat-
ural resources and current environmental problems.   Lists a
basic collection suitable for various grade levels.

59   CAUDILL, Harry.   My Land Is Dying.   New York: Dut-
         ton, 1971, $6.50, 144p
         L: HS & up   S: S
         Effective exposé of strip mining which puts to rest
the myth of land reclamation.   Includes devastating photos,
detailed explanation of impact of stripping on Ohio and Appalachia, and warns of what's in store for western states.

60   CHARTER, S.P.R.   Man on Earth: A Preliminary Evalua-
         tion of the Ecology of Man.   Sausalito, CA: Angel
         Island, 1962, $4.95, 272p; also avail in pap, New
         York: Grove, 1970, $1.70
         L: JHS & up   S: O
         Eighteen essays taken from the author's Pacifica
radio network lectures, 1960-1962.   Fascinating discussion
of the ecology of man.   Introduction by Aldous Huxley.

61   CHASAN, Daniel.   Klondike '70: The Alaskan Oil Boom.
         New York: Praeger, 1971, $6.95, 264p
         L: HS & up   S: Ol
         A history of oil exploration and exploitation in Alaska.
Chasan explains how the oil companies are involved in the
state's development and how, as a result, the state has grown

around and become dependent on oil interests. He traces the
big oil companies' influence, ending with the culminating
North Slope strike and the resulting pipe line controversy.

62   CHESTER, Michael.   Let's Go to Stop Air Pollution.
        New York: Putnam, 1968, $2.68 (PLB), 48 p, illus
        L: 2-4   S: Ap
        Review of the causes of air pollution and the alterna-
tive technological remedies for it such as electrostatic air
filters. Chester includes lots of good pictures that show
what air pollution looks like, where it comes from, and has
diagrams of technologies that reduce it. The diagrams show,
for instance, how a precipitator works and the mechanics of
a scrubber. A very good book for this age group.

63   _____. Let's Go to Stop Water Pollution. New York:
        Putnam, 1969, $2.86 (PLB), illus
        L: 2-4   S: Wp
        Like his Let's Go to Stop Air Pollution (62), an ex-
cellent text with supporting pictures and diagrams reviewing
the causes of water pollution, what it looks like, and devices
that can reduce it.

64   CHISHOLM, Anne.   Philosophers of the Earth: Conver-
        sations with Ecologists. New York: Dutton, 1972,
        $8.95, 201p
        L: HS & up   S: A
        Conversations with Environmentalists would more ac-
curately describe the contents, as the people interviewed are
concerned not only with the ecological aspect of biological
science, but with the entire environment. The book is extremely interesting, a book that the author says "attempts
to bridge the gap between the professional ecologist and the
interested layman." Includes conversations with Mumford,
Dubos, Boulding, F. F. Darling, Charles Elton, the Leopolds,
Commoner, Ehrlich, and ten other prominent figures in the
environment movement.

65   CITIZENS Advisory Committee on Environmental Quality.
        Community Action for Environmental Quality.
        Washington, DC: U.S. Gov. Printing Office, 1970.
        L: HS & up   S: Ps
        A citizens' guide for those individuals who wish to
get involved in practical action to make their communities
nicer places in which to live. The focus is on the main
avenues of approach, how to go about it, how people can
work together, what organizations and agencies to contact to
get help.

66 CLARKE, Robert. Ellen Swallow: The Woman Who
        Founded Ecology. Chicago: Follett, 1973, $7.95,
        288p, index
        L: HS & up   S: B/H
        Despite heavy romanticism, good cronicling of Swal-
low's involvement (late 1800's) with consumer protection, environmental education, and the beginnings of the ecology movement.

67 CLAWSON, Marion, et al. Land for the Future. (Re-
        sources for the Future.) Baltimore: Johns Hopkins
        University Press, 1960, $16.50, 570p, index, illus
        L: HS & up   S: Lu
        Dated, but extensive, very technical study of land
use and projections for the future involving the land and its
proper utilization. Clawson includes, for instance, how many
tons of coal are available, how many board feet of timber,
then projects how much will be needed to fill future needs.
An excellent source. Clawson was former director of the
Federal Bureau of Land Management and staff member of
Resources for the Future.

68 CLEPPER, Henry E., ed. Leaders of American Conser-
        vation. New York: Ronald, 1971, $10, 353p, index
        of contributors
        L: All   S: B/DBI
        A biographic directory of past and present leaders
and others involved in the conservation movement. A kind
of who's who in the conservation business, including a short
biography of each person mentioned. Not extensive enough
for encyclopedic reference, but good source for finding out
quickly the facts of everyone in the business.

69 _____, ed. Origins of American Conservation. New
        York: Ronald, 1966, $5, 193p, index
        L: JHS & up   S: H/Cn
        Short histories by respected authorities in the major
fields of conservation: wildlife, forests, fisheries, soil,
water, range, parks, historic sites. A good grounding point
that is considered an important work in the field of general
management of our natural resources.

70 COLINVAUX, Paul A. Introduction to Ecology. New
        York: Wiley, 1973, $12.50, 622p, index, illus
        L: College   S: Ec/Ed
        Colinvaux concentrates on the operation of natural
selection and evolution in ecology, focusing on basic population

and community ecology.   Can be used to advantage as an informative reference by teachers and advanced high school
students.

71   COLLIER, Boyd D. , Cox, George W. , Johnson, Albert W. ,
      and Miller, Philip C.   Dynamic Ecology.   Englewood
      Cliffs, NJ: Prentice-Hall, 1973, $11.95, 564p,
      index, illus
      L: College/Adv HS   S: Ec/Ed
      An evolutionary based approach to ecology.   Basically
a text book for college or very advanced high school students'
reference.   The authors assume that the student is familiar
with the processes of natural selection and proceed from this
base.

72   COMMONER, Barry.   The Closing Circle: Man, Nature,
      and Technology.   New York: Knopf, 1971, $6.95,
      326p, index; also avail in pap, New York: Bantam,
      1972, $1.95
      L: HS & up   S: O/T/H
      Lucid, well-written analysis by the dean of the Amer-
ican environmental movement and founder and director of
S.I.P.I.   Commoner's thesis: technology accounts for many
of our environmental woes.   The Closing Circle represents
the latest shot in the developing feud between Commoner and
Ehrlich, who believes that population is the major problem.
Good history of how scientists got involved in environmental
issues.

73   CONGRESSIONAL Quarterly, Inc.   Energy Crisis in
      America.   Washington, Congressional Quarterly,
      March 1973, $4 (pap), 96p
      L: HS & up   S: Ps/Eg
      Comprehensive overview of energy crisis background,
including such pertinent environmental issues as strip mining,
new sources of energy, pollution technology, environmental
problems.   Also lists relevant U.S. Supreme Court decisions
and congressional legislation.   "Recommended" by Library
Journal.   An excellent reference.

74   _____.   Man's Control of the Environment.   Washing-
      ton, D.C.: Congressional Quarterly, 1970 $4 (pap),
      91p.
      L: HS & up   S: Ps
      Review of the American environmental situation,
dealing primarily with government related aspects of federal
action and various lobbying groups.   Good reference to

8

75 COOLEY, Richard A. <u>Alaska: A Challenge in Conservation</u>. Madison: University of Wisconsin Press, 1966, $2.50 (pap), 170p, index, illus
L: 9-12   S: Lu/Ps
Assessment by the Conservation Foundation of Alaska's first decade of statehood and the state's treatment of the land and environment--most specifically the 104 million acres acquired from the Public Domain.

76 _____ and Wandesforde-Smith, Geoffrey, eds. <u>Congress and the Environment</u>. Seattle: University of Washington Press, 1970, $8.95, illus
L: HS & up   S: Ps/Cs/A
An anthology of original case studies taken from a year-long policy seminar at University of Washington. Details recent legislation put through Congress. Very thorough, good reference.

LE CORBUSIER see 221

77 COWAN, Edward. <u>Oil and Water: The Torrey Canyon Disaster</u>. Philadelphia: Lippincott, 1968, $6.95, 241p, index, illus
L: HS & up   S: Ol/Wp
A complete account of the Torrey Canyon wreck, March 1967, the resulting oil spill, devastating effects on the British and French coasts, and the governments' responses. Cowan gives a careful, detailed analysis of how it happened, how it affected the villages and the lives of the people who lived in them, and recounts day to day operations undertaken in cleaning it up. Interesting interviews with the captain and sailors.

78 CURRY-LINDAHL, Kai. <u>Conservation for Survival: An Ecological Strategy</u>. New York: Morrow, 1972, $6.95 ($3.25 pap), 335p, index
L: Adv HS & up   S: O/I
A world assessment by UNESCO's African ecology expert. Chapters on Conservation for Survival, the Air, the Sea, Fresh Water, the Soil, the Vegetation, the Animals, Man, Is Conservation a Losing Battle, Continental Problems of Today, the Future, and An Ecological Strategy.

79 DANSEREAU, Pierre, ed. <u>Challenge for Survival: Land, Air, and Water for Man in Megalopolis</u>. New York:

Columbia University Press, 1970, $2.75, 325p, index
L: HS & up   S: A/U
Experts' essays and commentaries on problems of
land, air, and water in heavily populated areas.

80 DARLING, Frank Fraser. Wilderness and Plenty. Bos-
    ton: Houghton Mifflin, 1970, $4.95, 84p; also avail
    in pap, New York: Ballantine, 1971, $0.95
    L: Adv HS & up   S: O
    Six short lectures introducing the key aspects of the
environmental crisis. A good starting point.

81 _____ and Milton, John P. Future Environments
    of North America. Garden City, NY: Doubleday
    (Natural History), 1966, $12.95 ($5.95 pap),
    767p, index
    L: Adv HS & up   S: O/Lu/A
    Speeches given at 1965 Conservation Foundation by 34
authorities. Topics are grouped under: The Organic World
and Its Environment; Regions: Their Development History
and Future; Economic Patterns and Processes; Social and
Cultural Purposes; Regional Planning and Development; and
Organization and Implementation. Very technical material.

82 DARLING, Lois and Darling, Louis. A Place in the Sun,
    Ecology and the Living World. New York: Morrow,
    1968, $4.50 ($4.14 PLB), 128p, illus, index, bibliog
    L: 7 up   S: Ec
    The Darlings explain the basic concepts of ecology by
using their own Connecticut farm as a laboratory and case
study. Also included in the book is a survey of man's interaction with nature, population, pesticides, pollution, the
balance of nature, evolving and adapting, the limits of life,
ecosystems of North America, man in the biosphere, pollution, poisoned ecosystems. A first-rate book.

83 DASMANN, Raymond F. Destruction of California.
    Riverside, NJ: Macmillan, 1970, $1.50 (pap)
    L: HS & up   S: Lu
    California's history chronicled as an environmental
case study: How the state deteriorated from its initial settlement to 1965.

84 _____. A Different Kind of Country. London: Col-
    lier-Macmillan, 1968, $5.95 ($1.95 pap, 1970),
    276p, illus
    L: 8 up   S: W/O

Clear delineation of basic ecological concepts and detailed plan for harnessing technology. Heavy concentration on wilderness problem, including what Dasmann calls the "urban wilderness." Dasmann points out that freedom is dependent upon a varied environment and examines citizens' roles in asserting their rights to such environmental freedom.

85 _____. Environmental Conservation. 3d ed. New
         York: Wiley, 1972, $10.50 ($6.95 pap), 473p, index
         L: HS & up   S: Cn/Ed
         Good, wide-coverage textbook study on soil, water,
timber, range, wildlife, fisheries, recreation, urban development, population, and politics.

86 _____. No Further Retreat: The Fight to Save
         Florida. New York: Macmillan, 1971, $6.95,
         index
         L: HS & up   S: Cs/Lu
         A detailed analysis of a state teetering between environmental success and destruction. Gives the state's development history and points out the need for citizen enlightenment of present problems. Specific case studies on Rookery Bay, the Everglades, the Florida Keys, and the proposed cross-Florida Barge Canal.

87 _____. Planet in Peril: Man and the Biosphere
         Today. New York: World, 1972, $8.95, 242p,
         index, illus
         L: HS & up   S: O/I
         A general overview of the environmental situation
and need for global action. Chapters on the Environmental Crisis; The Biosphere; the Impact of Man--Historical Records; Impact of Man--Recent Records; the Movement Toward Conservation; New Goals, New Decisions; and An International Program.

88 DAVIES, Brian. Savage Luxury: Slaughter of the Baby
         Seals. New York: Taplinger, 1971, $6.50, 214p,
         illus; also avail in pap, New York: Ballantine,
         1972, $1.25
         L: HS & up   S: Es
         The fight to prevent killing of baby and adult seals
for their fur. "An important book on a grim subject"--
Library Journal 6/1/71.

89 DAY, John A. , et al. Dimensions of the Environmental
         Crisis. New York: Wiley, 1971, $4.95 (pap)

L: Adv HS & up   S: A/P/Eg

An anthology stressing the interdisciplinary approach
to environmental problems. The authors examine the cultural
background, global aspects, some basic possible solutions,
and what they consider the key elements of the environmental
crisis: population and energy.

90 DE BELL, Garrett, ed. The Environmental Handbook.
New York: Ballantine, 1970, $5.95 ($0.95 pap),
367p, index

L: HS & up   S: A

One of the most widely read anthologies. Reflects
the intense "Let's get organized" vigor of the early 70's.
Excellent introductory survey book, a cram course on the
overall problem. Contains selections of the better environmental writers and a bird's eye perspective on everything
from pollution in the urban centers to resource conservation
to population control.

91 _____, ed. The Voter's Guide to Environmental
Politics. New York: Ballantine, 1970, $0.95 (pap),
305p.

L: HS & up   S: A/Ps

Anthology concentrating on the political issues and
political processes. Details how to get Congress and the
federal agencies to work for a better environment and lists
voting records of Senators and Congressmen on crucial environmentally oriented bills.

92 DIRECTORY of Consumer Protection and Environmental
Agencies. Orange, NJ: Academic Media, $39.50

L: All   S: DBI/Ps

Compilation of federal and state agencies involved
with environmental concerns and consumer protection.

93 DISCH, Robert, ed. The Ecological Conscience: Values
for Survival. Englewood Cliffs, NJ: Prentice-Hall,
1970, $2.45 (pap), 224p.

L: Adv HS & up   S: A/Et

A good anthology explaining the sociological ramifica-
tions of the environmental movement. Includes essays by
Allen Ginsberg, McHarg, Leopold, Shepard, Commoner,
Mumford, Paul Goodman, Buckminster Fuller, Allan Watts,
and Gary Snyder among others. Sixteen essays in all.

94 DOLAN, E. G. TANSTAAFL: The Economic Strategy
for Environmental Crisis. New York: Holt,

Rinehart & Winston, 1971, $3.50 (pap), 115p.
L: Adv HS & up   S: E
There Aint No Such Thing As A Free Lunch. Ad-
dressing his discussion to the layman and student, Dolan develops an ecologically sensitive system of economics that is
environmentally sound while at the same time viable. The
title refers to an old law of economics that wisely points out
that nothing is obtainable at no cost. There is a price, always, somewhere along the line, even if it is not immediately
evident.

95   DORFMAN, Robert and Dorfman, Nancy.   Economics of
     the Environment: Selected Readings.   New York:
     Norton, 1972, $10, 426p
     L: College   S: E
     A very technical anthology of economic approaches to
environmental sensibility and proposals for how environmental
considerations can be worked into economic systems.   Not for
the layman.

96   DORST, Jean.   Before Nature Dies.   Boston: Houghton
     Mifflin, 1970, $8.95, 352p, index; also avail in
     pap, Baltimore: Penguin, 1971, $2.45
     L: HS & up   S: H/I
     The impact of man on the whole earth from pre-
industrial times to the present.   Very comprehensive with
good specific case studies of problems throughout the world.

97   DOUGLAS, William O.   Muir of the Mountains.   Boston:
     Houghton Mifflin, 1961, $2.95, 179p, illus
     L: 7-11   S: B/H
     An excellent biography of the founder of the Sierra
Club and father of Yosemite Park.   Douglas is a mountain/
wilderness man himself and understands Muir, his ideas, and
his goals.

98   _____.   The Three Hundred Years War: A Chronicle
     of Ecological Disease.   New York: Random House,
     1972, $5.95, 215p, index
     L: HS & up   S: O
     Assessment of air, water, radiation, pesticides, gar-
bage, noise, estuaries, mining, wildlife, forest and wilderness, transportation and land use, and political action.   Organized by subjects.

99   _____.   A Wilderness Bill of Rights.   Boston: Little,
     Brown, 1965, $7.50 ($1.95 pap), 192p, index

L: Adv HS & up   S: Ps
The title is misleading. Actually a proposal for a federal Office of Conservation. Includes inventory of wilderness and recreation resources controlled by private, state, and federal agencies.

100 DUBOS, René. So Human an Animal. New York:
Scribner's, 1968, $8.85 ($2.45 pap), 267p, index
L: Adv HS & up   S: O/T
Dubos, a microbiologist who discovered germ fighting drugs can be obtained from microbes, argues that man is shaped not only by genetics but by his environment (man-made and natural). He states that man is unaware of the dehumanizing effects of our contemporary technologically-created environments, which are at the present time, working against him, and also that we must study the effects of the environmental forces man can control (urbanization and technology) in order to enhance our humanness.

101 DUFFY, Eric. Conservation of Nature. New York:
McGraw-Hill, 1970, $4.72 (PLB), illus
L: 5 up   S: Cn
A thorough discussion of conservation that does not talk down to children. Duffy covers the whole range of conservation topics: soil, water, forests, etc. Good illustrations.

102 DYE, Lee. Blowout at Platform A: A Crisis That
Awakened America. Garden City, NY: Doubleday, 1971, $5.95, 231p, index
L: HS & up   S: Ol/Wp
The first half chronicles the devastating Santa Barbara channel oilspill; the second half details the environmental impact of the oil industry as a whole.

103 EASTON, Robert. Black Tide: The Santa Barbara Oil
Spill and its Consequences. New York: Delacorte, 1972, $10, 336p, index
L: HS & up   S: Ol/Wp
A detailed narrative and analysis of the Santa Barbara oil spill of January 1969. Extremely well researched. Easton followed the whole fiasco as it was happening.

104 EHRENFELD, David. Conserving Life on Earth. New
York: Oxford University Press, 1972, $10, 360p, index, illus
L: HS & up   S: O

Listed as one of Library Journal's 100 Best Sci-
Tech Books of 1972. A holistic concept of conservation, defined as a way of life. But preserving all life on this planet
does not as Ehrenfeld sees it, necessitate returning to the
Dark Ages. It does, however, mean maintaining diversity in
the earth's natural systems. Ehrenfeld speaks from a broad
base of knowledge: a professional biologist, teacher, and re-
searcher, with degrees in history, medicine, and zoology.
Chapters include How Natural Communities are Threatened by
Man; Pollution; Industrial Accidents; Species Manipulations;
the Fate of the Blue Whale; Preservation of Natural Communities and of Species; and some sound conclusions. An
excellent book. Good illustrations.

105   ECOLOGY USA. New York: Special Reports, 1973, $125,
         624p
         L: HS & up   S: DBI
         This book is advertised as a comprehensive review
of everything that has happened in the environmental field
during the year 1973. If it lives up to its advanced notices,
it will provide an excellent source of reference.

106   EHRLICH, Paul R. The Population Bomb. New York:
         Ballantine, 1971, $0.95 (pap), 201p
         L: HS & up   S: P
         The original environmental doomsday book. Ehrlich
traces all environmental problems to exponentially expanding
population growth and, accordingly, proposes birth control and
ZPG as the most effective solutions to our environmental
problems. There is widespread disagreement to Ehrlich's
"population school of thought", but Barry Commoner notwith-
standing, The Population Bomb is a widely read book and a
definitive, rational force in the environmental movement.
Picked by Friends of the Earth as one of the best environmental books.

107   _____ and Ehrlich, Anne H. Population, Resources,
         Environment: Issues in Human Ecology. San
         Francisco: W. H. Freeman, 1972, 2nd ed., $9.95,
         383p, index, teacher's manual avail
         L: HS & up   S: P/Ed
         Summary text for school use on environment and
population. Scientifically oriented, in-depth, and technical.
The Ehrlichs explain how population, resources, and environment are interrelated and show the relationship between population and use of our limited natural resources. An excellent book.

108 _____ and Harriman, Richard. How To Be A Survivor (Orig. Title: How To Save Your Ass). New
York: Ballantine, 1971, $5.95, ($1.25 pap), 207p
L: HS & up   S: O/P/E
"A plan to save spaceship earth," organized around
a spaceship motif: Spaceship Operations, Size of the crew,
First Class Cabins (industrial world), Steerage, Control
Systems, and Spacemen. Ehrlich's concern: his favorite top
and his front-runner nominee for the environment's arch villain: overpopulation. Harriman's interest is new politics,
the political implications of ecological movements, and new
life styles. Emphasis on 60's radicalism and consideration
of economic development. Fine book.

109 ELLIOTT, Sarah M. Our Dirty Air. New York:
Messner, 1971, $3.95 ($3.79 PLB), 64p
L: 3-6   S: Ap
Good analysis for children of air pollution and proposed solutions.

110 _____. Our Dirty Water. New York: Messner,
1973, $5.25 ($4.79 PLB)
L: 3-6   S: Wp
Like her previous book, Our Dirty Air, published
two years earlier by Messner, a good book for young children. Elliott presents a clear, understandable analysis of
water pollution and explains the various proposals for solving
the problem.

111 EKIRCH, Arthur A., Jr. Man & Nature in America.
Lincoln: University of Nebraska Press, 1973,
$2.45 (pap)
L: Adv HS & up   S: H
The more important viewpoints of thinkers throughout United States history who concerned themselves with the
relationship of man to his environment and the way the growth
of American civilization has disrupted the harmonies of nature. Ekirch wisely includes excerpts from the original texts.

112 EMLEN, J. Merritt. Ecology: An Evolutionary Approach. Reading, MA: Addison-Wesley, 1973,
$14.95, 494p, index, illus
L: College   S: Ec/Ed
Basically, a college text, but good reference for
teachers. Provides excellent and thorough study of the process of natural selection and the levels of selection, covering

the basics of population and community ecology. The approach
to ecology is, of course, evolutionary; the stress on the operation of natural selection.

113   The Energy Crisis and the Environment. Ottawa:
            Carleton University Library, 1973, avail free from:
            Neil Brearly, Library, Carleton University, Colonel
            By Dr., Ottawa, Canada, KIS 5B6
            L: HS & up   S: DBI
            First in series of brief outlines for library use.
Includes books and review articles, journal articles, and
guidelines for more intensive research.

114   Energy, Environment, Economy. Avail from Enviro/
            Info., Box 115, Greenbay, WI 54305, $2
            L: HS & up   S: DBI
            Annotated bibliography of 109 U.S. federal govern-
ment publications concerning energy crisis and its environmental implications. Focus is on energy policy documents
and statistical substantiation.

115   The Energy Index: A Select Guide to Energy Informa-
            tion Since 1970. New York: Environmental Infor-
            mation Center, 1973, 400p, $50
            L: HS & up   S: DBI/Eg
            Catalogue of critical contemporary energy issues,
including resources and environmental impact and over 2000
abstracts on issues on everything from atomic power to zero
population growth.

116   Envirofiche. Avail from Microfiche Publications, 305
            E. 46th St., New York, NY 10017
            L: HS & up   S: DBI
            21 subject catalogues and Federal Register, cross
indexed by author, subject, industry, and accession number.
Available either by full subscription or by subjects.

117   ENVIRONMENTAL Action Association. Earth Day--The
            Beginning. New York: Arno/N.Y. Times-Bantam,
            1970, $5.95 ($1.25 pap), 233p
            L: HS & up   S: A
            A compendium of speeches (some of them contro-
versial--Rennie Davis calls for revolution within the environmental context), given on Earth Day, April 22, 1970. Lots
of big time environmentalists, politicians, radicals, even
Kurt Vonnegut. Book may turn out to be the environment's
Federalist Papers or an historical oddity.

118   ENVIRONMENTAL Action Bulletin and Organic Gardening
      & Farming. <u>Organic Guide to Colleges and Univer-
      sities.</u> Emmaus, PA: Rodale, 1973, $3.95 (pap),
      213p, index
      L: HS & up   S: DBI/Ed
      Most valuable for its listing of environmental pro-
grams at U.S. colleges and universities. Also includes sections on the environmental campus and how to make the cafe-
teria organic.

119   ENVIRONMENTAL Action Committee. <u>Earth Tool Kit.</u>
      New York: Pocket Books, 1971, $1.25, 369p
      L: HS & up   S: A/Ps/Ha
      The "tools" are politically oriented action law suits,
lobbying, elections, boycotts, picketing, marches, strikes,
harassments, etc. to combat highways, cars, airports, solid
wastes, pesticides, power, mining, noise, population, etc.
Eco-activists will love it; social science teachers will find
information linking the study of civics to environmental concerns.

120   ENVIRONMENTAL Information Center. <u>The Environ-
      mental Index '73: A Guide to the Key Environmen-
      tal Literature of the Year.</u> New York: The Cen-
      ter, 1973, $75, 750p
      L: HS & up   S: DBI
      Readers' guide to environmental literature published in
1973. Check also their guide for the previous years, <u>The Environmental Index '72</u> and <u>'71.</u> Name changed in 1974 to <u>Environ-
mental Access.</u> Monthly index and accession service available.

121   _____. <u>The Environmental Yearbook: A Chronicle
      of the Year's Events, Statistics, Politics, and Per-
      sonalities.</u> New York: Center, 1973, $50, 400p
      L: HS & up   S: DBI
      An annual reference cataloging events, trends, data.

122   ESPOSITO, John C. <u>Vanishing Air: The Report on Air
      Pollution.</u> (Ralph Nader Study Group Report.) New
      York: Grossman, 1970, $7.95 ($0.95 pap), 328p
      L: HS & up   S: Ap/Ps
      With customary Nader thoroughness, analyzes the
American air pollution problem. New York, Houston, and
Washington, D.C. are singled out for case study along with
major source of the problem: the automobile. Included also
is a detailed look at the National Air Pollution Control Administration.

123 EVERHART, William C. The National Park Service.
        New York: Praeger, 1972, $9, 276p, index
        L: HS & up   D: H/W
        A book for adults detailing the history of the Park
Service. Discusses the preservation vs. multiple use conflict
and the world-wide impact of this uniquely American idea.

124 EWALD, William R., Jr., ed. Environment for Man:
        The Next Fifty Years. Bloomington: Indiana Uni-
        versity Press, 1967, $6.95 ($2.95 pap), illus
        L: HS & up   S: A/O
        This collection of readings, along with his Environ-
ment and Policy: The Next Fifty Years (Bloomington: Indiana University Press, 1968, $10, $4.95 pap) is a valuable
adjunct reference or text. The environmental questions are
considered by the authorities in the field.

125 FABRICANT, Neil and Hallman, Robert M. Toward a
        Rational Power Policy: Energy, Politics, and
        Pollution. New York: Braziller, 1971, $8.95
        ($0.95 pap)
        L: Adv HS & up   S: Eg/Ps
        Analysis of the entire New York City energy picture
by the Environmental Protection Administration of New York
City.

126 FALK, Richard A. This Endangered Planet: Prospects
        and Proposals for Human Survival. New York:
        Random, 1971, $8.95 ($2.95 pap), 495p, index
        L: Adv HS & up   S: O/Ps
        Falk maintains that four basic principles underlie
the environmental crisis: war systems, overpopulation, depletion of our national resources through overuse and waste,
and general environmental deterioration. Argues that traditional governments are incapable of coping with a problem
that knows no boundaries and proposes a system of world
order and world government.

127 FALLOWS, James M. The Water Lords: Ralph Nader's
        Study Group Report on Industry and Environmental
        Crisis in Savannah, Georgia. New York: Grossman,
        1971, $7.95 ($1.95 pap), 294p, index
        L: Adv HS & up   S: Wp
        In-depth study centering on the pollution caused by
the Union Camp paperbag plant in Savannah.

128 FARB, Peter. Ecology. New York: Time-Life

(Silver Burdett), 1963, $7.60, 192p, index
L: JHS & up   S: Ec
One of the Time-Life Nature Library Series. Well
illustrated and well written. Farb covers the basic principles
of ecology, predators, food chains, biomes, habitats, etc.,
discussing the science of ecology, rather than explicit environmental considerations.

129 _____. The Land and Wildlife of North America.
New York: Time-Life (Silver Burdett), 1966,
$5.70 (PLB)
L: JHS & up   S: W/H/Lu
One of the Time-Life Nature Library Series. Shows
the land as it was like before the European settler arrived,
the build-up of the coast, the western deserts, mountain
ranges, foothills, western forests, the grasslands, and the
vanishing wilderness areas. A great deal of information is
included. A good reference.

130 FEIN, Albert. Frederick Law Olmsted and the American Environmental Tradition. New York: Braziller,
1972, $10 ($3.95 pap), illus
L: HS & up   S: H
Fein divides the book almost evenly between text
and illustrations. These include the original drawings and
renderings of Olmsted's plans for Central Park, Prospect
Park, and Stanford University. Charts and photographs cover
most of Olmsted's work. See Barlow's Frederick Law Olmsted's New York (16).

131 FERRY, B. W., et al., eds. Air Pollution and Lichens.
Toronto: University of Toronto Press, 1973,
$16.50, 389p, index, illus, maps, bibliog
L: Adv HS & up   S: Ec/Ap
Readable, well organized, non-specialty treatise on
how air pollution adversely affects lichens that are now being
considered as possible aids to measuring atmospheric contaminants. Also includes a good chapter on the harmful effect air pollution has on all vegetation.

132 FORTUNE Magazine. The Editors. Environment: A
National Mission for the Seventies. New York:
Harper & Row, 1969, $1.25 (pap), 220p
L: HS & up   S: E/A
A compilation of Fortune articles from the October
1967 and February 1970 issues. Treads middle ground be-
tween business and its critics. An excellent source for
pragmatic proposals.

133   FRASER, Dean.   People Problem: What You Should
          Know About Growing Population and Vanishing Re-
          sources.   Bloomington: Indiana University Press,
          1971, $6.95 ($2.95 pap, 1973), 248p, index
          L: Adv HS & up   S: P
          Discusses for the layman the population problem in
terms of mathematical and biological laws: describes the effect of exponential growth of resource use and the necessity
of limiting population to supportable levels.

134   FREEMAN, A. Myrick, ed.   The Economics of Environ-
          mental Policy.   New York: Wiley, 1973
          L: College   S: E
          Excellent, though fairly technical introduction to
problem of economics and environmental protection.

135   FULLER, R. Buckminster.   Approaching the Benign
          Environment.   University: University of Alabama
          Press, 1970, $6 ($1.25 pap), 121p (also avail
          New York: Macmillan)
          L: College & up   S: A/O
          Franklin Lectures in the Sciences and Humanities
at Auburn University.   Includes Fuller's Education for Com-
prehensivity, Eric A. Walker's Engineers and the Nation's
Future, and James R. Killan, Jr.'s Toward a Working Part-
nership of the Sciences and Humanities.

136   GABEL, Margaret.   Sparrows Don't Drop Candy Wrap-
          pers.   New York: Dodd, Mead, 1971, $3.95,
          unpag, illus
          L: 4-6   S: R/O
          A primer for the young child, detailing the do's
and don'ts for regaining and perpetuating healthy environments.   Gabel explains in simple terms that each person is
responsible for pollution, or at least some aspects of it, and
gives practical suggestions for individual action.   She includes
also good suggestions for group discussion.

137   GATES, David.   Man and His Environment: Climate.
          New York: Harper & Row, 1971, $5.95 ($3.25
          pap), index, illus
          L: Adv HS & up
          Like the other books in Harper & Row's Man and
His Environment series, an extremely well done, concise,
and thorough treatment, geared to provide the student with
the facts and basic concepts.   Also in the series: Wesley
Marx's Waste, Earl F. Murphy's Law, and Lester Brown

and Gail Finsterbush's Food. Also planned: Robert Cook's
Population and Lynton Caldwell's Policy and Administration.

138   GATES, Richard.   True Book of Conservation.   Chicago:
        Children's Press, 1959, $4.50 (PLB), 46p, illus
        L: 1-5   S: Cn/R
        An overview of what our land was like as wilder-
ness: a harmonious community of forests, grasslands, wildlife, and flowers.   Gates explains how man disrupted the
community, turning under grass, killing off wildlife, destroying topsoil; how the beginnings of the American conservation
movement gained momentum with Gifford Pinchot and Theodore
Roosevelt, and how conservation works and the way many
people are working to restore the forests and the wildlife.

139   GEORGE, Jean.   Who Really Killed Cock Robin: An
        Ecological Mystery.   New York: Dutton, 1973,
        $0.95 (pap), 149p
        L: 4-7   S: R/O
        Tony Isidoro takes delight in watching Cock Robin
and his mate build and tend their nest.   When, suddenly,
one day, Cock Robin dies, Tony sets out with his friend
Mary Alice to track down the killer.   The author follows
their relentless pursuit of the killer pollutant, examining the
contaminants in air, soil, and water, involving the reader in
the cycles of nature and the problems of living in an industrial, urban world.

140   GILLAM, Harold.   For Better or for Worse: The
        Ecology of an Urban Area.   San Francisco:
        Chronicle Books, 1972, $5.95, 183p, illus
        L: HS & up   S: Lu/Cs
        In-depth study of the problems confronting the San
Francisco Bay area.   Gillam has done a series of books on
the San Francisco Bay area.   This and his earlier book,
Between the Devil and the Deep Blue Bay (San Francisco:
Chronicle Books, 1969, $2.95 pap), concentrate on the en-
vironment.

141   GOLDMAN, Marshall I.   Controlling Pollution: The
        Economics of a Cleaner America.   Englewood
        Cliffs, NJ: Prentice-Hall, 1967, $1.95 (pap),
        175p
        L: Adv HS & up   S: E/I
        An anthology.   Explores the nature of the problem,
economic analysis, current cases, Soviet parallel, and national solutions.

142 _____ . The Spoils of Progress: Environmental Pol-
        lution in the Soviet Union. Cambridge, MA: MIT
        Press, 1972, $7.95, 372p, index
        L: Adv HS & up   S: I
        Rapid industrial growth has visited the Soviet Union,
as it has other highly industralized nations, with the inevitable
by-products of water, air, and waste pollution. Goldman
analyzes the forces that have brought about the current situation and describes both the drawbacks and advantages of state
control of conservation. He focuses on the pollution of Lake
Baikal in Siberia. Appendix includes environmental laws in
the U.S.S.R., the Conservation law of the Russian Republic
1960, and the Water Law 1970.

143 GOLDSMITH, Edward and Ecologist editors. Blueprint
        for Survival. Boston: Houghton Mifflin, 1972,
        $5.95, 189p
        L: HS & up   S: O/I
        Overview of the current British environmental prob-
lems by Goldsmith and the editors of Ecologist, a British
magazine.

144 GOLDSTEIN, Jerome. Garbage As You Like It.
        Emmaus, PA: Rodale, 1969, $5.95, 243p
        L: HS & up   S: Wt
        "A plan to stop pollution by using our nation's
wastes." The answer lies in composting and recycling, as-
suming, of course, that non-recyclables, plastics, packaging,
etc. are eliminated entirely. Rodale Press is very much involved in health foods, organic farming and gardening, etc.,
and the emphasis of this book, not surprisingly, is on cutting
down on the amount of garbage that must be disposed of and
composting all organic wastes.

145 _____ . How To Manage Your Company Ecologically.
        Emmaus, PA: Rodale, 1971, $1.95 (pap), 119p.
        L: Adult   S: E
        A handbook for the executive that points out ex-
amples of how good ecology is good economics, how a company can get involved in community projects, how it is good
public relations to do this, how recycling reduces corporate
expenditures, etc. Goldstein gives practical ways of doing
what he recommends, so the book is not merely about why
companies should adopt environmentally-sensitive practices,
but how they can.

146 GORDON, Suzanne. Black Mesa. New York: John

Day, 1973, $8.95 ($4.95 pap), 113p
L: HS & up   S: Eg/Ap/Cs
The destruction of sacred Hopi and Navajo land by
a smoke-belching, coal-gobbling power plant to benefit Las
Vegas, Los Angeles, and other cities hundreds of miles away.
A devastating, combination of photographs and text to provide
an excellent, effective case study.

147 GRAHAM, Frank, Jr. Man's Dominion: The Story of
        Conservation in America. New York: Evans & Co.,
        1971, $8.95, 339p, index
        L: HS & up   S: H
        An excellent history of American conservation. In-
cludes in-depth narratives on the Audubon plume-bird flight in
Florida, Teddy Roosevelt's political action, the Ballinger-
Pinchot affair, Hetch Hetchy, Steven Mather, T.V.A., and
more.

148 _____. Since Silent Spring. Boston: Houghton
        Mifflin, 1970, $6.95, 288p; also avail in pap,
        New York: Fawcett, 1970, $0.95.
        L: HS & up   S: Pc/H
        Classic follow-up to Silent Spring. Examines the
impact of Silent Spring through the 1960's, detailing governmental and popular response to the pesticide problem.

149 _____. Where the Place Called Morning Lies. New
        York: Viking, 1973, $7.95, 238p
        L: HS & up   S: Lu
        Lament for the quickly disappearing way of life in
the state of Maine and a plea to enlighten man's ignorance of
ecological balance and correct problems created by modern
technology. Exposes the lumbering industry's contribution to
the state's problems and its effects on lobstering, fishing,
and agriculture. And for what? No longer for masts for
the king's ships, but for paper napkins. Highly recommended
by Library Journal.

150 GROSSMAN, Mary L. and Hamlet, John N. Our
        Vanishing Wilderness. New York: Grosset &
        Dunlap, 1969, $14.95, 324p, index, illus
        L: 7 up   S: Ec/W
        Up-to-date, scientifically oriented exploration of the
basic concepts of ecology. Good text and photographs. Excellent for junior and high school students.

151 GROSSMAN, Shelly and Grossman, Mary L. How and

Why Wonder Book of Ecology. New York: Grosset
and Dunlap, 1971, $1.50 ($2.29 PLB) ($0.65 pap),
illus; also avail, New York: Wonder, $1.50
($2.29 PLB), illus
L: 4-6   S: Ec
Clear, easy-to-understand study of the Chain of
Life, the Habitats, the Seasons, the Biomes, the Eastern
Forests, the Grasslands, the Hot Deserts, the Cold Desert,
the Mountains, the Coastlines, Problems and Alternatives
(discussion of the use of DDT, etc.). Excellent illustrations.

152 HAFNER, Everett M. and Committee. Environmental
     Education. New York: Scientists' Institute for
     Public Information, 1970
     L: Adult   S: Ed
     Margaret Mead was formerly S.I.P.I. president,
and Barry Commoner is now its president and driving force.
The primary function of the Institute is to put out science/
environmental education information. Write 30 E 68th Street,
New York, NY for details and listings of publications.

153 HAHN, James and Hahn, Lynn. Recycling: Reusing
     Our World's Solid Wastes. New York: Watts,
     1973, $3.95 (PLB), 128p, illus
     L: 5 up   S: Wt
     A good book, directed specifically to children, tell-
ing them of their responsibilities. Hahn discusses the problem of getting rid of wastes and examines the process of recycling. Good photographs. Glossary.

154 HAINES, Madge and Morrill, Leslie. John Muir: Pro-
     tector of the Wilds. Nashville: Abingdon, 1957,
     $2.25, illus
     L: 4 up   S: B/H
     Children's biography of John Muir (1838-1914), the
founder of the Sierra Club, father of Yosemite, and active
California environmentalist.

155 HALACY, D. S., Jr. Habitat: Man's Universe &
     Ecology. Philadelphia: Macrae Smith, 1970,
     $4.50, 186p, index
     L: 7 up   S: O
     This is the second in a series entitled The Nature
of Man. Halacy considers man's role in his habitat and presents a scientifically (rather than socially or philosophically)
oriented whole earth overview of this relationship of man to
his surroundings. Useful, basic, well written book. Good
illustrations.

156 _____. Now Or Never: The Fight Against Pollution.
New York: Scholastic Book Service, 1971, $5.95
($5.62 PLB), 203p, illus
    L: 5 up   S: Ap/Wp
A very good survey of all pollution problems with
suggestions for reader action.

157 _____. The Water Crisis: A Background Study
Analyzing Ways and Means of Supplying Water for a
Growing World. New York: Dutton, 1966, PLB
($4.95), 192p, illus.
    L: 7 up   S: Wp
Well rounded study of past, present, and future
water use. Good detail on pollution.

158 HAMILTON, David. Technology, Man and the Environment. New York: Scribner's, 1973, $9.95, 356p,
illus
    L: HS & up   S: T
Technology: what it is and its effects on our everyday lives, how it is changing our world, and the problems it
causes.

159 HAMILTON, Michael, ed. This Little Planet. New
York: Scribner's, 1971, $6.95 ($2.45 pap), 241p
    L: Adv HS & up   S: Et
Six essays in three sections entitled Pollution,
Scarcity, and Conservation. Discussion by the Canon at
Washington Cathedral of the concept that our Judeo-Christian
heritage does not encourage exploitation of the earth's re-
sources.

160 HANSON, Herbert C. Dictionary of Ecology. Washington, DC: Philosophical Library, 1962, $10, 382p,
bibliog
    L: 5 up   S: DBI
Dictionary of the more widely used ecological terms
for use by, as the author advises, "students, teachers, and
investigators in ecology and related fields such as range management, forestry, wildlife, conservation, agronomy, and
limnology." Definitions, however, do not always adhere to
the precise, scientific explanations, but indicated the generally accepted connotation implied in contemporary usage.
Nonetheless, useful. The definitions are simple and clear
so that even younger children will be able to understand their
meaning.

161   HARDIN, Garrett.   Exploring New Ethics for Survival:
         The Voyage of the Spaceship Beagle.   New York:
         Viking, 1973, $1.45 (pap), index
         L: Adv HS & up   S: O/Et
         Hardin expands on the "commons" problem in a
science fiction parable.   Suggests a unified approach to pollution control, resource use, and population control that he
says demands "mutual coercion, mutually agreed upon."

162   HARMER, Ruth M.   Unfit For Human Consumption.
         Englewood Cliffs, NJ: Prentice-Hall, 1971, $6.95,
         374p, index
         L: HS & up   S: Pc/Fp
         Centers on pesticides and their effect on food.
Very comprehensive and well integrated science/narrative.
Good reading.

163   HARRINGTON, Carol, et al.   If You Want To Save the
         Environment: Start at Home!   New York: Haw-
         thorn, 1971, $2.50, 56p
         L: HS & up   S: Ha
         Pamphlet detailing what individuals can do in their
daily routines to stop environmental pollution.

164   HARRISON, C. William.   Conservation: The Challenge
         of Reclaiming Our Plundered Land.   Rev. ed.   New
         York: Julian Messner, 1973, $5.95 ($5.29 PLB),
         191p, index
         L: 7 up   S: Cn
         The book details, with text and illustrations, the
history of American conservation.   By tracing the history,
Harrison attempts to teach the basic principles of soil, water,
and wildlife conservation, showing how man treated these aspects of his environment in the past and how his past mistakes were successfully remedied.

165   HARRISON, Gordon.   Earthkeeping: The War With
         Nature and A Proposal for Peace.   Boston:
         Houghton Mifflin, 1971, $5.95, 276p, index
         L: Adv & up   S: O/T
         An essay by the head of the Ford Foundation's Con-
servation Program on the Environmental Revolution.   Harrison keeps in mind, and urges that all people keep in mind,
what the goals of technology are and what are the people's
goals in creating or implementing a new technology.   He
views the environmentalist, therefore, as a planner, assessing the merits and demerits of a technology before creating it.

166 HAYS, Samuel P. Conservation and the Gospel of Efficiency: The Progressive Conservation Movement 1890-1920. Cambridge, MA: Harvard University Press, 1959, $11.50, 297p, index; also avail in pap, New York: Atheneum, $2.95
L: Adv HS & up   S: H/Cn
History of the era when conservation was linked with good business and when scientists and technicians, rather than the nature lovers, championed conservation. Considered a path-breaking analysis, outlining the first great surge of conservation which began during the Progressive Era. For further reading, see Elmo R. Richardon's The Politics of Conservation: Crusades and Controversies, 1897-1913 (Berkeley: University of California Press, 1962).

167 HEADY, Eleanor B. and Heady, Harold F. High Meadow. New York: Grosset & Dunlap, 1970, $4.50 ($4.59 PLB), 120p, index, illus
L: 5-8   S: Ec
The story of the ecology of a mountain meadow, how the various elements of nature depend on each other. The Headys begin with the Ice Age when a glacier forms a lake that, eventually, fills into the meadow. In time the animal populations and the plant species mesh into a closed, natural system. A good case study of a localized area.

168 HEINDL, L. A. The Water We Live By: How To Manage It Wisely (orig title: Our Water Resources). New York: Coward McCann, 1971, $4.49 (PLB), 127p, illus
L: 6-9   S: Wp/I
A good survey of international water pollution for the late elementary grades and junior high school students. Excellent photographs support the text.

169 HELFMAN, Elizabeth S. Our Fragile Earth. New York: Lothrop, 1972, $4.95 ($4.59 PLB), 160p, index, illus
L: 5-9   S: Lu/H
A very complete survey of soil use and abuse and good history of American soil problems. Includes Dust Bowl, TVA, etc.

170 HELFRICH, Harold W. , Jr. , ed. Agenda for Survival: The Environmental Crisis--2. New Haven: Yale University Press, 1970, $10 ($2.95 pap), illus
L: Adv HS & up   S: A/O

Sequel to The Environmental Crisis (below).
1969-1970 Yale School of Forestry lecture series organized
by Stewart Udall.   Includes: Brower, Paul McCloskey,
Charles Luce, Harry Caudill, Gaylord Nelson, Laurence
Halperin, and others. Sixteen lectures in all.

171 _____, ed. The Environmental Crisis: Man's Strug-
      gle to Live with Himself. New Haven: Yale Uni-
      versity Press, 1970, $2.25 (pap), 187p
      L: Adv HS & up   S: A/O
      1968-1969 Yale School of Forestry lectures.   In-
cludes Ehrlich, Boulding, Sax, and others.

172 HERBER, Lewis. Crisis in Our Cities: The Shocking
      Truth About the Urban Epidemic. Englewood Cliffs,
      NJ: Prentice-Hall, 1965, $7.95, 239p, index
      L: HS & up   S: U/Ap
      Analyzes cities and pollution brought on by great
concentrations of people and industry. Details Donora, London, and Los Angeles.

173 HERNDON, Booton. The Great Land. New York:
      McKay, 1971, $6.95, 241p, index
      L: HS & up   S: Ol/Lu
      The North Slope of Alaska, its history, and analy-
sis of the impact of the oil discovery.

174 HIBBARD, Benjamin H. A History of Public Land
      Policies. New York: Macmillan, 1924; reprinted,
      Madison: University of Wisconsin Press, 1965,
      $4.25 (pap)
      L: Adv HS & up   S: H/Lu
      Good source illuminating the relationship of federal
land policy and the public domain to the emerging environmental and conservation movements. See also E. Louise
Peffer's The Closing of the Public Domain: Disposal and
Reservation Policies 1900-1950, Marion Clawson and Burnell
Held's The Federal Lands: Their Use and Management
(1056), Clawson's Man and Land in the United States (a more
simplified survey), and Vernon Carstensen's The Public
Lands: Studies in the History of the Public Domain, a
collection of the more important essays written on the
public domain.

175 HICKEL, Walter. Who Owns America? Englewood
      Cliffs, NJ: Prentice-Hall, 1971, $6.95 ($9.95
      large print PLB, 1972, G. K. Hall); avail in

pap, New York: Warner, 1972, $1.50
L: HS & up   S: Pn/Ps
Hickel's memoirs of Alaskan political life and his
career as Secretary of the Interior. Unfortunately not the
story behind the story, but a good description of his day-to-
day activities as Secretary. Once Governor of Alaska,
Hickel's nomination as Nixon's Secretary of the Interior was
bitterly opposed by environmentalists. But they came to regard him as one of their champions and one of their few
friends within the Nixon administration.

176 HILL, Gladwin and Bernstein, Theodore M., eds. Mad-
     man in a Lifeboat: Issues of the Environmental
     Crisis. New York: John Day, 1972, $5.95 ($1.95
     pap), 118p, index
     L: Adv HS & up   S: O
     Hill, the Environmental Correspondent for the New
York Times, foresees the environment becoming a political
issue. Titles of chapters: Population, Land Resources, Air
Pollution, Water Pollution, Solid Waste, Myth: "We Can't
Afford To Be Clean", States, Industry, Government, Inter-
national Action, Citizen Action.

177 HILTON, Suzanne. How Do They Get Rid of It? Phila-
     delphia: Westminster, 1970, $5.25, 117p, index,
     illus
     L: 7 up   S: Wt
     Hilton details how various items are disposed of:
the baling of junked cars, for instance, the reuse of airplane
parts and railroad equipment, new life for old ship hulks, the
art of building demolition, container disposal, wood by-products use, recycling books and paper, factory wastes, making
garbage useful, sewage treatment, and nuclear waste disposal.
Each method of recycling or disposal is thoroughly and inter-
estingly presented.

178 HIRSCH, S. Carl. Guardians of Tomorrow: Pioneers
     in Ecology. New York: Viking, 1971, $4.95
     ($4.53 PLB), 192p, index, illus
     L: 7 up   S: H/B
     Excellent short biographies of American environ-
mentalists: Thoreau, Marsh, Olmsted, Muir, Pinchot,
George Norris, Aldo Leopold, Carson.

179 _____. The Living Community: A Venture Into
     Ecology. New York: Viking, 1966, $4.50 ($4.13
     PLB), 128p, index, illus

L: 7 up   S: Ec
        A non-technical narrative on ecology and examination
of Darwin, nature, and man-made pollution. A good history
of world-wide environmental devastation with assessment of
the present American situation. Good chapter on pesticides
and what happens when man begins to tamper with the balance
of nature.

180   HITCH, Allen S. and Sorenson, Marian.   Conservation
        & You.   New York: Van Nostrand Reinhold, 1964,
        $4.95, 126p, index, illus
        L: 7 up   S: Cn/H
        A very good history of world devastation and as-
sessment of present American status. Focus, however, is
on conservation, not pollution.

181   HOGNER, Dorothy C.   Conservation in America.   Phila-
        delphia: Lippincott, 1958, $4.95, 240p, index
        L: 7-9   S: Cn/Hs
        The story (from 1492 to the mid-20th century) of
man's struggle to preserve the resources of America from
both natural and human depredations.   Hogner depicts what
private and public agencies and certain industries are doing
to restore some of our despoiled landscapes and to preserve
what remains of those yet untouched.   She discusses also un-
renewable resources, wildlife, the Great Dust Bowl, and the
American Forest.

182   HOKE, John.   Ecology: Man's Effects on His Environ-
        ment and Its Mechanisms.   (A First Book.)   New
        York: Watts, 1971, $3.75 (PLB), 96p, index
        L: 4-6   S: Ec
        Divided into two sections: the first on the science
of ecology; the second on man's effect on the environment.
Good, not simple, but clear and well suited to the age group.

183   HOLDREN, John and Herrera, Philip.   Energy: A
        Crisis in Power (orig title: Megawatt).   San Fran-
        cisco: Sierra Club, 1972, $2.75 (pap), 256p
        L: HS & up   S: Eg
        Part One (Holdren), is a general overview of the
various energy sources: fossil fuels, nuclear power, etc.
with explanations of their environmental impact.   Part Two
(Herrera), gives case studies of controversies involving these
different energy sources.   A Sierra Club Battlebook.

184   HUNGERFORD, Harold R.   Ecology: The Circle of

Life. Chicago: Childrens, 1971, $4.75 (PLB),
95p, index, illus
L: 5 up   S: Ec
A simple and well-illustrated overview of the science
of ecology for the elementary level.

185 HURD, Edith T. Wilson's World. New York: Harper
     & Row, 1971, $4.50 ($4.79 PLB), illus
     L: K-3   S: R
Wilson can paint any kind of world he likes, so
after tracing the development of history up to the present
and finding that he doesn't like the present, he paints a more
pleasing environment.

186 HUTCHINS, Ross E. The Last Trumpeters. Chicago:
     Rand McNally, 1967, $3.50, illus
     L: 2-5   S: Es
A heartrending story of the life of a pair of swans.
A fine account by a prolific writer of children's books and
guaranteed to cause both tears and anger.

187 HUTH, Hans. Nature and the American: Three Cen-
     turies of Changing Attitudes. Lincoln: University
     of Nebraska Press, 1972, reprint of 1957 Univer-
     sity of California Press ed, $2.95 (pap), 250p,
     index, illus
     L: HS & up   S: H/At/En
Thorough cultural history of American attitudes
toward the land and nature. Special attention to authors,
artists, and creative thinkers. Excellent analysis of the development of the public's appreciation of natural beauty during
the 19th century. An extremely good source.

188 HUXLEY, Aldous. Brave New World. New York: Har-
     per & Row, 1932, $5.95 ($4.43 PLB), ($0.95 pap),
     177p
     L: HS & up   S: En
Futuristic landmark work by the spiritual father of
contemporary environmental awareness. (Many of his pre-
dictions are being fulfilled.) An excellent vehicle for an
English teacher for combining the study of environmental considerations, especially the oft-touted "controlled society,"
with analysis of a great novelist's foremost work. Also suggested is Huxley's lecture, "Tangents of Technology/Concepts
of Ecology," from the Center for the Study of Democratic Institutions, Santa Barbara, CA.

189 HYDE, Margaret O. For Pollution Fighters Only. New
       York: McGraw-Hill, 1971, $4.95 ($4.72 PLB),
       157p, index
       L: 7 up   S: Ec
       An excellent book filling both cognitive and manipu-
lative needs of this age group. Activity oriented, supple-
menting environmental theory with easily performed experiments. Full of good source material.

190 _____. This Crowded Planet. New York: McGraw-
       Hill, 1961, $4.33 (PLB), 159p, index, illus
       L: 7 up   S: P
       Detailed discussion of the problems and possible
solutions for providing for mushrooming populations.

191 HYLANDER, Clarence J. Wildlife Community: From
       the Tundra to the Tropics in North America.
       Boston: Houghton Mifflin, 1966, $6.95, 342p,
       index, illus
       L: 7 up   S: Ec
       An ecology text with thorough analysis of each
biome. No discussion of pollution, etc. ; just ecology, with
good illustrations and charts.

192 ISENBERG, Irwin, ed. The City in Crisis. (The
       Reference Shelf, vol 40, no 1.) New York: H. W.
       Wilson, 1968, $4.50, 246p
       L: HS & up   S: U/A
       A survey of the principal urban troubles which con-
front us and an examination of some of the proposed remedies
for solving them. Isenberg introduces each section with a
brief background description of the subsequent article. Subjects covered range from dirty air, to breakthroughs in mass
transit, to how European cities combat urban sprawl; writers
represented include James Ridgeway, Lyndon B. Johnson, and
regular contributors and staff writers of publications such as
the New York Times, the Wall Street Journal, etc. , from
which most of the selections are taken. One of the more interesting chapters is the Case for Building 350 New Towns
(p211) and How Europe Combats Urban Sprawl (p224).

193 JACOBS, Jane. The Death and Life of Great American
       Cities. New York: Random House, 1961, $10
       ($1.25 pap) ($2.95 Modern Library ed), 458p,
       index
       L: Adv HS & up   S: U
       Tells all about American cities--their problems,

politics, pollution, overdevelopment, and overpopulation.

194   JACOBY, Henry D. and Steinbruner, John.   Clearing
      the Air: Federal Policy on Automotive Emissions
      Control.   Cambridge, MA: Ballinger, 1973, $15,
      228p
      L: Adv HS & up   S: Ap/ Ps
      A policy analysis of decisions that the government
faces in executing its automotive emissions control policies.
Discusses alternatives to present governmental policies and
comparative costs and environmental impact of these options.

195   JARRETT, Henry, ed.   Comparisons in Resource
      Management.   Gloucester, MA: Peter Smith,
      $3. 75, 271p, index
      L: College   S: Lu/ I
      Describes management programs in England, Wales,
Sweden, West Germany, Canada, and France, their approaches
to national park administration, small forest holdings, natural area preservation, river pollution, multi-purpose land
and water districts, and regional development.

196   _____.   Perspectives on Conservation: Essays on
      America's Natural Resources.   Baltimore: John
      Hopkins University Press, 1971, $9 ($2. 95 pap),
      258p, index
      L: HS & up   S: Cn
      Includes proceedings of the Resources for the Fu-
ture symposium which was held in 1958.   Several noted
scholars knowledgeable in the fields of conservation, environment, and natural resources are represented.   A good source.

197   JENNINGS, Cary.   The Shrinking Outdoors.   Philadel-
      phia: Lippincott, 1972, $5. 50, 192p, index
      L: 7 up   S: O
      Good, fast-reading, hard-punching overview of life
on earth today, what it once was, the cluttered landscape,
vanishing wildlife, withering greenery, the despoiled waters,
polluted skies, overpopulation, the people (especially in government and industry), who seem not to care.   But he cites
the courageous groups and individuals who do and what they
have done already.   He goes on, then, to inform his reader
just what he or she can do as a young citizen and future
voter.   His suggestions are far superior to the usual "get
involved" advice.   An excellent book.

198   JOHNSON, Cecil E. , ed.   Social and Natural Biology:

Selections from Contemporary Classics. Princeton,
NJ: Van Nostrand Reinhold, 1968, $3.75 (pap),
illus
     L: Adv HS & up   S: A
     Excellent collection of articles by, among others,
L. S. B. Leakey, Aldous Huxley, Garrett Hardin, John
Steinbeck, Rachel L. Carson, John Muir, John Burroughs,
Henry David Thoreau, Loren Eiseley. See Johnson's Eco-
Crisis (199).

199 _____, ed. Eco-Crisis. New York: Wiley, 1970,
     $3.75 (pap), 182p
     L: Adv HS & up   S: A
     Sixteen excerpts from the best of the thinkers and
writers on ecology, conservation, pollution. Many of the
essays included are not widely known, but are of unusual interest. Johnson's introduction sets a frightening stage, but
one that we are becoming all too familiar with. His brief
biographies of the authors at the beginning of each selection
and quick description of the subsequent text will be helpful to
orient the student. Among the better known works included
are portions of Carson's Silent Spring, Ehrlich's The Population Bomb, and Aldous Huxley's The Politics of Ecology: The
Question of Survival. An excellent and highly recommended
introductory anthology.

200 JONES, Claire, Gadler, Steve, and Engstrom, Paul.
     Pollution: The Air We Breathe; Pollution: The
     Food We Eat; Pollution: The Balance of Nature;
     Pollution: The Dangerous Atom; Pollution: The
     Noise We Hear; Pollution: The Population Explo-
     sion; Pollution: The Land We Live On. Minneapo-
     lis: Learner Publications Co. , 1971-72, $3.95
     each (PLB), illus
     L: 5-12   S: Ap/Fp/Ec/Np/P/Lu
     Good basic coverage of each topic by the members
of the Minnesota Environmental Control Citizens Association.
Extremely well done.

201 JONES, Holoway R. John Muir and the Sierra Club:
     The Battle for Yosemite. San Francisco: Sierra
     Club, 1964, $10
     L: HS & up   S: H
     A history of the founding of the Sierra Club, the
battle for Yosemite, and the tragic loss of Hetch Hetchy
Valley to "multiple use." Amply illustrated with contemporary photographs, maps, some newspaper cartoons and

photographs, and Sierra Club flyers.

202 KASH, Don E. , White, Irvin L. , et al. A Technology
    Assessment of Outer Continental Shelf Oil and Gas
    Operations. Norman: University of Oklahoma
    Press, 1973, $10 ($4.50 pap), 350p, illus, tables
    L: Adv HS & up   S: Eg/Ol/T
        Study (sponsored by the National Science Founda-
tion), on whether or not our technology can meet future
energy needs and still preserve the environment.

203 KAUFFMANN, John M. Flow East: A Look at Our
    North American Rivers. New York: McGraw-Hill,
    1973, $7.95, 284p, bibliog, index
    L: HS & up   S: Wp/Cn/Pn
        Naturalist and canoeist Kauffmann shares his and
others' adventures on the Atlantic coastal rivers. Describes
the effects of pollution, development, dam building, and
argues for saving what is left of our river resources and
proposes how it can be done. Read in conjunction with Roy
Mann's Rivers in the City.

204 KAVALER, Lucy. Dangerous Air. New York: John
    Day, 1967, $4.95, 143p, illus
    L: 8 up   S: Ap
        A comprehensive, smoothly narrated review of air
pollution. Kavaler gives a great deal of background information, references to the London 1952 disaster, Donora, and
pertinent technical data. A useful source, readable history,
and far from pleasant account of the possible futures we face
in our poisoned atmosphere.

205 KELLEY, Ben. The Pavers and the Paved. New York:
    Scribner's, 1971, 183p, index
    L: Adv HS & up   S: Lu
        An assault on the highway trust fund by a renegade
PR man for the Highway Administration. Out of print, but
enlightening.

206 KELLY, Katie. Garbage: The History and Future of
    Garbage in America. New York: Saturday Review
    Press, 1973, $7.95, 232p, index
    L: HS & up   S: Wt
        The complete story of garbage and its removal,
including: how we spend 3.7 million dollars to get rid of
our garbage--more than twice what we spend on medical research. Entertaining, informative, and thorough. The

author even includes a chapter on the infamous garbage rifler
A. J. Weberman, renowned most notably for his ransacking
of Dylan's garbage pails.

207 KERR, Robert S. Land, Wood and Water. New York:
     Fleet, 1960, $6, illus
     L: Adv HS & up   S: Cn/H
     Polemical account of conservation movement. Con-
centrates on water conservation: hydropower production, irrigation, and flood control. An excellent source.

208 KILGORE, Bruce, ed. Wilderness in a Changing World.
     San Francisco: Sierra, 1972, $6.50, 253p, illus
     L: Adv HS & up   S: W
     A compilation of speeches from the ninth Biennial
Wilderness Conference with contributions (among many others)
from Paul B. Sears, Ashley Montagu, Luna B. Leopold,
Clinton P. Anderson, James Bonner, and Sigurd F. Olson.
Good photographs, including several very effective ones by
David Brower and Ansel Adams.

209 KORMONDY, Edward J. Concepts of Ecology. Engle-
     wood Cliffs, NJ: Prentice-Hall, 1969, $8.50
     ($4.95 pap), 209p, index
     L: Adv HS & up   S: Ec
     A text type book on ecology with minimum technical
jargon and good diagrams and charts. Useful for the general
reader. Kormondy is a professor of biology at Oberlin.

210 KREBS, Charles J. Ecology: The Experimental
     Analysis of Distribution and Abundance. New
     York: Harper & Row, 1972, $14.95, 694p, index,
     illus
     L: College   S: Ec/Ed
     Krebs bases his ecology study on evolution and
natural selection, but he assumes that the processes are self-
evident and familiar to all students and does not describe the
basics underlying his examinations and conclusions. The
book, therefore, should be used as an advanced level text,
by teachers, or by advanced high school students as a reference, but only if they are familiar with the elementary under-
pinnings of the evolutionary ecological approaches.

211 KUCERA, Clair L. and Rochow, John J. The Challenge
     of Ecology. St. Louis: Mosby, 1973, $5.95, 226p,
     illus
     L: HS & up   S: Ec

The authors advocate solving society's problems
through relating the ecological processes (which must be
thoroughly understood), to human crises. In the book, they
relate the science of ecology to community organization,
species, and the ecosystems, covering among other topics
biotic diversity, energy relationships, soil environment, and
an original, socio-economic approach to ecosystem simulation.

212 LANDAU, Norman J. and Rheingold, Paul D., eds.
     The Environmental Law Handbook. New York:
     Ballantine/Friends of the Earth, 1971, $1.25 (pap),
     496p
     L: HS & up   S: L/A
     A companion to De Bell's The Environmental Hand-
book (90). Sensible primer and extremely informative source
book on important and often misunderstood legal aspects of
the environmental movement. It is not a how-to-get-corporate-
polluters-without-a-lawyer-and-collect-big-bounties-book.

213 LANDSBERG, Hans, Fischman, Leonard, and Fisher,
     Joseph. Resources in America's Future: Patterns
     of Requirements and Availabilities 1960-2000.
     Baltimore: Johns Hopkins University Press/Re-
     sources for the Future, 1963, $20, 1017p, illus
     (abridged pap ed avail, title: Natural Resources
     for U.S. Growth: A Look Ahead to the Year 2000,
     $2.45)
     L: Adv HS & up   S: Lu
     Very technical data on past uses and projected fu-
ture needs for resources, parks, packaging, etc. Fine graphs
and tables. Complete assessment; excellent source.

214 LATHAM, Jean Lee. Rachel Carson: Who Loved the
     Sea. Champaign, IL: Garrard, 1973, $2.84 (PLB),
     80p, illus
     L: 2-4   S: B/H
     A short, but factual and interesting career biography
of Rachel Carson that explains how Silent Spring grew out of
Carson's battle against the careless use of chemicals.
Latham gives some conservation/ecology background, also,
but fails to explain fully the theories Carson presents in
Silent Spring--perhaps understandably given the age level she
is writing for. Latham does stress Carson's sensitivity to
nature, along with the travails of her writing career. Large
print.

215 LAYCOCK, George. Air Pollution. New York:

Grossett & Dunlap, 1972, $4.95 ($3.99 PLB), 81p,
index
L: 4-6   S: Ap
Detailed analysis of air pollutants and solutions for
the pollution problem. Illustrations useful in explaining text
and identifying the various sources of air contaminants.

216 _____. Alaska: The Embattled Frontier. Boston:
Houghton Mifflin, 1971, $6.95, 205p, index
L: Adv HS & up   S: Lu/Cn
Analysis of Alaskan conservation, past, present,
and future. Details the conflict between exploitation and
preservation. (Audubon Library, Vol. I)

217 _____. America's Endangered Wildlife. New York:
W. W. Norton, 1969, $4.95 ($4.51 PLB), 226p,
illus
L: 5-9   S: Es
Good, extensive coverage with excellent photographs.

218 _____. Animal Movers: A Collection of Ecological
Surprises. Garden City, NY: Doubleday (Natural
History), 1971, $4.50, illus, 107p, index
L: 1-7   S: Ec
Explains the oftentimes dire consequences of re-
locating animal species (such as sparrows, rabbits, etc.) to
an alien environment where they have no predators and,
therefore, flourish to the point of becoming pests, risking
famine, etc.

219 _____. The Diligent Destroyers. Garden City, NY:
Doubleday, 1970, $5.95; also avail in pap, New
York: Ballantine, $1.25
L: HS & up   S: Lu/Ps
Discussion of corporations, politicians, and govern-
ment agencies who, for short-term gain, ravage the landscape
with highways, dams, strip mines, etc. and ideas on how to
stop them.

220 LEAF, Munro. Who Cares? I Do. Philadelphia:
Lippincott, 1971, $3.59 ($1.95 pap)
L: PS-3   S: R
Exposes the Spoilers, Droppers, and Wreckers who
litter the environment. The Spoilers include two sub-groups:
the Droppers who litter unconsciously; the Wreckers who
know very well what they are doing. They are the vandals.
But both types ruin the environment for all of us, and all of

us should take care we do not fall into either category.

221 LE CORBUSIER. The Athens Charter. New York:
        Grossman, 1973, $11.50, 111p, illus
        L: Adv HS & up   S: U
    Milestone avant-gardist manifesto in the development
of urban planning which came out of the fourth meeting of
CIAM (International Congress for Modern Architecture) in
1933. Sets down comprehensive outlines of problems and
workable solutions for urban centers in Chapter II which
should be required reading for city planners, environmentalists, politicians--anyone who is seriously interested in
concrete proposals for creating healthy, livable environments.
What is perhaps the most noteworthy achievement of this
work is that it is a multi-disciplined effort: a product
mainly of architects and city planners, but inspired, too,
by sociologists, economists, philosophers, educators, doc-
tors, and artists.

222 LEFKOWITZ, R. J.   Water for Today and Tomorrow.
        New York: Parents' Magazine Press, 1973, $3.97
        (PLB), 64p, index illus
        L: 2-4   S: Wp
    Lefkowitz analyzes city reservoir systems, the
process of cleaning drinking water supplies, general water
pollution problems, and water conservation. He incorporates
questions into the text that will stimulate classroom discussion. Ink drawings complement the narrative.

223 LEINWAND, Gerald, ed.   Air and Water Pollution.
        (Problems of American Society series.) New
        York: Washington Square Press, 1969, $0.75 (pap)
        L: 9-12   S: Wp/Ap
    Good introduction to the overall subject of air and
water pollution: its origins, its effects on all life, why we
have the problem of air and water pollution and what has to
be done about it.

224 LEOPOLD, Aldo.   A Sand County Almanac and Sketches
        Here and There. New York: Oxford University
        Press, 1949, $1.95 (pap), 226p, illus; also avail,
        New York: Ballantine, 1970, $0.95 (pap)
        L: HS & up   S: Pn
    One of the Conservation/Environmental "classics."
The Almanac details in personal narrative form how Leopold,
a professor of game management at the University of Wisconsin, and his family restored a worn-out and abandoned sand

farm in Wisconsin. In the first section, Leopold describes
what he and his family did weekends to restore the farm, arranging his "shack sketches" seasonally as a "Sand County
Almanac. " In the second part, "Sketches Here and There,"
he tells of those events in his own life that taught him,
gradually, that man is out of step with nature, and in the
third and last section, "The Upshot," he tells how we can
get back into step. Leopold warns in the introduction that
many will shun confrontation with the hard philosophical questions he raises in the last section, but this is the core of
the book and the rationale behind his thesis that land is to be
"loved and respected," not regarded as a mere commodity to
be passed between people for financial gain. A wonderful
book, and as timely today as it was when first published in
1948.

225 LEWIS, Alfred. Clean the Air: Fighting Smoke, Smog,
       and Smaze. New York: McGraw-Hill, 1965,
       $3.83 (PLB), 96p, index, illus
       L: JHS & up   S: Ap
       A sectional study, scientifically oriented, but not
overly technical. Good photographs supplement the text which
is good reference for grades seven and up.

226 LEYDET, Francois, ed. Tomorrow's Wilderness. San
       Francisco: Sierra Club, 264p (text) 32p (illus)
       L: JHS & up   S: W/A
       Eighth Biennial Wilderness Conference speeches, in-
cluding (among others), those of Paul Brooks, Fairfield Osborn, Wallace Stegner, Nathaniel Owings, and Stewart Udall.
Evaluates today's wilderness resources from the vantage points
of various prejudices and projects what lies ahead for our
wilderness areas' future. Out of print, but a good reference
with many fine photographs.

227 LILLARD, Richard G. The Great Forest. New York:
       Da Capo, 1973, reprint of 1947 Knopf ed, $15,
       399p, illus
       L: Adv HS & up   S: H/F
       Good history of the forest by an English professor
and amateur ecologist. His study of man's impact on the
American environment and the impact the American natural
environment has had on man's development is brilliant.
Highly recommended.

228 LINE, Les, ed. What We Save Now: An Audubon
       Primer of Defense. Boston: Houghton Mifflin,

1973, $10, 438p, index, illus
L: Adv HS & up   S: A/W
An excellent summary. Includes essays by Joseph
Wood Krutch, Archie Carr, Alvin Josephy, Jr., and Hal
Borland, all knowledgeable contributors. Basically, Line ex-
plores how to defend what wilderness still remains.

229 LINTON, Ron M. Terracide: America's Destruction of
     Her Living Environment. Boston: Little Brown,
     1970, $7.95, 354p; also avail in pap, New York:
     Paperback Library, 1971, $1.25
     L: Adv HS & up   S: O
     Linton examines human reactions to our fouled en-
vironment, the effects of commerce, industry, and the new
technology on the environment, and the proposed solution for
curing our current problems.

230 LITTLEWOOD, Cyril. The World's Vanishing Birds.
     New York: Arco, 1973, $5.95 (PLB), 63p, color
     illus and maps by D. W. Ovendeen
     L: 4 & up   S: Es
     Illustrations and descriptions of 60 endangered
species of rare birds, giving order, family, and physical appearance, birds' plight and background.

231 LIVINGSTON, John A. One Cosmic Instant: Man's
     Fleeting Supremacy. Boston: Houghton Mifflin,
     1973, $5.95, 240p, index
     L: Adv HS & up   S: H
     A capsule history of man's developing attitude
toward nature and his apparent need to dominate it.

232 LONGGOOD, William. The Darkening Land. New York:
     Simon & Schuster, 1972, $9.95, 572p, index
     L: HS & up   S: O
     A comprehensive report on all aspects of pollution;
a global approach but with emphasis on United States. Covers
water, air, poisons, population, wastes, power, despoilers,
and the choice of cataclysm or reform. Author is a Pulitzer
Prize winner.

233 LORD, Russell. The Care of the Earth. New York:
     Nelson, 1962, $0.95 (pap)
     L: Adv HS & up   S: W
     An excellent study of human impact on the American
wilderness and the effect of the wilderness on American
thought.

234 LOWENTHAL, David. <u>George Perkins Marsh: Versatile
     Vermonter.</u> New York: Columbia University Press,
     1958, $9
     L: HS & up   S: B/H
     The one and only biography of the father of ecology.
Lowenthal, an expert on Marsh, edited the Harvard reprint of
<u>Man and Nature</u>. Marsh was born in post-revolutionary Ver-
mont (1801), a man of uncommon intellect and unquenchable
thirst for knowledge. A professional and intellectual eclectic,
he accumulated a wide range of knowledge by reading (he began at the age of six by reading Reese's Encyclopedia), spoke
over twenty languages, and was a lawyer, professor, congressman, and eventually a diplomat. From his wide knowledge accrued through reading and travel, he put together what
he concluded was the synthesis and interdependency of nature
--the web of life--and what we now call ecology.

235 McCAMY, James L.   <u>The Quality of the Environment.</u>
     New York: The Free Press, 1972, $7.95, 320p,
     index
     L: Adv HS & up   S: O
     A topical review with analysis of the response by
the institutes of social change.

236 McCLELLAN, Grant S. , ed.   <u>Protecting Our Environ-
     ment.</u> (Reference Shelf, vol 42, no 1.) New York:
     Wilson, 1970, $4.50, 210p
     L: HS & up   S: O/A
     Compilation of articles reprinted from noted na-
tional periodicals that reflect the recent notion of man as
custodian of spaceship earth, a finite, perishable planet.
The first section deals with the global aspects of the overall
problem of pollution; the second part deals primarily with
American environmental problems: air pollution, saving our
waterways, and how we should deal with our natural landscape. The last section studies our national attempts to
handle environmental issues effectively and examines foreign
and international steps being taken to protect the global environment.

237 McCLUNEY, William R. , ed.   <u>Environmental Destruc-
     tion of South Florida: A Handbook for Citizens.</u>
     Coral Gables, F L: University of Miami Press,
     1971, $1.95 (pap), 134p
     L: HS & up   S: A/Lu/Cs
     Twenty-one non-technical essays with emphasis on
the Everglades and the wide range of pollution problems
threatening its survival.

238 McCLUNG, Robert M. Lost Wild America: The Story
     of Our Extinct and Vanishing Wildlife. New York:
     William Morrow, 1969, $5.95, 240p, index, illus
     L: 7 up   S: Es
     Good discussion, species by species, of the past,
present, and future outlook for America's wildlife. Excellent
pen and ink drawings.

239 _____. Mice, Moose, and Men: How Their Popula-
     tions Rise and Fall. New York: William Morrow,
     1973, $4.25 ($3.94 PLB), 64p, index, bibliog,
     illus
     L: 5-7   S: Ec/P
     Fine book of instruction in ecology, conservation,
and natural history. Explains how weather, water, and food
supplies affect animal populations and draws the obvious conclusions of how they must therefore affect human populations
also. See his other books, also published by Morrow: Caterpillars and How They Live, 1965 and Moths and Butterflies
and How They Live, 1966.

240 McCOY, J. J. Shadows Over the Land. New York:
     The Seabury Press, 1970, $4.95, 152p, index
     L: 5 up   S: O
     A comprehensive study of the environmental crisis
and a brief history of how it developed. The reading level
and information is not simplified, and it will, in most cases,
challenge even junior high school readers. McCoy discusses
the view of the whole earth as seen from the moon, then
separately, water, air, pesticides, farming, wildlife, wilderness, estuaries, cities, and finally, an analysis of the "new"
conservation. He includes a glossary, suggested readings,
recommended films, and a listing of the major conservation
groups. Other books of interest that he has written (1212,
1213) are listed in Section II.

241 McDONALD'S Corporation. Ecology Action Pack.
     Dayton, OH: Dayton Museum of Natural History,
     1973, 24p, illus
     L: 4-6   S: Ec/Ed
     Developed by the Dayton Museum of Natural History
to aid the teacher in teaching environmental awareness to
young children. The materials, according to the museum's
director E. J. Koestner, "may be used to introduce existing
units of study, may serve as high-interest supplements to a
textbook, or as a source of special projects." They are intended to stimulate thinking and activity in the area of

environmental problems, activities, and solutions. There are
five units within the pack: Make Your Own Ecology Mini-
Spinner; Let's Look at a Food Chain; Drip the Water Drop:
Save Me!; A Very Short History of Trash: How Paper Is
Recycled; and Be an Ecology Champion. Contained within
the booklet are 12 spirit duplicating masters, an overhead
transparency, and 10 pages of background information and
teaching suggestions. For further information write: A. E.
Doyle, 7th Floor, McDonald's Corp. , One McDonald's Plaza,
Oak Brook, IL 60521.

242 McGEARY, M. Nelson. Gifford Pinchot, Forester-
       Politician. Princeton, NJ: Princeton University
       Press, 1960, $13.50
       L: HS & up   S: B/H/F
       Biography of America's first forester and the father
of conservation. Excellent source on the origins of conservation with good coverage of the Ballinger-Pinchot affair and
Hetch Hetchy.

243 McHALE, John. The Ecological Context. New ed.
       New York: Braziller, 1970, $7.95, 188p, illus
       L: HS & up   S: O
       McHale is the director of the Center for Intergrative
Studies at the Binghamton campus of S. U. N. Y. His book
deals with earth's "life support" systems: energy and materials. Many graphic charts, documents, depiction of ecological systems and cycles, and cogent analysis, McHale
gives a very visible foundation for environmental planners
(both professional and lay), to work from. Chapters include
the Ecological Context, Man in the Biosphere, Population and
Food, Energy, Materials, and Ecological Redesign. An excellent source.

244 McHARG, Ian L. Design with Nature. Garden City,
       NY: Doubleday (Natural History), 1971, $19.95,
       ($5.95 pap), 197p, index, illus
       L: HS & up   S: Lu/U/At
       McHarg analyzes his own designs, how he takes
into consideration all aspects of the natural environmental
conditions into which his own physical development schemes
are to fit. He contends that landscape architecture and community design must be implemented only after full and careful
resource and ecological analysis of the region to be altered.
A good start towards sane physical development. See Le
Corbusier's The Athens Charter (221).

245 McHENRY, Robert, ed., with Charles Van Doren. <u>A</u>
     <u>Documentary History of Conservation in America.</u>
     New York: Praeger, 1972, $13.50 ($5.95 pap),
     422p, author index
     L: HS & up   S: H/A
     211 excerpts from original documents detailing the
origins of the American environmental movement from the
1200's to the present. Starts with English literary works
which influenced later American thought. Strongly suggested
for any history teacher. A superlative source book or adjunct text for cultural history classes.

246 McHUGH, Tom. <u>The Time of the Buffalo.</u> New York:
     Knopf, 1972, $10, 339p
     L: HS & up   S: H/Es
     A history of the buffalo, his relationship with the
American Indian, and his near extinction at the hand of white
man. This is an excellent book; the illustrations are superb.

247 McNAUGHTON, S. J. and Wolf, Larry L. <u>General</u>
     <u>Ecology.</u> New York: Holt, Rinehart & Winston,
     1973, $13, 710p, index, illus
     L: College   S: Ec/Ed
     Yet another text based on evolution and adaptation
of species, taking for granted that the student is familiar
with the basic processes of natural selection. This aspect
of ecology, therefore, is not explicitly discussed. McNaughton
and Wolf assume its validity, using it as a base on which they
build their own arguments.

248 McNULTY, Faith. <u>Must They Die? The Strange Case</u>
     <u>of the Prairie Dog and the Black Footed Ferret.</u>
     Garden City, NY: Doubleday, 1971, $4.95; also
     avail in pap, New York: Ballantine, 1972, $0.95,
     96p
     L: HS & up   S: Es/Ps
     Exposes American Government's dichotomous atti-
tude and cross-purpose operations with regard to the prairie
dog. Some agencies are trying to protect it; others, to ap-
pease ranchers, poison it. See also author's <u>Whooping</u>
<u>Crane: The Bird That Defies Extinction</u> (1217).

249 McPHEE, John. <u>Encounters with the Archdruid.</u> New
     York: Farrar, Straus & Giroux, 1971, $6.95;
     also avail in pap, New York: Ballantine, 1972,
     $1.25
     L: Adv HS & up   S: O/Pn

A recounting of dialogues between David Brower
(head of Friends of the Earth), a developer, a dam engineer,
and a mineral engineer who journey together on three separate occasions through the wilderness. They discuss their
jobs and their own particular concerns. The book is an interesting exposure of their conflicting interests and priorities.

250 MADDOX, John. The Doomsday Syndrome. New York:
     McGraw-Hill, 1972, $6.95, 293p (pap, 1973,
     $2.95)
     L: HS & up   S: C
     Graceful, sophisticated pricking of some over-blown
eco-evangelistic balloons and well-founded plea against the
dangerous pessimism that can result from the all-is-lost
syndrome. Not an anti-environmental book, rather a gal-
vanizing message of hope: we can set it right again if we
get busy and do it.

251 MALTHUS, Thomas Robert. On Population. Ed. and
     introduced by Gertrude Himmelfarb. New York:
     Random (Modern Library), 1960, 602p, $2.45,
     index
     L: Adv HS & up   S: P/H
     Malthus (1766-1834) shattered in 1798 the unfounded,
yet popular, notion that the destiny of man could follow the
course of unlimited progress. The problem, he argued, is
that while both food and the need to procreate are essential
for human existence, food increases arithmetically and population geometrically. This book includes his original 1798
essay on the Principle of Population, and discusses among a
great many other things, the difficulties arising from population growth, the different ratios in which population and food
increase, the effects of this difference, the hunter versus the
shepherd-type society, the principal checks to population in
less civilized nations (in past times, and in the different
states of modern Europe), and the future possibilities if the
evils stemming from unchecked population growth were re-
moved. A classic, as timely today as it was, undoubtably,
when Malthus wrote it.

252 MARINE, Gene. America the Raped. New York:
     Simon & Schuster, 1969, $5.95, 312p, index
     L: 8-12   S: Lu
     A selection of case studies illustrating how the en-
gineering mentality of many Americans, its compulsion to
build without regard for either the peoples' welfare or that
of the land, has devastated the North American continent.

A good source for getting closer to the source of our problems. Marine is an editor of Ramparts.

253 _____ and Van Allen, Judith. Food Pollution: The Violation of Our Inner Ecology. New York: Holt, Rinehart & Winston, 1972, $8.95 ($2.95 pap), 385p, index
     L: HS & up   S: Fp
     This extremely thorough and well-documented treatise on food additives was one of the 100 Best Sci-Tech Books of 1972 according to Library Journal.

254 MARSH, George Perkins. Earth As Modified by Human Action (orig title, Man and Nature). St. Clair Shores, MI: Scholarly Press, 1970 (reprint of 1874 ed), $21
     L: Adv HS & up   S: H/Ec
     Revised edition of next entry.

255 _____. Man and Nature. Facsimile edition, ed. by David Lowenthal. Cambridge, MA: Harvard University Press, 1965, $12.50, 472p, index
     L: Adv HS & up   S: H/Ec
     The book that put everything together by the first American to understand the importance of what we now call ecology. Marsh's primary thesis is that man should work in harmony with nature, not at odds with it. He divides his book into sectional discussions: the first on woods lays a firm foundation for the later efforts of American foresters; the second on "The Transfer, Modification, and Extirpation of Vegetable and Animal Species" deals with man's conscious and unconscious alterations of nature; another on water deals with the uses and effects of dikes, aqueducts, etc.; "The Sands" analyzes the origin, composition, and distribution of the great dunes and their relationship to bodies of water; and "Projected or Possible Geographical Changes by Man" contains practical and long range applications of his theories, the probable effects on nature of man's technology. A stunning and formidable work.

256 MARSHALL, James. The Air We Live In--Air Pollution: What We Must Do About It. New York: Coward, McCann & Geoghegan, 1969, $4.49 (PLB), 95p, illus
     L: 6-9   S: Ap
     The whys, hows, and technological solutions to air pollution. Includes excellent photographs and provocative text

that encourages the child to draw some of his own conclusions
and think about what he can do to help stop air pollution.
Part of the New Conservation Series.

257 _____ Going to Waste: Where Will All the Garbage
        Go? New York: Coward, McCann & Geoghegan,
        1972, $4.49 (PLB), 92p, illus
        L: 7-11   S: Wt
        A well balanced treatment of garbage and packaging.
Good illustrations. Thorough coverage. Encourages young
reader to think further and deeper into the subject and about
what he or she can do to help alleviate the solid waste problem. Part of the New Conservation Series.

258 MARTIN, Cy. Saga of the Buffalo. New York: Hart,
        1973, $4.95 (pap), 188p, illus
        L: HS & up   S: Es/H
        Describes the Indian's relationship to the buffalo,
the buffalo's decimation by the white man who in fifty years
reduced its numbers from 75 million to a mere 2500. The
white extermination squads included the Army, who wanted to
wipe out the Indian's food supply, the hide-hunters, railroad
builders, and so-called "sportsmen" and trophy hunters.

259 MARX, Leo. The Machine in the Garden: Technology
        and the Pastoral Ideal in America. New York:
        Oxford University Press, 1964, $11.50 (pap, 1967,
        $2.95)
        L: Adv HS & up   S: H/T
        Excellent cultural history which sheds light on the
deep and often conflicting values that permeate American culture. A great help in understanding American attitudes
toward the natural world.

260 MARX, Wesley. The Frail Ocean. New York: Ballan-
        tine, 1969, $0.95 (pap), 274p; hardbound ed avail,
        New York: Coward, McCann, 1970, $6.95, 240p
        L: HS & up   S: Wp
        Marx brilliantly dynamites two rampant myths:
(1) that the ocean's resources will eventually solve the so-
called food problem, and (2) that the dreams of visionaries
for underwater cities, farms, etc., can come true. The
sea, Marx explains, is not a new frontier waiting to be ex-
ploited; it is not an untapped goldmine. It is rather the
largest source of the earth's oxygen supply and destroying
its delicate ecological balance will destroy man as well as
the other oxygen-dependent creatures. A superb book.

261 _____. Man and His Environment: Waste. New
        York: Harper & Row, 1971, $6 ($3.25 pap),
        179p, index, illus
        L: Adv HS & up   S: Wt
        A concise non-technical examination of all waste
emissions. Marx's view is comprehensive, his treatment
approached from a variety of viewpoints which he weaves
deftly into a smoothe, comprehensible account, giving an
overall perspective of the total impact on the environment
of all wastes: liquid, gaseous, solid, noise, radiation. He
examines the methods of control, their limitations, and the
relationship of waste generation and our present methods of
trying to control it to our methods of resource utilization.
His purpose is to provide the student with the basic concepts
of the problem and to give him some of the necessary insights to apply them. He includes a farsighted examination
of behavioral changes individuals and society alike may have
to undergo to adequately control wasteful depletion of resources
and waste pollution and also details a semi-enclosed system
of resource utilization that includes recycling wastes, and
low pollution methods of transportation, energy, and pest control. Also in this Man and His Environment series: Lester
Brown and Gail Finsterbush's Food (45), David Gates's Climate (137), and Earl Finbar Murphy's Law (279). Books on
population (Robert Cook) and policy and administration (Lynton
Caldwell) are also planned.

262 _____. Oilspill. San Francisco: Sierra Club, 1972,
        $2.75 (pap), 139p
        L: HS & up   S: Ol
        The causes, effects, and political ramifications of
oilspills. Marx analyzes the scientific and ecological aspects
of the issue and explains how political and economic considerations also are involved. An excellent source.

263 _____. The Protected Ocean: How to Keep the Seas
        Alive. (New Conservation Series.) New York:
        Coward, McCann, 1972, $4.86 (PLB), 195p, illus
        L: 7 up   S: Wp
        An analysis of ocean resources and how the ocean's
delicate balance is threatened by pollution.

264 MASON, George F. The Wildlife of North America.
        New York: Hastings House, 1966, $4.17 (PLB),
        87p, illus
        L: 6-9   S: Es/Wp
        Basically a nature/wildlife book, but includes also

a lucid discussion of water pollution's effects on wildlife and remedial suggestions available through conservation. Mason examines, also, the first land animals, mammals, birds, and insects.

265   MAY, Julian.   Blue River.   New York: Holiday House,
      1971, $4.95
      L: K-3   S: R/Wp
      A good early reader.   Tells of a polluted river and
how it was cleaned by the townspeople living in the village
through which the river flows.

266   MEADOWS, Dennis, et al.   The Limits to Growth: A
      Report for the Club of Rome Project on the Pre-
      dicament of Mankind.   New York: Universe Books,
      1972, $6.50 ($2.75 pap), 207p, illus
      L: Adv HS & up   S: O/T/I
      A series of computer simulations of the world's
natural and economic systems programmed by a team of
M.I.T. scientists.   By varying different factors, imposing
alternate sets of controls, and then allowing the system to
run its course, the Meadows group illustrates the consequences of our present growth patterns.   Most of the simula-
tions result in economic collapse well within the next century.
Only by reorganizing our priorities, economic systems, etc.,
can it be avoided.   The impact is devastating.   Useful not only
in social studies, environmental studies, and science classes,
but in mathematics and economics classes as well.   Chosen as
one of the best environmental books by Friends of the Earth.

267   MILLARD, Reed and Science Book Associates Editors.
      Clean Air--Clean Water for Tomorrow's World.
      New York: Julian Messner, 1971, $4.29 (PLB),
      190p, index, illus
      L: 7 up   S: Ap/Wp
      Excellent, detailed discussion of air and water pol-
lution and the many possible alternative remedies.   Scientifically oriented.

268   MILNE, Lorus and Milne, Margery.   Arena of Life:
      The Dynamics of Ecology.   Garden City, NY:
      Doubleday, 1972, $15, 351p, index, illus
      L: HS & up   S: Ec
      A copiously illustrated summary of the science of
ecology, characteristically well-presented by this prolific
writing team.   See also their Nature of Life: The Earth,
Plants, Animals and Man and How They Affect Each Other.
(New York: Crown, 1970, $17.50, illus, gr 6 up) and Balance

of Nature (New York: Knopf, 1960, $6.95, HS & up).

269   MINES, Samuel.   The Last Days of Mankind.   New
         York: Simon & Schuster, 1971, $7.95, 320p,
         index
         L: HS & up   S: O
      An excellent series of overview cases which view
man as an endangered species. Covers water, woods, wildlife, urban ecology, roads, pesticides, and the Public Domain.

270   MINNESOTA Environmental Sciences Foundation.   En-
         vironmental Discovery Units.   Washington, DC:
         National Wildlife Federation, 1973, price of in-
         dividual units either $1 or $1.50
         L: 1-11   S: Ed
      Individual units, including order no. and grade level:
         79007   Plants in the Classroom   3-6
         79016   Vacant Lots Studies   5-9
         79025   Differences in Living Things   4-8
         79034   Shadows   1-8
         79043   Wind   3-6
         79052   Snow and Ice   1-6
         79061   Man's Habitat--The City   4-9
         79070   Fish and Water Temperature   4-9
         79089   Oaks, Acorns, Climate and
                    Squirrels   1-6
         79105   Nature Hunt   (Spec Ed)   K-1
         79098   Sampling Button Populations   3-9
         79114   The Rise and Fall of a Yeast
                    Community   6-9
         79123   Genetic Variation   4-9
         79132   Soil   2-9
         79141   Tile Patterns and Graphs   1-2
         79150   Plant Puzzles   1-6
         79169   Brine Shrimp and Their Habitat   1-5
         79178   Nature's Part in Art   3-6
         79212   Contour Mapping   4-9
         79187   Change in a Small Ecosystem   5-9
         79196   Transect Studies   3-9
         79203   Stream Profiles   4-9
         79221   Color and Change   K-2
         79230   Outdoor Fun for Students   1-11
      For a free brochure describing activities in the in-
dividual units, write: The National Wildlife Federation, Educational Servicing, 1412 16th St., N.W., Washington, DC
20036.   Each unit comes with a teacher's preparation booklet
which gives thorough directions on how to use the unit.   The

units themselves comprise a series of experiments that illustrate how the various subjects are important in the overall
environment.   For instance with snow, there is not only a
study of the scientific properties of snow (how it is formed,
etc.), but an explanation of its ecological properties as an
insulator, how animals stay alive in it, etc.

271   MITCHELL, John G. and Stallings, Constance L., eds.
      Ecotactics: The Sierra Club Handbook for Environ-
      mental Activists.   New York: Trident, 1970, 288p,
      $6.95; also avail in pap, New York: Simon &
      Schuster, 1970, $1.95, and New York: Pocket
      Books, 1970, $0.95
      L: HS & up   S: A/O
      "Ecotactics," as the authors define it, is "the
science of arranging and maneuvering all available forces in
action against enemies of the earth." It also means teach-
ins, confrontations with industrial polluters, activating community concern, boycotts, education, advertising, etc.   Includes chapters on three activists: Stephanie Mills, Gary
Snyder, and December Duke--a 19-year-old girl who demon-
strates in front of General Motors.   For the young and/or
radical, but with many sound suggestions for the more con-
servative also.

272   MIZMURA, Kazue.   If I Built a Village.   New York:
      Crowell, Collier, 1971, $4.50, illus, unpaged.
      L: K-3   S: R/U
      "If I built my village, my town, and my city--
there would be people who care and share with all living
things the land they love." It would be a natural city with
whales and eagles, a nice place to live.   This is a gentle,
but useful book for young (very young) children, as it gives
them the notion that a city can and should be a pleasant place
to be and it should be natural, or at the very least, accom-
modate natural things.

273   MONTAGUE, Katherine and Montague, Peter.   Mercury.
      (Battlebook #2.)   San Francisco: Sierra Club,
      1972, $2.25, 158p
      L: HS & up   S: Fp/Wp
      Analysis, through case studies, of mercury poison-
ing, its effects, and its causes.   Focuses on the case of the
Huckleby family in New Mexico whose pork was poisoned by
mercury polluted grain and includes case of Minamata, Japan.
Devastating account.

274 MOORCRAFT, Colin. <u>Must the Seas Die</u>? Boston: Gam-
        bit, 1973, $6.95, 194p, index, illus
        L: HS & up   S: Wp
        <u>Library Journal</u> recommends it for most libraries.
A frightening account of finite limits of our oceans' resources
and need for world governments to work in concert to save
them. Moorcraft describes in detail for the layman the extent of pollution and dumping, as well as the finiteness and
fragility of the world's oceans.

275 MOWAT, Farley. <u>Never Cry Wolf</u>. Boston: Little,
        Brown, 1963, $5.75, 176p; also avail in pap,
        New York: Dell, 1963, $0.75
        L: HS & up   S: Es/Pn
        The real story of wolves is not in <u>Little Red Riding</u>
<u>Hood</u>, it is here. Mowat punctures the myth of the vicious,
ferocious wolf. A good story.

276 _____. <u>A Whale for the Killing</u>. Boston: Little,
        Brown, 1972, $6.95, 239p; also avail in pap,
        Baltimore: Penguin, 1973, $1.50; condensed in
        <u>Reader's Digest</u>, February 1973
        L: HS & up   S: Es/Pn
        The powerful story of a trapped Fin whale which
unthinking Newfoundlanders make into a living target gallery
for the fun of it. Farley, a non-native and "outsider" tries
to save the whale by launching a public campaign in her defense. "Moby Joe" dies, climaxing a moving, agonizing de-
nouement, but the encounter between animal, man, and community makes for thought-provoking reading and class discussion once the tears subside. Throughout the narrative, fur-
thermore, Mowat infuses information on the present plight of
all whales.

277 MUMFORD, Lewis. <u>The City in History: Its Origins,</u>
        <u>Its Transformations, and Its Prospects</u>. New York:
        Harcourt, Brace, Jovanovich, 1961, $15 ($4.95
        pap), 657p, index, illus
        L: Adv HS & up   S: U/H/Lu
        The complete analysis of cities throughout history.
An excellent source for finding out how our urban dilemmas
develop and how some cities have successfully coped with the
problems inherent in urban concentrations. Extremely
thorough and worthwhile study.

278 MURPHY, Earl F. <u>Governing Nature</u>. New York:

Watts, 1970, $2.95 (pap), 333p, index
    L: Adv HS & up   S: O/Ps
    A summary of past and present interaction between
government and nature, focusing on what Murphy describes as
the "life cycle" resources: air, water, and land.

279 _____. Man and His Environment: Law. New York:
         Harper & Row, 1971, $3.25 (pap), 168p, index
         L: Adv HS & up   S: L
         Like the other books in Harper & Row's Man and
His Environment series, an extremely well done, concise,
nontechnical treatment of the subject, geared to give the student a thorough background, the facts, and the ability to apply the
basic concepts. Also in the series: Wesley Marx's Waste
(261), Lester Brown and Gail Finsterbush's Food (45), David
Gates's Climate (137). Books on population (Robert Cook) and
policy and administration (Lynton Caldwell) are also planned.

280 NASH, Roderick. The American Environment: Readings
         in the History of Conservation. Reading, MA:
         Addison-Wesley, 1966, $3.25 (school price $2),
         236p, bibliog
         L: HS & up   S: H/Cn
         Nash explores the development of the American con-
servation movement both as a concept and as a reality, extending his scope beyond the strict defining limits of the term
"conservation" to include the total environment of historical
sites, roads, even cities. He divides the book into four
parts: the Conservation Impulse, the Progressive Conservation Crusade, Conservation Between the Wars, and Conservation as Quality of the Environment. Included are comments
by the contemporary historians on leading conservation writers
as well as the writings of these men themselves. Thirty-six
conservationists are represented, among them: Catlin,
Thoreau, Marsh, Theodore Roosevelt, Pinchot, Muir, Rachel
Carson, Leopold, Lyndon Johnson, and Udall. An excellent
book.

281 _____. Wilderness and the American Mind. Rev.
         ed. New Haven: Yale University Press, 1973,
         $10 ($2.95 pap), 256p, index
         L: Adv HS & up   S: H/W
         Strictly speaking, a social history, but Nash does
much more than simply trace social attitudes: he explores
the roots of American awareness of its wilderness areas
and, beginning with the first settlement, tracks through American thought how we have treated our land during our 350

year development.   He begins with a study of the Old World
and the significance of wild country from the days of the Old
Testament through the time where peoples' appreciations of
wilderness increased as its dimensions shrank--this along
with the Romantics and the new religious and ethical concepts
and the call to preserve our dwindling forests in the public's
own interest.   Among topics included: the condition of the
wilderness, Old World roots of opinion, the American wilderness, Thoreau, Preservation, John Muir, Hetch Hetchy, and
Aldo Leopold.

282 _____, ed. The Call of the Wild. (American Cul-
        ture Series.) New York: Braziller, 1970, $7.50
        ($3.95 pap)
        L: HS & up   S: H
        A cultural history of the era 1900-1916, with very
good sections on America's changing attitudes toward the environment.   The change was brought about by the emerging
conservation movement and Theodore Roosevelt's presidency.
Nash shows how conservation pervaded the culture of the
time, one example being Frank Lloyd Wright's naturalist architecture, the blending of physical forms into the surrounding
natural environment.

283 NATIONAL Academy of Sciences and National Research
        Council. Resources and Man: A Study and Recom-
        mendations by the Commission on Resources and
        Man. San Francisco: W. H. Freeman, 1969,
        $5.95 ($2.95 pap), illus
        L: HS & up   S: O
        An introduction to the problem of our national re-
sources, covering the ecology and geography of resources,
demographic trends, and whether or not there are adequate
resources of food, minerals, and energy to meet present and
future needs of man.

284 NATIONAL Audubon Society. Ecosystems. New York:
        The Society, 1972, 16p, bibliog, illus
        L: 6 up   S: Ec/Ed
        An excellent booklet, containing description and il-
lustrations of the seven North American biomes.   Also included is a fold-over rendering of a rural American ecosystem
with several plastic overlays diagramming food chains, the
nitrogen cycle, the carbon cycle, and the water cycle.   The
booklet is extremely well done and makes a complex subject
easily comprehensible.   Children will love the illustrations
of the animals.   The reading level is for junior high school

students, but the teacher can use it as an effective teaching
aid with younger children.   For details and other teaching
aids, write the National Audubon Society, 950 Third Ave.,
New York, NY 10022.

285 _____. A Place to Live.   New York: The Society,
        1970, 64p, (52p teacher's manual avail), illus
        L: 2-4   S: Ec/Ed
        A discovery workbook on urban ecology, stressing
the child's relationship to his immediate, local surroundings.
Works on the basic concept that man is but one animal within
the ecosystem.   An excellent curriculum aid for the urban
child.   Teacher's manual is very comprehensive and helpful.
Write to National Audubon Society, 950 Third Ave., New
York, NY 10022 for details and other educational materials.

286 NATIONAL Environmental Education Development [NEED]
        Program.   Adventure in Environment.   New York:
        Silver Burdett, 1971 (includes teacher's guide and
        Outdoor Book)
        L: 5-9   S: Ec/Ed
        Emphasis on explaining to students how their atti-
tudes and habits will determine their own future environmental
quality.   Book is structured around five excellent principles:
(1) Variety and Similarity, (2) Patterns, (3) Interaction and
Interdependence, (4) Continuity and Changes, and (5) Adaptation and Evolution.

287 NAVARRA, John G.   The World You Inherit: A Story
        of Pollution.   Garden City, NY: Doubleday (Natural
        History), 1970, $5.50, 192p, index, illus
        L: 6-9   S: O
        An excellent overview of the entire pollution problem
by a world-renowned scientist.   Dr. Navarra is a professor of
geoscience and former chairman of the division of science at
Jersey City State College.   His appeal for common sense in
dealing with our environment, buttressed by sometimes shocking photographs (even now, when we have become hardened to
chemical effluents in rivers, belching smokestacks, etc.) and
documentable evidence of air, water, and soil pollution will
ring a sympathetic chord with any reader.   Navarra's prose
is readable, and his arguments sound.   An extremely good
book.

288 NELKIN, Dorothy.   Nuclear Power and Its Critics:
        The Cayuga Lake Controversy.   Ithaca, NY: Cor-
        nell University Press, 1971, $6.50 ($1.75 pap),
        128p, index, illus

L: College   S: N/Cs
A very detailed, technical study of a proposed nu-
clear power plant on Lake Cayuga near Cornell University.
Not easy reading, but an excellent study.

289 NICHOLSON, Max. Environmental Revolution: A Guide
        For the New Masters of the Earth. New York:
        McGraw-Hill, 1970, $10
        L: HS & up   S: P/F
        Nicholson is former head of the Nature Conservancy.
This book is a comprehensive world view of the present state
of the environment and the emerging so-called environmental
revolution. Nicholson's focus, however, is on British and
American environmental history, problems, etc.

290 NICKELSBURG, Janet. Ecology: Habitats, Niches, and
        Food Chains. Philadelphia: Lippincott, 1969,
        $4.43, 128p, index, illus
        L: 7 up   S: Ec
        A survey of all the principles of ecology. Explores
various biomes in the United States, the habitats within the
biomes, the many organisms' roles within the biomes, and
food chains.

291 _____. Field Trips: Ecology for Youth Leaders.
        Minneapolis: Burgess, 1966, $3.95 (pap), 120p,
        illus
        L: Adult   S: Ec/Ed
        A concise review for fieldtrip leaders. Covers all
the ecological biomes and shows how the leader can draw
upon them to educate his students. The coverage is general,
perhaps unavoidably so, but the principles are sound and
easily applicable to specific trips.

292 NOBILE, Philip and Deedy, John. The Complete
        Ecology Fact Book. Garden City, NY: Doubleday,
        1972, $10, 472p, index, illus
        L: 7 up   S: DBI
        A better title would be the "Complete Environmental
Almanac." Includes statistics and tables on population, endangered species, pollution, detergents, food, pesticides,
solid wastes, and mineral wastes. An excellent source.

293 NYE, Russel B. This Almost Chosen People: Essays
        in the History of American Ideas. East Lansing,
        MI: Michigan State University Press, 1966, $7.50,
        index

L: College/Adv HS research   S: H
Scholarly account of Americans' experience with nature.   Especially relevant for the student of America's attitudes towards the natural environment is his chapter entitled
"The American View of Nature." Basically a college reference, but useful also for advanced high school students re-
searching this aspect of America's cultural history.

294   ODUM, Eugene P.   Fundamentals of Ecology.   3d ed.
      Philadelphia: Saunders, 1971, $11.75, 574p, index,
      illus
      L: Adv HS & up   S: Ec/Ed
An in-depth ecology text for school use, but it can
also be used to great advantage as a source book for the interested layman.   Covers three basic units: I: Basic Ecological Principles and Concepts; II: The Habitat Approach;
and III: Applications and Technology.   But the book, basically, is three books in one.   Book One (Chapters 1-4, 9,
15, 16, and 21), gives the "big picture" of the relationship
of ecology and human affairs and serves as a review of
ecology for concerned citizens and non-scientific students of
the environment.   It is also a useful, adjunct reference for
"man in the environment" or "human ecology" courses.
Book Two (Chapters 1-10, 15, 16, and 21), serves as a text
for the college undergraduate ecology course and Book Three
(the whole book), is recommended as a comprehensive reference or graduate text on principles, environments, and ecological technology.

295   OGDEN, Samuel R. , ed.   America the Vanishing:
      Rural Life and the Price of Progress.   Brattleboro,
      VT: Greene, 1969, $6.95 ($3.95 pap), 241p, illus
      L: HS & up   S: A/H
An historical anthology of environmental writers, in-
cluding (among others), Audubon, Parkman, Muir, Twain, the
Milnes, Commoner, and Carson.

296   OLSEN, Jack.   Slaughter the Animals, Poison the Earth.
      New York: Simon & Schuster, 1971, $6.95, 287p,
      illus
      L: HS & up   S: Es/Pc/Ps
Olsen concentrates on the extermination of the
coyote, but examines how all wildlife is being systematically
poisoned in the Western United States by stockmen and
ranchers working in cooperation with government agencies.
The policy has driven the wildcats, wolves, eagles, bears,
mountain lions, and coyotes--the great predators--to virtual

extinction.   A chilling indictment of man.

297 OLYMPUS Research Corporation.   Career Education in
     the Environment: A Handbook.   Washington, DC:
     U. S. Government Printing Office, approx 485p
     L: HS & up   S: Ed/Cr
     This handbook is, according to the compilers, "de-
signed to be used in secondary schools to explore environmental problems and solutions and to provide information on
existing and emerging career opportunities in this field.   It
is directed toward and intended to be used by school administrators, curriculum planners, life sciences and social sciences
instructors, vocational counselors, librarians, and students. "
The first section on career education and the environment reviews the nature and extent of environmental pollution, giving
social, technical, and cultural reasons for it as well as some
solutions.   The second chapter, Environmental Careers, lists
the various career possibilities in environmentally related
fields.   They are categorized, the jobs described, earning
potentials cited, etc.   Chapter Three: Environmental Education Curriculum, contains two sources of environmental education, including lesson plans, teacher's manual, etc. , and
Chapter Four: Bibliography, includes selections on general
and specialized environmental topics.

298 The ORYX GROUP, Inc.   Environment U. S. A. A. Guide
     to Agencies, People, and Resources.   Ann Arbor:
     Bowker (The Oryx Press), 1973, $15. 95, 416p
     L: HS & up   S: DBI
     Includes almost 6000 of the most important sources
of environmental information in the United States, such as
what and where to get conservation films, local agencies, environmental libraries, job opportunities, state, federal, citizen, and professional agencies, essays on environmental law,
fund raising, and more.

299 OSBORN, Fairfield.   Our Plundered Planet.   Boston:
     Little, Brown, 1948, $4. 50; also avail in pap,
     New York: Pyramid Publications, 1970, $0. 95
     L: HS & up   S: O
     A postwar world assessment that (while obviously
dated), contains some fascinating material and is an excep-
tionally good review.

300 PACKARD, Vance.   The Waste Makers.   New York:
     McKay, 1960, $7. 95 ($0. 95 pap)
     L: 9 up   S: Wt

A hard look at the contemporary American--i. e.
the consumer: the waster, litterer, polluter, etc.   Popular,
good reading, and even after 14 years in print a widely read
book.

301   PEDDIWELL, J. Abner.   Saber-Tooth Curriculum.   New
         York: McGraw-Hill, 1939, $3.90 ($1.95 pap)
         L: Adult   S: Ed
         As valuable today as it was 35 years ago.   A clas-
sic study of the problems of confronting the environment with
curriculum and the curriculum with the environment.

302   PERCIVALL, Julia and Burger, Pixie.   Household
         Ecology.   Englewood Cliffs, NJ: Prentice-Hall,
         1971, $5.95, 230p, index
         L: HS & up   S: Ha
         Practical methods and materials for the house-
keeper that avoid damage to the environment but which are,
nonetheless, effective and get the job done.

303   PERERA, Thomas B. and Orlowsky, Wallace.   Who
         Will Clean the Air?   New York: Coward McCann,
         1971, $3.86 (PLB), illus
         L: 2-3   S: Ap
         Review of all aspects of air pollution and the pos-
sible technological remedial methods now available.   See also
his companion book, Who Will Wash the River? (New York:
Coward McCann, 1970, $3.86 PLB, illus, gr K-3).

304   PERRY, John.   Our Polluted World: Can Man Survive?
         New York: Watts, 1972, $5.95 ($4.95 PLB), 237p,
         index
         L: 7 up   S: O
         Details the progress against pollution made in the
last five years.   Covers all forms and how they are and
should be treated.   His outlook, however, is pessimistic.

305   PINCHOT, Gifford.   Breaking New Ground.   Seattle:
         University of Washington Press, 1972, reprint of
         1945 ed, $10.50, illus
         L: HS & up   S: B/H/I
         Pinchot's autobiography, relating his Forest Service
career, progressive politics, relationship with Theodore
Roosevelt, and his philosophy of conservation.   Analyzes the
Ballinger-Pinchot Affair, but discretely avoids Hetch Hetchy.

306   _____.   The Fight For Conservation.   Seattle:

University of Washington Press, 1967, reprint of
1910 ed, $7.50 ($2.45 pap), 152p, index
L: HS & up   S: H
A summary of conservation by the man who invented
the term. Excellent for use as an original source. Bonus:
condensed discussion of progressive thought during the first
decade of this century.

307 PLATT, Rutherford. The Great American Forest.
Englewood Cliffs, NJ: Prentice-Hall, 1971, $2.95
(pap), 271p, index, illus
L: HS & up   S: W/F
Platt describes the forests, their make-up, development, function, their importance, and what man does to them.
Included is a chapter on Alexander MacKenzie and his 3000-
mile round trip journey on the MacKenzie River (1789) and
his 1793 conquest of the Rocky Mountain coast range country
between the canoe country and the Pacific. Most important
(for the student of the environment), is his explanation of the
importance of our forests in relation to the total environment,
as water collectors, evaporation inhibitors, and protectors of
the ground from the direct rays of the sun. He also illustrates the importance of the forests to man both materially
and spiritually. His writing is forceful, artistic; the message is clear. A fine book.

308 PODENDORF, Illa. Every Day Is Earth Day. Chicago:
Children's Press, 1971, $4.50 (PLB), 48p, illus
L: 2-3   S: R/Ap/Wp/En
Podendorf was formerly chairman of the Science
Department of the Laboratory Schools, University of Chicago.
In his books, he emphasizes the processes of observing,
classifying, communicating, measuring, inferring, and pre-
dicting--all important elements in activating a child's thinking
processes. This book includes examples of written and
verbal communicating techniques, shows how to use the drawings and graphs, and provides opportunities for making pre-
dictions and inferences. Also tells what the young child can
do to further environmental awareness. An excellent book.

309 POMERANTZ, Charlotte. The Day They Parachuted
Cats on Borneo: A Drama of Ecology. Reading,
MA: Addison-Wesley, 1971, $4.75 (PLB), illus,
unpag
L: 3-7   S: Ec/Pc/En
A true story (New York Times: 11/13/69) that
Pomerantz has adapted into a play for young school children.

The island of Borneo is sprayed with DDT to kill malarial
mosquitoes, but the poison makes its way up the food chain
through the cockroaches, caterpillars, and lizards to the cats.
The cats die, and the rats then multiply at such an alarming
rate that the Government decides to parachute to the rescue
an army of parapussycats. A wonderful, absorbing story.

310 POTTER, Jeffery. Disaster by Oil: Oil Spills, Why
        They Happen, What They Do, How We Can End
        Them. New York: Macmillan, 1973, $7.95, 301p
        L: HS & up   S: Ol/Wp
        An analysis of tanker accidents and off-shore blow-
outs. Examines suggested technical solutions, the energy
crisis, and potential Atlantic off-shore drilling.

311 PRINGLE, Laurence. Ecology: Science of Survival.
        New York: Macmillan, 1971, $4.95 ($1.96 pap)
        text, illus
        L: 7 up   S: Ec
        Concentrates on organisms and their interaction
with surrounding habitat. Includes the various cycles and
some references to pollution and its effects.

312 _____. Into the Woods: Exploring the Forest Eco-
        system. New York: Macmillan, 1973, $4.95
        (PLB), illus, 64p
        L: 3-6   S: Ec/F
        Pringle explains the forest to young children--its
make-up, levels of life within it, how people should care for
it. His focus is on plants and animals of forests in the
temperate zones, though he touches, also, on the tropical
and rain forests.

313 _____. One Earth, Many People: The Challenge of
        Human Population Growth. New York: Macmillan,
        1971, $4.95 ($1.96 pap), 86p, index, illus
        L: 5 up   S: P
        Explains population, the problems it creates, and
the limits to the earth's support capabilities--i. e., the reasons behind the necessity for zero population growth.

314 _____. The Only Earth We Have. New York:
        Macmillan, 1969, $4.50 (pap, 1971, $0.95)
        ($1.96 'text ed'), 86p, index, illus
        L: 4-8   S: O
        Focus is on pollution, but includes interesting ma-
terial on ecology too. Strikes a good balance between text

and excellent supplementary photographs, giving a concise, well-grounded statement of man's abuse of his natural environment. Good introduction to the overall problem for young children.

315 PRYDE, Philip R. Conservation in the Soviet Union.
     New York: Cambridge University Press, 1972,
     $12.50, 301p, index, illus
     L: Adv HS & up   S: I
     A complete survey of the present status of the
Soviet Union's environment and programs for its renewal.

316 QUIGG, Philip W., ed. World Directory of Environ-
     mental Education Programs. New York: Bowker,
     1973, $14.95, 289p
     L: HS & up   S: DBI/Ed
     Prepared by the International Institute for Environ-
mental Affairs in cooperation with the Institute of International
Education. Comprehensive guide to over 1000 environmental
study programs offered by U.S. and foreign schools. Includes college degree programs, brush-up courses, and everything in between--all of which are fully described with eligi-
bility requirements, length of courses, number of faculty,
language of instruction, degree awarded, tuition, scholarships
available, etc.

317 RAE, John B. The Road and the Car in American Life.
     Cambridge, MA: M.I.T. Press, 1971, $12, 408p,
     index
     L: Adv HS & up   S: T/Lu
     Surveys the relationship throughout history between
vehicles and thoroughfares that serve them. Enlightening
contrast of American and European experience.

318 RAMPARTS Magazine, Editors of. Eco-Catastrophe.
     New York: Harper & Row, 1970, $3.95 ($2.95
     pap), 158p, illus
     L: Adv HS & up   S: A
     Reprints of Ramparts articles, including exposé of
the California aqueduct and the Santa Barbara student riots
that they maintain were environmentally inspired. Sometimes
good, sometimes suspect muckraking.

319 RASKIN, Edith. Pyramid of Living Things. New York:
     McGraw-Hill, 1967, $4.33 (PLB), 192p, index
     L: 7 up   S: Ec
     Raskin approaches the study of ecology through

examining the various biomes.   Excellent, in-depth coverage.

320 RASMUSSEN, Frederick A. , Holobinko, Paul, and
      Showalter, Victor M. Man and the Environment.
      Boston: Houghton Mifflin, 1971, $6.60, 417p,
      index, illus, glossary
      L: JHS & up   S: Ec/Ed
      Extremely good junior high school textbook that
teaches sciences through the investigation of ecology and the
environment. The book is unique in that it helps students to
investigate on their own--to learn about life science through
their own activities by setting up experiments to test ideas
about the behavior of plants and animals (and man), to find
out what conditions affect living things, and to plan ways to
solve the problems that face contemporary man. There are
four units, each of which is subdivided into separate "investigations. " The first unit is concerned with investigating living
things; the second, the environment and how it affects living
things; the third, how living things affect each other; and
fourth, how man affects his environment. Specific subjects
include the effects of pollution on people and plants, thermal
pollution, the fate of the redwoods, red tide, earth management, managing wildlife, how to make scientific observations,
and many, many others.

321 RATHLESBERGER, James, ed. Nixon and the Environ-
      ment: The Politics of Devastation. New York:
      Village Voice Book, 1972, $2.45 (pap), 279p, index
      L: HS & up   S: Ps/H
      A review, written by the League of Conservation
voters, of the Nixon administration's environmental record,
1968-1972. Extensive coverage on recent legislation and the
administration's circumvention of statutes such as the 1899
Refuse Act.

322 REID, Keith. Nature's Network: Interdependence in
      Nature. Garden City, NY: Doubleday (Natural
      History), 1970, $6.95, index, illus
      L: 7 up   S: Ec
      Wonderfully illustrated with many color pictures,
multi-colored graphs and diagrams to support a clear and
well-organized text describing the intricate, inter-related,
interdependent network of all living things. Topics covered
include ecology in general, energy, the differences between
autotrophs and heterotrophs, associations between organisms,
energy flow in the ecosystem, the chemical environment
(macronutrients, micronutrients, water cycle, the oxygen

cycle, carbon, nitrogen, phosphorus, and sulphur cycles,
limiting factors and tolerance, the growth of ecosystems,
the relation of man to his natural environment, and the
world's main biomes. There is also a glossary of ecological
terms. Keith Reid is a zoologist and ecologist and a Fellow
of the Royal Entomological Society. An excellent text.

323 REVELLE, Roger and Landsberg, Hans, eds. America's
       Changing Environment (Daedalus Library, vol 15.)
       Boston: Houghton Mifflin, 1970, $6.95, 314p,
       index
       L: Adv HS & up   S: A/Ec/U/Lu/Ap/Wp/Et/E/Ed
       An anthology divided into the following sections:
Ecology as an Ethical Science; Air, Water, and Land; Eco-
nomics and Politics; The Humane City; Playgrounds for
People; and the Roles of Education.

324 RICKLEFS, Robert E. Ecology. Newton, MA: Chiron,
       1973, $15, 862p, index, illus
       L: College   S: Ec/Ed
       An ecology textbook that stresses the interaction be-
tween population and community. Ricklefs explores influence
of natural selection and evolutionary approach, asking "What
determines the outcome of competitive relationships between
species and the ability of populations to specialize on different
resources?"

325 RIDGEWAY, James. Politics of Ecology. New York:
       Dutton, 1971, $6.95 ($1.75 pap), 222p, index
       L: HS & up   S: Ps
       An exposé of current pollution control practice,
sewers, fuel trusts, the Santa Barbara Oil Spill, and the
Army Corps of Engineers.

326 RIENOW, Robert and Rienow, Leona T. Moment in the
       Sun: A Report on the Deteriorating Quality of the
       American Environment. New York: Dial, 1967,
       $6, 286p, index
       L: HS & up   S: O
       One of the best pioneer works representing environ-
mental renaissance. Still widely read and anthologized, it
gives a well-written, lucid overview of the entire subject.
Highly recommended for high school use.

327 ROBBINS, Roy M. Our Landed Heritage: The Public
       Domain 1776-1936. Gloucester, MA: Peter Smith,
       19 , $5; also avail in pap, Lincoln: University

of Nebraska, 1962, $2.45; illus; both reprints
from 1942 Princeton University Press ed
L: Adv HS & up   S: Lu/ H
Scholarly treatment and exploration of the relationship of the public domain and federal land policy to environment and conservation movements. Basically for college use,
but good also for advanced high school research and reference.

328 ROGERS, George, W. , ed. Change in Alaska: People,
       Petroleum, and Politics. Seattle: Universities of
       Washington and Alaska, 1970, $7.95, 213p, index,
       illus
       L: Adv HS & up   S: A/ Lu/ Ps
       Eighteen papers taken from the 20th Alaska Con-
ference held in 1969. Analysis of the state, its people,
politics, and the effects of the oil discovery.

329 ROOSEVELT, Nicholas. Conservation: Now or Never.
       New York: Dodd, Mead, 1970, $5.95, 238p, index;
       also avail in pap, New York: Apollo editions,
       $1.95
       L: HS & up   S: Pn/ Cs
       Roosevelt's personal memoirs of conservation land-
mark battles: Jackson Hole, the Forest Service, the Lewis
and Clark trail, Storm King Mountain, Redwoods, Colby
College vs. the Interstate and others. Good vignettes and a
worthwhile study.

330 ROSENBAUM, Walter A. The Politics of Environmental
       Concern. New York: Praeger, 1973, $9 ($3.95
       pap), 298p
       L: Adv HS & up   S: Ps
       An historian's analysis of recent environmental
politics. Thorough and sound.

331 ROSS, William M. Oil Pollution as an International
       Problem; A Study of Puget Sound and the Strait
       of Georgia. Seattle: University of Washington
       Press, 1973, $12, 224p, illus
       L: Adv HS & up   S: Ol/ Cs
       Analyzes oil spill problems, laws and agreements
now in existence, and gives recommendations for future controls.

332 ROTH, Charles E. The Most Dangerous Animal in the
       World. Reading, MA: Addison-Wesley, 1971,
       $4.50, 127p, index, illus

L: 6 up   S: O
The most dangerous animal, of course, is man.
Roth, the Director of Education for the Massachusetts Audubon Society, focuses on man, his environment, his development of that environment, and the resulting dilemma of this
development. An energetic, worthwhile book.

333 ROUECHE, B. What's Left: Reports on a Diminishing
     America. Boston: Little, Brown, 1969, $5.95,
     210p; also avail in pap, New York: Berkley, 1970,
     $0.95
     L: HS & up   S: Pn
     Culled from Roueche's New Yorker articles.
Breezily written treatise, detailing his encounters with our
remaining wilderness. Not overly informative, but pleasant
reading.

334 RUDD, Robert L. Pesticides and the Living Landscape.
     Madison: University of Wisconsin Press, 1964,
     $10 ($2.50 pap)
     L: HS & up   S: Pc
     One of the best compilations of information on pesti-
cides. Each category of pesticides is examined for its effect
on various forms of life. Includes the most notorious of the
pest and pesticide problems with well documented case studies.

335 RUSSELL, Helen R. Earth, The Great Recycler. Nash-
     ville, TN: Nelson, 1973, $5.95, 160p, index
     L: 5 up   S: Ec
     Explores the life cycles on earth and the natural re-
cycling processes. Also discusses our contemporary environmental problems and what the reader can do about them.

336 RUSSELL, W. M. Man, Nature, and History. Garden
     City, NY: Doubleday (Natural History), 1969,
     $6.95, 252p, index
     L: Adv HS & up   S: H
     An excellent review of man's interaction, throughout
history, with his environment, including the influences of
diseases, food, plagues, etc. Emphasis is on problems of
the past, scant on contemporary problems.

337 SALE, Larry L. and Lee, Ernest. Environmental Edu-
     cation in the Elementary School. New York: Holt,
     Rinehart & Winston, 1972, $4.95; Winston Mine
     Editions, 1972, $5.28
     L: Adult   S: Ed

A review of learning problems and solutions for
these difficulties. Includes excellent information and hints
for working environmental studies into teaching strategies.

338   SALTONSTALL, Richard, Jr.   Your Environment and
         What You Can Do About It.   New York: Ace,
         1972, $1.25 (pap), 299p, index
         L: Adv HS & up   S: O/Ps
         Includes all the basic information on environmental
quality and what the citizen can do about improving it: which
private groups and government agencies to contact and what
the citizen's rights are concerning water, air, noise, waste,
economic growth, garbage, land use, shorelines, farming,
gardening, and law.

339   SAX, Joseph L.   Defending the Environment: A
         Strategy for Citizen Action.   New York: Knopf,
         1971, $6.95 ($1.95 pap), 255p, index
         L: Adv HS & up   S: L
         Sax, an expert in environmental law, explains why
citizens should reassert their right to determine the condition
and fate of their environment and how to do it.   He shows
how citizens can take their grievances into the courtroom and
by doing so restore democracy to environmental disputation.

340   SCHOENFELD, Clay.   Everybody's Ecology: A Field
         Guide to Pleasure in the Out-of-Doors.   Cranbury,
         NJ: A. S. Barnes, 1971, $7.95, 316p, index,
         illus
         L: HS & up   S: O/Ec
         Collection of writings on the outdoors, mainly from
Field and Stream and the Journal of Environmental Education.
Good discussion on the environmental hazards such as snow-
mobiles and power boats.   Especially thorough coverage of
Wisconsin issues.

341   SCIENTIFIC American Editors.   The Biosphere: A
         Scientific American Book.   San Francisco: W. H.
         Freeman, 1970, $3.25, 134p, index, illus
         L: HS & up   S: Ec
         A survey of ecological cycles, covering energy,
water, carbon, oxygen, nitrogen, minerals, food production,
energy production, and materials production.   Thorough, concise, and clear.

342   SEARS, Paul B.   Living Landscape (expanded version of
         Where There Is Life, 1962).   New York: Basic,

1966, $5.95, 199p, illus
L: HS & up   S: O
Sears introduces reader to the subject of modern
ecology and the need for water, breathable air, careful management of land. After explaining what he describes as the
"Rules of the Game," earth's fitness, the new science (that
embraces all organisms, including man, into its realm), the
atmosphere, hydrosphere, geosphere, and soil, Sears steers
the reader into drawing some frightening conclusions. He
urges us to see beyond what we would like to see and not to
confuse growth of urban centers with health or judge economic
soundness on the basis of maximum quick returns. An excellent book. Sear's background: Professor at Yale University, former Director of the Yale University Conservation
Program, and once Chairman of the Board of the National
Audubon Society.

343 SEGERBERG, Osborn, Jr. Where Have All the Flowers
        Fishes Birds Trees Water and Air Gone? What
        Ecology Is All About. New York: McKay, 1971,
        $6.95 ($2.95 pap), 320p
        L: Adv HS & up   S: O/Ec
        A detailed analysis of the roots and ramifications
of the environmental crisis. Section I details "The System"--
the ecological environment; II portrays man's attempt at
"Beating the System."

344 SHANKLAND, Robert. Steve Mather of the National
        Parks. Rev. ed. New York: Knopf, 1971, $8.95,
        370p, index, illus
        L: HS & up   S: B/H
        A well-done adult biography of the man who left the
presidency of 20-Mule-Team Borax to head the National Park
Service. He applied his managerial skills and talents to make
the Park Service a professional, effective organization.

345 SHANKS, Ann Z. About Garbage and Stuff. New York:
        Viking, 1973, $5.95 (PLB), illus
        L: K-5   S: Wt
        How one family amasses garbage, how it is disposed
of, and the need to conserve and recycle. Shanks explains
the need for conservation to save our natural resources for
the essentials, thus reducing the wastes we throw away in
our garbage, and the need to recycle those things that we
throw away that can be recycled. "A strong, effective photo-
sermon"--Library Journal.

346 SHANLEY, J. Lyndon. The Illustrated Walden, with
       photographs from the Gleason Collection. Prince-
       ton, NJ: Princeton University Press, 1973,
       $12.50, 66 illus, boxed
       New edition with never before published photographs
of areas Thoreau described.

347 SHELFORD, Victor E. The Ecology of North America.
       Urbana: University of Illinois Press, 1963, $10,
       610p, species and locality indexes, bibliog, illus
       L: College/Adv HS ref   S: Ec/Ed
       Extremely thorough ecology textbook for college
level ecology course. Excellent graphs, pictures, and diagrams supplement the text, the purpose of which according
to the author "is to describe North America from an ecological point of view as it appeared in the period A.D. 1500
to 1600 before European settlement." The first chapter provides excellent reference and analysis defining habitat, community, ecosystems, food chains, pyramids of numbers, community development, etc. Chapter 2 and 3 explain the temperate deciduous forest biome in the northern and southern
regions, Chapter 4 the floodplain forest and grassland biomes;
5, the Boreal Coniferous forest; 6, Montane Coniferous Forest and Alpine Communities; 7, the Tundra Biome; 8, the
Northern Pacific Coast Rainy Western Hemlock Forest Biome
and Mountain Communities; 9, the summer Drought or Broad
Sclerophyll-Grizzly Bear Community; 10, Cold Desert &
Semidesert Communities; 11, Ecotone Woodland and Bushland
Communities; 13-14, the Northern and Southern Temperate
Grassland; 15, the Hot Desert; 16, the Tropical Rain Forest;
17, Tropical Deciduous Forest and Related Communities with
a Dry Season; 18, the Oak-Pine Forests, Cloud Forest, and
other Mountain Communities; and 19, the Communities of
Southern Florida, Cuba, and the shores of the Mainland.

348 SHEPARD, Paul. The Tender Carnivore and the Sacred
       Game. New York: Scribner's, 1973, $9.95, 302p,
       index
       L: Adv HS   S: O
       An account of how man's past history affects his
present attitudes and treatment of his natural environment.
Shepard argues for the abandonment of agriculture in favor
of a technological/hunter-gatherer society. Whether or not
one agrees with his unorthodox proposals, Shepard's book
provokes stimulating thought and classroom discussion.

349 _____ and McKinley, Daniel, eds. The Subversive

Science: Towards an Ecology of Man. Boston:
Houghton Mifflin, 1969, $6.50, 453p, illus
L: Adv HS & up   S: A
One of the few anthologies without an essay by
Barry Commoner. Does include Watts, Dubos, Hardin,
Darling, McHarg, and Leopold. But it is not the usual re-
shuffling of the environmental essay's deck of cards, rather
a fascinating collection of 36 essays covering all disciplines.
Includes: Men as Populations, The Environmental Encounter,
Men and Other Organisms, Men in Ecosystems, and Ethos,
Ecos, and Ethics.

350 SHUTTLESWORTH, Dorothy E. Clean Air--Sparkling
Water: The Fight Against Pollution. Garden City,
NY: Doubleday, 1968, $4.95 ($0.95 pap), 95p,
index, illus
L: 3-5   S: Ap/Wp
A good combination of photographs and text covering
all types of air and water pollution. She divides the book
into three sections. The first section describes (in thinly
veiled terms New York City and a suburb in New Jersey),
air and water pollution in the city and its suburb, how the
suburb generates its own pollution and how it is affected,
also, by that of the adjacent big city. The second section
discusses the origins of air and water pollution throughout
America, Asia, and Europe and the general pollution problems all three continents presently face. Part three describes how man is fighting back, largely through technology.
Vivid photographs greatly enhance an already excellent text.

351 _____ and Cervasio, Thomas. Litter: The Ugly
Enemy; An Ecology Story. Garden City, NY:
Doubleday, 1973, $4.95 ($5.70 PLB), 62p,
illus
L: 3-5   S: Wt
Focuses on problem of waste disposal as it affects
the environment and how it can be reduced. Traces the
story of Rita and Ralph who have moved to a small city and
become upset when new industries come in and cause pollution in their new habitat. They work through school programs, service clubs, and city government agencies to initiate
clean-up programs. Book includes, also, reports of programs
in several cities, programs which, in many cases, were
started by school children. Gives practical guides for student
action.

352 SILVERBERG, Robert. John Muir: Prophet Among the

Glaciers. New York: Putman, 1972, $4.69, 249p
     L: 6 up   S: B/H/W
     One of the best biographies of America's foremost
conservationist, depicting Muir's fights to preserve the wilderness areas he loved, his pursuits, later involvement in politics to gain his ends, his writing career, etc.

353 _____. Vanishing Giants: The Story of the Sequoias.
     New York: Simon & Schuster, 1969, $4.50 ($4.29
     PLB), 160p, illus
     L: 7 up   S: H/Cs/F/W
     A good case study of the tallest trees and Muir's
campaign to save them. (This campaign is still going on to
this day.) Good illustrations support well-presented text.

354 SIMON, Hilda. Our Six-Legged Friends and Allies:
     Ecology in the Backyard. New York: Vanguard,
     1972, $4.95, illus
     L: 6-12   S: Ec/Pc
     Simon thoroughly covers each insect, how it looks,
its lifestyle, what it does, etc. and illustrates each with
careful pen and ink drawings. But more importantly, she
explains how these six-legged allies can do the job of insecticides, just as well and without the hazardous effects.
As long as the proper balance is maintained, no one species
becomes a hazard. Insects described include dragonflies,
parasite wasps, and ladybugs.

355 SIMON, Seymour. Science Projects in Ecology. New
     York: Holiday House, 1972, $4.50, 127p, index
     L: JHS   S: Ec/Ed
     Very good, easily executed experiments for junior
high school ecology students. Simon also has another book
out (similar to this), for grades four through nine. Well
recommended.

356 _____. Science Projects in Pollution. New York:
     Holiday House, 1972, $4.50, 118p, index
     L: 5-10   S: Ec/Ed/Wp/Ap
     Good experiments for the easy detection of air and
water pollutants in surrounding atmosphere and environments.
Has a second book, also, for grades 4-9.

357 SMALL, George L. The Blue Whale. New York:
     Columbia University Press, 1971, $9.95 ($3.95
     pap), 216p
     L: Adv HS & up   S: Es

A National Book Award winner. An excellent historical and economic analysis of the modern whaling industry and warning of the impending extermination of the largest creature ever to inhabit the earth.

358 SMALLWOOD, William Martin and Smallwood, Mabel C.
     Natural History and the American Mind. New York:
     Columbia University Press, 1941, $11
     L: College/Adv HS ref   S: H
     An interesting, well done description of the impact
of the early "naturalist" on America's cultural life. Basically oriented towards the college level student, but is a good reference for the more advanced high school student.

359 SMITH, Frances C. The First Book of Conservation.
     Rev. ed. New York: Watts, 1972, $3.95 (PLB),
     69p, index, illus
     L: 4-6   S: Cn
     A good, basic introduction to the history and concepts of the conservation movement and what the student can do to help it along. Smith begins by explaining the principles of ecology, the interdependency of plant and animal species, the work of insects, usefulness of the ostensibly problem animals (moles, mice, etc.), definition of environment versus ecology, environmental history, the beginnings of soil, forests, water, animal conservation, insect management, the environmental crisis, what children can do, and glossary of conservation terms. A fine little book.

360 SMITH, Frank E.   Conservation in the United States:
     A Documentary History. New York: Van Nostrand
     Reinhold, 1971, 5 vols, $30 each or $150 for set
     L: Adults & up   S: H
     Vol I, Water and Air Pollution, 824p, index;
vol II, Land and Water, pt 1, 911p, index; vol III, Land and Water, pt 2, 778p, index; vol IV, Minerals; vol V, Recreation. A complete documentation of the historical development of American conservation policies in water, air, land, minerals, and recreation. Includes guidelines for individuals, schools, and industries that they can adopt to help in the conserving of natural resources.

361 _____. The Politics of Conservation. New York:
     Pantheon, 1966, $7.95; also avail in pap, New
     York: Harper & Row, 1971, $2.96
     L: HS & up   S: H
     The political development of American conservation

with heaviest concentration on public works. Smith traces
the development of federal policies from 1789 to the mid
1960s. Sometimes rough going, but an extremely thorough
study and invaluable source for the history teacher. Smith
was a Representative from Mississippi for 12 years and then
director of the Tennessee Valley Authority.

362 SMITH, Guy-Harold, ed. Conservation of Natural Re-
     sources. 3d ed. New York: Wiley, 1971, $12.95,
     533p, bibliog, index
     L: Adv HS & up   S: Cn/Ed
     One of the leading textbooks on conservation and
resource management, straightforward, dealing with the subjects of conservation, soil, air, water, minerals, forests,
wildlife, recreation, city planning, pollution, and national
planning in a traditional manner rather than from the particular vantage point of pollution. Excellent bibliography for
additional literature in the field.

363 SMITH, Henry Nash. Virgin Land: The American West
     as Symbol and Myth. New York: Random, 1957,
     $1.95 (pap); also, Cambridge, MA: Harvard Uni-
     versity Press, 1970, $12.45 (pap)
     L: Adv HS & up   S: H
     Another invaluable aid to understanding American
attitudes towards the natural environment. Lucid enlightening
look into the entire conception of the "frontier."

364 STERLING, Philip. Sea and Earth: The Life of Rachel
     Carson. New York: Crowell, 1970, $4.50, 213p,
     index, illus
     L: 5-8   S: B/H
     Sterling draws much of Carson's biography from the
recollections of her friends and colleagues to give a good picture of this gifted writer and dedicated scientist's life, her
devotion to her work, her friends and family, and the natural
world she sought to defend and preserve.

365 STEVENS, Leonard. Town That Launders Its Water
     (orig title, The Santee Water Project). New York:
     Coward, McCann, 1971, $4.49 (PLB), 122p, index,
     illus
     L: 6-9   S: Wp
     The story of Santee, California's unique sewage
system that recycles used (but still precious) water which
normally would have been dumped into the Pacific. Using
percolation beds and oxidation ponds, the sewage is cleaned--

105

enough so that the final oxidation ponds are used for swimming, boating, fishing, and other water sports. The Santee sewage system has proven a public asset that not only beautifies the town and raises land values, but provides a total water recycling system. Strongly recommended for both children and adults.

366 STEWART, George R. Not So Rich As You Think.
     Boston: Houghton Mifflin, 1967, $6.95; also
     avail in pap, New York: New American Library,
     1968, $0.95
     L: HS & up   S: Wp/Ap
     Discussion of American pollution and its waste of
natural resources. Points out that these two by-products of
industry negate what we optimistically and incorrectly call
progress.

367 STILL, Henry. The Dirty Animal. New York: Haw-
     thorn, 1970, 298p, bibliog, index
     L: HS & up   S: O
     Thorough documentation in terse, tough reporter
style of our polluted land, water, and air which the dirtiest
animal (man, of course), has desecrated and all but ruined
with his garbage, industrial wastes, physical structures which
create urban congestion, his carelessness, and his greed.
The author focusses one section on the automobile which he
considers one of the primary contributors to air pollution,
litter, and our unsightly landscapes. He outlines, also, the
abatement programs for all pollution that government and industry, aware at last of the disastrous consequences of unchecked pollution, are trying to get underway.

368 STORER, John. The Web of Life. New York: New
     American Library, 1972, $0.95 (pap), 160p; also,
     Old Greenwich, CT: Devin-Adair, 1972, $2.75
     (pap), illus, index
     L: HS & up   S: O
     An overview which examines how the environment
influences population, food, natural resources, employment,
economics, government, and individual rights. Divided into
sections that cover: Background for Today, Today, and
Tomorrow. Concise, highly readable account of how everything in life is dependent and related to everything else.

369 STOUTENBURG, Adrien. A Vanishing Thunder: Extinct
     and Threatened American Birds. Garden City, NY:
     Doubleday (Natural History), 1967, $3.95, 124p,
     illus

L: 7-9   S: Es
Good narrative and history of the plights of the
passenger pigeon, ivory billed woodpecker, great auk, California condor, American egret, and whooping crane.

370 STRONG, Ann L. Planned Urban Environments: Swe-
     den, Finland, Israel, the Netherlands, France.
     Baltimore: Johns Hopkins University Press, 1971,
     $20, 406p, index
     L: Adv HS & up   S: U/I
     Case studies of successful European urban planning
experiences and their possible application for American urban
environmental revitalization.

371 STRONG, Maurice, ed. Who Speaks For Earth? New
     York: Norton, 1973, $6.95 ($1.75 pap), 173p,
     index
     L: Adult   S: A/I
     Lectures from the International Institute for Environ-
mental Affairs in cooperation with the Population Institute.
Overviews by Barbara Ward, René Dubos, Gunnar Myrdal,
Carmen Miro, and Aurelio Pecci, and others.

372 SWAIN, Donald C. Wilderness Defender: Horace M.
     Albright and Conservation. Chicago: University
     of Chicago Press, 1970, $10.75, 347p, index,
     illus
     L: HS & up   S: B/H
     A biography of Horace M. Albright, the foremost
leader of the American Park Service, the man who carried
out the traditions of Steve Mather.

373 SWAN, Malcolm D. , ed. Tips and Tricks in Outdoor
     Education. Danville, IL: Interstate, 1970, $3.95
     L: Adult   S: Ed
     Better than the title indicates. One of the best
handbooks of environmental teaching techniques. It is concerned specifically with environmental instruction.

374 SWATEK, Paul. The User's Guide to the Protection of
     the Environment. New York: Ballantine, 1970,
     $1.25 (pap), 312p, index
     L: HS & up   S: Ha
     A nuts and bolts guide for the environmentally con-
scious consumer but including information that every modern
home economics and shop teacher should be aware of--as
should we all. It has stood up well against all the "change-

the-world's-consciousness" books. Highly practical, also, for the social studies teacher, as it includes vast information on the environmental impact of American contemporary consumption practice.

375 SWIFT, Hildegarde H. Edge of Peril: A Biography of John Burroughs. New York: Morrow, 1957, $5.95, illus
        L: 9 up   S: B/H
      Excellent, straightforward biography of John Burroughs, famous early naturalist writer and nature analyst who wrote during the late 19th and early part of the 20th centuries.

376 _____. From the Eagle's Wing: A Biography of John Muir. New York: Morrow, 1962, $4.95, 287p, illus
        L: 7 up   S: B/H/W
      Excellent biography of John Muir, the father of Yosemite and eminent, charismatic, zealous preservationist. Muir was perhaps the most colorful of the transcendental wilderness lovers, often politically active in his later years. He also wrote prolifically and romantically of the wilderness areas he fought throughout his life to defend and preserve. A fascinating subject and a good treatment of it.

377 TALBOT, Allan R. Power Along the Hudson: The Storm King Case and the Birth of Environmentalism. New York: Dutton, 1972, $7.95, 244p, index, illus
        L: Adv HS & up   S: Eg/Cs/Ps
      Talbot begins with the 1963 decision by Con Edison to build a hydroelectric power generator at Storm King Mountain on the Upper Hudson. He details the citizen campaign waged against the project and that of the Hudson River Expressway project. Talbot traces the Hudson River's use since the building of the Erie canal and the Sierra Club's fight against the Mineral King California project.

378 TAYLOR, Gordon R. The Doomsday Book. New York: World, 1970; avail in pap, New York: Fawcett, 1971, $1.25, 335p, index
        L: HS & up   S: P
      Taylor believes that uncontrolled population growth will, in the end, doom the earth as we know it.

379 TAYLOR, Theodore B. and Humpstone, Charles C.

The Restoration of the Earth. New York: Harper
& Row, 1973, $7.95, 223p, illus
L: Adv HS & up   S: O
A blueprint for environmental management.   Taylor
and Humpstone state their cases for the "containment principle" that holds that environmentally related activities should
be confined to areas dedicated for those stipulated activities
exclusively.

380 TERRY, Mark. Teaching for Survival. New York:
     Ballantine, 1971, $1.25
     L: Adult   S: Ed
     Makes the case for and provides ideas and means
for incorporating environmental studies and the understanding
of environmental problems into all education.   Maintains cor-
rectly that all education is environmental education and that
our educational practices should be altered to incorporate this
point of view.   It is now out of print, but well worth finding.

381 THEOBALD, Robert. Habit and Habitat. Englewood
     Cliffs, NJ: Prentice-Hall, 1972, $8.95, 277p,
     illus
     L: Adv HS & up   S: Ec
     By applying systems analysis, Theobald strikes a
blow to neo-Keynesian economics, describing it as a "system
of controlled scarcity." He shows, however, that conservation is economically feasible by using a systematic approach.

382 THOMPSON, Dennis L. , ed. Politics, Policy, and
     Natural Resources. New York: Macmillan (Free
     Press), 1972, $12.95, 452p, index
     L: Adv HS & up   S: A/Ps
     A detailed anthology describing the interplay of
forces and conflicts of political interests and environmental
needs.

383 THOMPSON, Donald N. The Economics of Environ-
     mental Protection. Englewood Cliffs, NJ: Prentice-
     Hall (Winthrop), 1973, $6.95 ($3.95 pap), 278p,
     index
     L: Adv HS & up   S: Ec/Cs
     Written for students; provides solid, readable intro-
duction to economics of environmental deterioration and pro-
tections.   Uses case studies to advantage in illustrating water,
air, and chemical pollution and its problems.

384 THOREAU, Henry David. Walden. New York: New

American Library, 1954, $0.60 (pap), 156p; also
avail in a number of other editions: 'young adult'
ed (grades 9-12), Apollo, $2.25; large type ed,
Watts (7 up), $8.95 PLB; 1969 text ed $6.96 and
$0.95 pap text ed, Merrill; Dutton, $3.50; AMSCO
School Publications, $0.90 pap text ed; AMSCO
School Publications, $1.25 pap text for grades 7-
12; Bantam $0.95 (pap); College and University
Press illus ed, 1951, $2.95; Doubleday pap ed,
$1.45
L: 7 up   S: Pn/En
  A classic and the epitome of transcendentalism:
how one man reacts to his environment. After 120 years, it
is as timely as ever--as the number of editions suggest.
Picked by Friends of the Earth as one of the best environ-
mental books.

385 TURNER, Frederick Jackson.   The Frontier in American
  History. New York: Holt, Rinehart and Winston,
  1962 (orig 1920), $5.95 ($5.50 pap), 375p; also
  Gloucester, MA: Peter Smith, $7.50
  L: Adv HS & up   S: H
  Landmark works of Turner compiled in book form.
The original essays published in the late 19th century stirred
little interest, but within the decade, Turner's revolutionary
thesis pointing to the differences between American and European civilizations galvanized a flurry of intellectual debate
that has never completely died down.   Turner dislodged the
comfortable and generally held belief that American cultural
roots dig solely and deeply in the European experience, citing
the unique American environment (the frontiering experience)
as the overlooked element that radically altered the European
immigrant and his progeny.   He saw the frontier as but one
of the many forces shaping the Americans' destiny, but he
maintained that it was undeniably a liberating force from
which is traced the uniquely American characteristics of individualism, exuberance, aggressive foreign policy, strength,
inquisitiveness, etc.

386 UDALL, Stewart.   The Quiet Crisis. New York: Holt,
  Rinehart and Winston, 1963, $6.95, 209p, index;
  also avail in pap, New York: Avon: 1964, $1.25,
  224p, index
  L: HS & up   S: H/B
  A biographical history of the American environmen-
tal/conservation movement from the early American Indians
and the first settlers to the Kennedy Administration.   Udall

emphasizes the rise of the conservation ethic, tracing the
ideas and works and accomplishments of Marsh, Pinchot,
Muir, Thoreau, and other environmental pioneers. An excellent, beautifully written book, considered among the best,
if not the best, of the general survey studies written by an
active leader in the movement. Udall was Secretary of the
Interior under Kennedy and Johnson.

387   U. S. Congress. Joint Economic Committee. The
        Economy, Energy, and the Environment. Washing-
        ton, DC: Legislative Reference Service, Library
        of Congress, 1970.
        L: Adv HS & up   S: Eg/Ec
        Background study of the existing literature on the
various technical aspects of the production of electric power.
The emphasis is basically on the supply of the various fuels
that are used in producing electric power and on the environmental consequences of energy conversion. A good survey.

388   U. S. Council on Environmental Quality. Environmental
        Quality: First Annual Report. Washington, DC:
        Government Printing Office, 1970, $1.75
        L: Adv HS & up   S: O/Ps
        Survey of the present conditions of the environment;
identification of the major trends, problems, and present programs underway to improve the overall quality of the United
States environment. Review of federal legislation included,
with focus on water, air, weather and climate, solid wastes,
noise, pesticides, radiation, population, and land use.

389   VAN DEN BOSCH, R. and Messenger, P. S. Biological
        Control (Ecology). Scranton, PA: Intext, 1973,
        $8.50 ($4.50 pap), 180p, index, illus
        L: Adv HS & up   S: Ec/Ps
        Intended for advanced undergraduate students, but
an excellent introduction for interested layman on the control of
pests through ecologically-safe biological controls. Authors
are personally involved in developing such biological controls
to hold down the populations of undesirable insect pests.

390   VAN DERSAL, William R. The Land Renewed: The
        Story of Soil Conservation. Rev. and enl. ed.
        New York: Walck, 1968, $6.50, 160p, illus
        L: 7-9   S: Cn/H
        Straightforward account of soil conservation including
studies of the Dust Bowl and the Soil Conservation Service.
Dry, but competent. Good illustrations.

391 VIVIAN, V. Eugene. Sourcebook for Environmental
       Education. St. Louis: Mosby, 1973, $5.95, 206p,
       illus
       L: Adult   S: Ed
       Vivian gives guidelines for the teaching of environ-
mental sciences. He includes, also, a series of unit plans
comprised of exercises for the several grade levels and
actual case studies that show students how they might conduct
an in-depth study of their own.

392 VOSBURGH, John. Living with Your Land. New York:
       Scribner's, 1972, $6.95 ($2.65 pap), 191p, index,
       illus
       L: HS & up   S: Lu
       An excellent guide to land use for the private prop-
erty owner. He explains how to attract wildlife to your land
and in beautifully descriptive chapters, tells what types of
animals you will be able to entice to share your property
with you. A fine book.

393 WAGNER, Kenneth A. , et al. Under Siege: Man, Men,
       and Earth. New York: Abelard, 1973, $10.95,
       386p; also avail, text ed for $10 with teacher's
       manual (Intext); illus, bibliog, index
       L: Adv HS & up   S: O
       An attempt to make reader aware of new problems
constantly confronting man before they become critical. Includes good and plentiful sprinkling of illustrations, graphs,
lists of sources for further readings, and detailed index.
Note particularly sections outlining materials in assessing the
population problem and the quest for an environmental ethic.

394 WAGNER, Philip L. The Human Use of the Earth.
       New York: Free Press, 1960, $6.95, 270p, index
       L: Adv HS & up   S: O/Lu
       Good survey for advanced high school students.
Covers wide range of environmental aspects as illustrated by
chapter headings: Human Interaction with Earth; Conditions
of Human Life; Man's Place in the World; Human Societies
as Geographic Forms; the Economic Bond; the Means of
Production; Artificial Environments; Ways of Livelihood;
the Commercial Environment; A Geographic Outlook.

395 WAGNER, Richard. Environment and Man. New York:
       Norton, 1971, $7.50, illus
       L: Adv HS & up   S: Ec/Ed
       The book was written primarily as a science

textbook for "poet's" biology courses (survey science courses
for nonscience majors) that are offered at most colleges.   It
is useful too, however, to advanced high school students in
an environmental studies class or as an adjunct to more traditional biology classes.   In any case, an informative source
that should be made available at least for reference purposes,
if not as a text.

396 WALKER, Laurence C.   Ecology and Our Forests.
     Cranbury, NJ: A. S. Barnes, 1973, $7.95, 175p,
     index, illus
     L: HS & up   S: Ec/F
     Useful introduction (for the layman) to forest ecol-
ogy, with explanation of forest's role in total ecological picture.   Includes a history of the better known American trees
and forests and explanation of forest management practice in
America.

397 WARD, Barbara and Dubos, René.   Only One Earth:
     The Care and Maintenance of a Small Planet.   New
     York: Norton, 1972, $6, 225p, index
     L: Adv HS & up   S: O/I
     The original manuscript was sent to 152 experts in
all environmental fields for their review and comments that
were then included in the final draft.   The book served as a
jumping off point for discussions during the 1972 Stockholm
Conference and gives, therefore, an up-to-date and very
thorough overview of the world's environmental situation.   A
children's edition is also planned.   A fine reference.

398 WARNER, Matt.   Your World--Your Survival.   New
     York: Abelard, 1970, $4.25, 128p, illus, bibliog,
     index
     L: 5-10   S: O/I
     A close look at the problem of pollution which has
become critical the world over.   Warner points out that the
health hazards of a polluted environment are as incalculable
as they are devastating, and we must, to survive, quickly
protect our life-supporting air and water supplies and guard
our natural resources.   He also encourages readers to get
actively involved in community conservation efforts.   Includes
some very effective photographs.

399 WEATHERSBEE, Christopher and Weathersbee, Bonnie.
     The Intelligent Consumer: A Handbook for the Con-
     sumer Who Wants to Make Peace with the Earth.
     New York: Dutton, 1973, $10.95 ($5.96 pap),
     384p, index

L: HS & up   S: Ha

How to curb pollution through altering daily habits (in shopping, home heating, clothing, working, vacationing, etc.). Includes recommendations of books for cosmetics and wine making, gardening, and brand name products to avoid. Interesting, helpful, and readable book.

400 WHALE Fund of the New York Zoological Society. The
     Whale Fund Manual. New York: New York
     Zoological Society, 1971, donation, 32p
     L: 8 up   S: Es

Dr. Roger Payne, of "Song of the Humpback Whale" fame, directed the writing and compilation of this manual that is put out by his Whale Fund of the New York Zoological Society. It includes a brief analysis of the present plight of the earth's remaining whale population and incorporates the economic as well as the humane arguments for preserving the whales. Good economic analysis and supportive statistical data.

401 WIDENER, Don. Timetable for Disaster. Los Angeles:
     Nash, 1972, $6.95, 277p
     L: JHS & up   S: O/Cs

The author wrote and produced the Emmy Award winning television program The Slow Guillotine. This book, basically, is a review of the many hazards of smog, leaded gasoline, DDT, etc., and includes also the major environmental landmark problems such as Lake Erie's water pollution and the Everglades jetport. It is written on the level of a TV documentary: clear, easy to understand, straightforward, and entertaining.

402 WILLE, Lois. Forever Open, Free and Clear: The
     Struggle for Chicago's Lakefront. Chicago:
     Regnery, 1972, $7.50, 224p, illus
     L: HS & up   S: H/Lu/Cs

The history of the Chicago lakeside parks, their origins, and the constant battle that is waged to keep out commercial and public development. Wille details particular actions such as the McCormick Place arena that the environmentalists fought against, but which they eventually lost to the developers.

403 WILSON, J. W. People in the Way: the Human As-
     pects of the Columbia River Project. Toronto:
     University of Toronto Press, 1973, $12.50, 200p,
     illus, bibliog, index

L: HS & up   S: Lu/Cs
Case study, as Wilson describes, for students on
the 1964 Canadian-American agreement to redevelop the
Columbia River.   The three dams built flooded the valleys,
affecting the lives of hundreds and hundreds of peoples whose
farms, homes, and whole towns were destroyed.

404 WILSON, Thomas W., Jr.   International Environmental
        Policy: A Global Survey.   New York: Dunellen,
        1971, $12.50, 364p
        L: Adv HS & up   S: L/I
        An environmental "state of the world" survey con-
ducted by the Aspen Institute for Humanistic Studies.   Emphasis principally on international law and political activity
affecting environmental problems.

405 WILSON, William K., Dowd, Morgan D., and Sholtys,
        Phyllis A.   World Directory of Environmental Re-
        search Centers.   2d ed.   Ann Arbor, MI: Oryx
        Press in assoc with R. R. Bowker, 1973, $19.50,
        450p
        L: HS & up   S: DBI/Ed
        Includes over 5000 organizations in the United
States and abroad that are engaged in research on the environment.   Organized separately under subject and geographic
sections, giving names, addresses, director, size, and special interest of each organization.

406 WOOD, Nancy.   Clearcut.   San Francisco: Sierra
        Club, 1971, 151p, $2.75, illus
        L: HS & up   S: F
        Third in the Sierra Club Battlebook Series and a
chilling account of the Forest Service that, with the retire-
ment of the old Progressives by the middle of the 1950's,
degenerated into what Michael McCloskey (who wrote the
Foreword), describes as "industrial farmers trained by the
forestry schools to maximize income from forest crops."
In their wake they leave the forests a baren wasteland, and
Nancy Wood describes every detail with documentable evidence, appalling photographs, and telling quotes from profit-
hungry foresters.   She challenges both government and industry to call a halt to this on-going raid of our forest resources,
the scalped land policy, the obliteration of soil, watersheds,
wildlife, and recreation facilities.   An excellent book.

407 YATES, Elizabeth.   The Road Through Sandwich Notch,
        with drawings by Nora S. Unwin.   Brattleboro, VT:

Greene, 1973, $5.95, 122p, illus
L: JHS & up   S: Pn/Lu/Cn
Though the pass through the New Hampshire White
Mountains has no major historical significance, Yates's under-
stated plea against developing it for commercial use rings an
almost heroic universal note: the road and regional area
symbolize a continuity with the past and should be preserved.
The story traces Yates's walk with her dog through the pass
and back, but it embodies, also, both a nostalgia for a fast
vanishing life style and a regional study of yet another one
of America's threatened rural areas.

408 ZWICK, David and Benstock, Marcy. Water Wasteland:
     The Report on Water Pollution. (Ralph Nader's
     Study Group Reports.) New York: Grossman,
     1971, $7.95, 414p, index; also avail in pap, New
     York: Bantam, 1972, $1.50
     L: HS & up   S: Wp
     A thorough "Nader's Raiders" documented analysis
that concentrates on the industrial poisoning of Lake Erie.
Refutes the optimistic but mistaken notion that water pollution
is being cleaned up.

Section II

FURTHER READING AND RESEARCH GUIDE

PRELIMINARY NOTE

This section comprises a list of unannotated titles (though a few are briefly reviewed), many of which we could not obtain. All possible information we could find, however, is included. Levels are indicated where cited in Books in Print 1973 and the main subject of the book is indicated. The level and subject codes are as in Section I.

Late additions to this list, fully indexed, will be found in Appendix 3 numbered (i. e. , "1006a") according to where they would have appeared in the present list.

Books included are the following:

(1) Extremely technical books that are useful only for reference or by specialists.

(2) Books that are in print but can be found only in the larger public and university libraries.

(3) Superior books that are presently out of print such as Richard Highsmith's Conservation in the United States (1145), one of the leading textbooks in conservation and resource management.

(4) Books whose titles are so obvious that any comment would be superfluous. Indexes and directories to narrow fields of interest fall within this category.

(5) Those books of noted naturalist, environmental, conservation, and ecology writers that are either out of print or whose focus is not directly relevant to environment. The many books of John Muir on his youth, his travels through the Sierra, and on Yosemite are examples, along with those such as Dorothy Shuttleworth's Sense of Wonder (1327a). While she includes the works of famous environmentalists such as Rachel Carson, John Muir and Henry Thoreau, the emphasis is on the fascination of nature, not on ecology or environment.

116

FURTHER READING AND RESEARCH GUIDE

1001   ABISCH, Roz. Around the House That Jack Built: A
       Tale of Ecology. New York: Parents Magazine,
       1972, $4.50 ($4.19 PLB), illus (L: K-3) (S: R/Ec);
       an early reader with an ecological theme.

1002   ADELSTEIN, Michael E. and Pival, Jean G., eds.
       Ecocide and Population. New York: St.
       Martin's, 1971, $2.50 (pap), teacher's manual avail (S: P/Ed).

1003   ALEXANDER, Taylor R. and Fichter, George S.
       Ecology. New York: Western, 1973, $1.95 (pap)
       (S: Ec).

1004   AMERICAN Association of School Administrators. Con-
       servation: In the People's Hands. Washington, DC:
       American Association of School Administrators,
       1964, $6 (pap) (S: Cn).

1005   AMERICAN Museum of Natural History. Encountering
       the Environment. New York: Van Nostrand
       Reinhold, 1971, $3.95 (pap) (S: O).

1006   ANDERSON, David D., ed. Sunshine and Smoke:
       American Writers and the American Environment.
       Philadelphia: Lippincott, 1971, $5.50 (pap), in-
       structor's manual avail (S: En/Ed).

1007   ARVILL, Robert. Man and Environment: Crisis and
       the Strategy of Choice. Gloucester, MA: Peter
       Smith, $4.25 (also avail in pap, Baltimore: Pen-
       guin, 1970, $1.65), illus (S: O).

1008   ATWATER, Montgomery. Adventures in Conservation.
       Philadelphia: Macrae, 1973, $5.95 (L: 4 up)
       (S: Cn).

1009   AUDUBON, John James. Audubon in Florida, 1831-
       1832, comp. by Kathryn H. Proby. Coral Gables,
       FL: University of Miami Press, 1973, $8.95,
       460p, illus (S: B/H).

1010   BAER, Jean G. Ecology of Animal Parasites. Ur-
       bana: University of Illinois Press, 1951, $5
       (S: Ec).

1011 BAER, Marian E. Pandora's Box: The Story of Con-
      servation. Ann Arbor, MI: Finch Press, reprint
      of 1939 ed, $12 (S: Cn).

1012 BAKKER, Elna. An Island Called California: An
      Ecological Introduction to Its Natural Communities.
      Berkeley: University of California Press, 1971,
      $11 ($2.95 pap), illus (S: Ec).

1013 BARBOUR, Michael G., et al. Coastal Ecology:
      Bodega Head. Berkeley: University of California
      Press, 1973, $12.95, illus (S: Ec).

1014 BARON, W. M. Nature Conservation: A Practical
      Handbook. New York: Barnes & Noble, 1971,
      $3 (pap), illus (S: Cn).

1015 BECK, Alan M. Ecology of Stray Dogs: A Study of
      Free-Ranging Urban Animals. Baltimore: York,
      1973, $9.50 (S: Ec).

1016 BEHRENS, June. Earth Is Home: The Pollution
      Story. Chicago: Children's Press, $5.85 (L:
      4-7) (S: Wp/Ap).

1017 BERG, George C. Water Pollution. New York:
      Scientists' Institute for Public Information, 1970,
      $1 (S: Wp).

1018 BERGER, Melvin. Jobs That Save Our Environment.
      (Exploring Careers Series.) West Caldwell, NJ:
      Lothrop, 1973, $5.50 ($3.95 pap) ($3.78 PLB),
      illus (L: 5 up) (S: Cr).

1019 [no entry]

1020 BETHEL, May. How to Live in Our Polluted World.
      New York: Pyramid, $0.95 (pap) (L: 7 up)
      (S: Wp/Ap).

1021 BIGART, Robert, ed. Environmental Pollution in
      Montana. Missoula, MO: Mountain Press Pub.
      Co., 1972, $8.50 ($5.95 pap) ($3.95 pap text
      ed), 350p (L: 9-12) (S: Ap/Wp).

1022 Biological Sciences Curriculum Study. University of
      Colorado, P.O. Box 930, Boulder, CO 80302;

includes current projects along environmental lines;
newsletter also available (S: Ed).

1023 BLAKE, Peter. God's Own Junkyard; The Planned
      Deterioration of America's Landscape. New York:
      Holt, $4.50 ($2.95 pap) (S: Lu).

1024 BLAUSTEIN, E. H. Ecology for the Junior High
      School Student. Dobbs Ferry, NY: Oceana, 1973,
      $6 ($4.75 pap) (L: 6-8) (S: Ec/Ed).

1025 _____, et al. Ecology for the Senior High School
      Student. Dobbs Ferry, NY: Oceana, 1973, $6.75
      ($5.50 pap) (L: HS) (S: Ec/Ed).

1026 BOOKCHIN, Murray and Ecology Action East. Ecology
      and Revolutionary Thought. Washington, NJ: Times
      Change Press, 1971, $1.25 (pap) (S: Ec/Ps).

1027 BOSSEL, Hartmut H. Solid Waste: Problems and
      Solutions. Santa Barbara: Mechanical Engineering
      Department, University of California, 1970. Sur-
      veys solid waste problem in the United States and
      other advanced societies; discusses present methods
      of solid waste disposal and necessity of developing
      methods of waste reduction and conversion (S: Wt).

1028 BOUGHEY, Arthur S. Contemporary Readings in
      Ecology. (Contemporary Thought in Biological
      Science Series.) Belmont, CA: Dickenson, 1968,
      $8.65 (pap) ($6.95 pap 'text ed') (S: Ec).

1029 _____. Ecology of Populations. Rev. ed. New
      York: Macmillan, 1973, $3.95 (pap), illus (S: Ec).

1030 _____. Fundamental Ecology. Scranton, PA:
      Intext, 1971, $4.25 (pap) (S: Ec).

1031 _____. Man and the Environment: An Introduction
      to Human Ecology and Evolution. New York:
      Macmillan, 1971, $10.95 ($6.95 pap) (S: Ec).

1032 _____. Readings in Man, the Environment, and
      Human Ecology. New York: Macmillan, 1973,
      $6.95, illus (S: Ec).

1033 BOULDING, Kenneth E. and Stahr, Elvis J., eds.

Economics of Pollution. (The Charles C. Moskowitz
lectures.) New York: New York University Press,
$6.50 (L: Adv HS & up) (S: E/A).

1034 BRAINERD, J. W. Nature Study for Conservation.
New York: Macmillan, 1971, $5.25 (pap) (S: Cn).

1035 BREHMAN, Thomas R. Environmental Demonstrations,
Experiments, and Projects for the Secondary School.
Englewood Cliffs, NJ: Prentice-Hall, 1973, $8.95
(S: Ed).

1036 BRESLER, Jack B., ed. Environments of Man.
Reading, MA: Addison-Wesley, 1968, $4.75
($3.60 school price) (L: 9-12) (S: A/O);
anthology of 24 articles.

1037 BRIGGS, Peter. Water: The Vital Essence. New
York: Harper & Row, 1967, $5.95, illus (L: 7 up)
(S: Wp).

1038 BRINK, Wellington. Big Hugh: The Father of Soil
Conservation. New York: Macmillan, 1951
(S: B/H).

1039 BROWER, David, et al. Only a Little Planet: A
Friends of the Earth Book. New York: Herder &
Herder, 1972, $12.50, illus (S: O/A); basically
photographs, supported by a rather poetic text.

1040 BURCH, William R., Jr. Daydreams and Nightmares:
A Sociological Essay on the American Environment.
New York: Harper & Row, 1971, $3.95 (pap)
(S: O).

1041 _____, et al., eds. Social Behavior, Natural Resources, and the Environment. New York: Harper
& Row, 1972, $5 (pap), 374p (S: O/A).

1042 BURTON, Maurice. Animals of Europe: The Ecology
of Wildlife. New York: Holt, Rinehart & Winston,
1973, $10.95, illus (L: 7 up) (S: Ec).

1043 CAILLIET, G., et al. Everyman's Guide to Ecological
Living. New York: Macmillan, 1971, $0.95 (pap),
119p (S: Ha).

1044 CALDER, Nigel, ed. Nature in the Round: A Guide
      to Environmental Science. New York: Viking,
      1973, $8.95, maps, diagrams (S: Ec).

1045 CARLOZZI, Carl A. and Carlozzi, Alice A. Conser-
      vation and Caribbean Regional Progress. Kent, OH:
      Kent State University Press, 1968, $4 (S: Cn).

1046 CARPENTER, J. R., ed. Ecological Glossary. New
      York: Hafner Press, 1971, reprint of 1938 ed,
      $7.95 (S: DBI).

1047 CARSON, Rachel. Edge of the Sea. Boston: Houghton
      Mifflin, 1955, $6.95 (L: 7 up) (S: Pn).

1048 _____. The Sea Around Us. New York: New
      American Library, 1954, $1.25 (pap) (L: 7 up)
      (S: Pn).

1049 _____. Sense of Wonder. New York: Harper &
      Row, 1965, $6.50 ($2.95 pap) ($5.52 PLB) (L:
      7 up) (S: Pn).

1050 _____. Under the Sea Wind: A Naturalist's Picture
      of Ocean Life. New York: Oxford University Press,
      1952, $7.50 (L: 7 up) (S: Pn).

1051 CARVAJAL, Joan and Munzer, Martha. Conservation
      Education: A Selected Bibliography. Danville, IL:
      Interstate, 1968, $2.50 (pap) (1971 suppl avail
      $0.75) (S: Ed/DBI).

1052 CLANCY, Dan and Jensen, Karen. Ecological Living
      Handbook. Pacheco, CA: Center for Ecological
      Living, 1971, $1 (pap) (S: Ha).

1053 CLARKE, George L. Elements of Ecology. Rev. ed.
      New York: Wiley, 1965, $11.45 (S: Ec).

1054 CLARKE, L. R., et al. Ecology of Insect Populations
      in Theory and Practice. New York: Halsted, 1967,
      $8.75 (S: Ec).

1055 CLAUS, George and Bolander, Karen. Ecological
      Overkill. New York: McKay, 1973, $7.95.

1056 CLAWSON, Marion and Held, Burnell. Federal Lands:

Their Use and Management. Lincoln: University
of Nebraska Press, 1965, $2.95 (pap), illus (S:
H/ Lu).

1057   CLAYTON, Kenneth C. and Huie, John M. Solid
       Waste Management: A Regional Solution. Cam-
       bridge: Ballinger, 1973, $12.50, 144p, illus
       (S: Wt).

1058   COBB, J. B., Jr. Is It Too Late: A Theory of
       Ecology. St. Paul, MN: Bruce Pub. Co., 1971,
       $1.95 (pap) (S: Ec).

1059   COMMONER, Barry. Science and Survival. New
       York: Viking, 1966, $1.25 (pap) (also avail, New
       York: Ballantine, 1970, $1.25 pap) (S: O).

1060   CONSERVATION Education Association. Critical Index on
       Man and His Environment. Danville, IL: Inter-
       state, 1972, $1.25 (pap) (S: DBI/ Ed).

1061   COOK, R. S. and O'Hearn, George T. Process for a
       Quality Environment. Green Bay: University of
       Wisconsin Press, $2.50 (S: Ed/A); papers pre-
       sented to the National Conference on Environmental
       Education.

1062   COOKE, Joseph J. and Wisner, William J. Blue
       Whale: Vanishing Leviathan. New York: Dodd,
       Mead, 1973, $3.95, illus (L: 3-8) (S: Es).

1063   COOLEY, Richard A. Politics and Conservation: The
       Decline of the Alaska Salmon. New York: Harper
       & Row, 1963 (S: Es/ Ps).

1064   COOPER, Margaret and Mantel, Linda. The Balance
       of Living: Survival in the Animal World. Garden
       City, NY: Doubleday, 1971, $5.95, illus (L: 6-8)
       (S: Ec).

1065   COOPER, M. and Silverman, I. Pioneers of Ecology.
       Maplewood, NJ: Hammond, 1972, $4.39, illus
       (L: 7 up) (S: H/B).

1065a _____ and _____. Your Environment and You:
       Level 1. Dobbs Ferry, NY: Oceana, 1973
       (L: 3-6) (S: O/ Ed).

1066   COX, George W. , ed. Readings in Conservation
        Ecology. New York: Appleton, 1969, $6.25 (pap),
        illus (S: Ec/A).

1067   COYLE, David Cushman. Conservation: An American
        Story of Conflict and Accomplishment. New Bruns-
        wick, NJ: Rutgers University Press, 1957 (S: Cn/
        H); undocumented but reliable survey of the con-
        servation movement.

1068   CREED, Robert. Ecological Genetics and Evolution.
        New York: Appleton, 1972, $25.85 (1973 text ed
        $24.50), illus (S: Ec).

1069   CUBBEDGE, Robert E. Destroyers of America.
        New York: Manor, 1971, $0.75 (pap) (S: O/Lu).

1070   CULBERTSON, J. M. , ed. Economic Development:
        An Ecological Approach. New York: Knopf, 1971,
        $7.95 (S: E).

1071   CURTIS, Richard and Hogan, Elizabeth. The Perils
        of the Peaceful Atom: The Myth of Safe Nuclear
        Power Plants. Garden City, NY: Doubleday,
        1969, $4.59 (S: N).

1072   CUTRIGHT, Paul Russell. Theodore Roosevelt, the
        Naturalist. New York: Harper, 1956 (S: B/H).

1073   DANA, Samuel T. Forest and Range Policy: Its
        Development in the United States. (The American
        Forestry Series.) New York: McGraw-Hill, 1956,
        $12.95 (S: F/H).

1074   DARNELL, Rezneat. Ecology and Man, ed. by Peter
        Volpe. Dubuque, IA: Brown, 1973, $2.50 (pap)
        (S: Ec).

1075   DASMANN, Raymond F. The Last Horizon. New
        York: Macmillan, 1971, $2.95 (pap), 279p (S: O).

1076   _____, et al. Ecological Principles for Economic
        Development. New York: Wiley, 1973, $5 (pap)
        (S: E/A).

1077   DAVIS, James Garrett. Environmental Planning Recom-
        mendations. Environmental Science Center, 5400

Glenwood Avenue, Golden Valley, MN 55422 (S:
Ed). Collection of practical selections for establishing and utilizing an outdoor environmental study area
at the Blake School in Hopkins, MN; valuable information for schools interested in setting up a similar
system, using the surrounding locale for environmental studies.

1078 DETWYLER, Thomas R. Man's Impact on Environment.
New York: McGraw-Hill, 1971, $6.95 (S: O).

1079 Directory of Natural History, Conservation and Environmental Organizations in Canada. Reprinted from
the Canadian Field-Naturalist, Box 3264, Postal
Station C, Ottawa, Ontario (S: DBI).

1080 DODD, Ed. Careers for the Seventies: Conservation.
New York: Macmillan, 1971, $4.95, illus (L: 7-
12) (S: Cr).

1081 DUBOS, René. Man Adapting. New Haven: Yale University Press, 1965, $15 ($3.75 pap), illus (L: HS
& up) (S: O); focuses on man and his health, but
the entire relation of man to his environment is, if
not covered, implied.

1082 DURRENBERGER, Robert W. Environment and Man:
A Bibliography. Palo Alto, CA: National Press,
1970, $1.95 (pap) (S: DBI).

1083 DWIGGINS, Don. Spaceship Earth: A Space Look at
Our Troubled Planet. Los Angeles: Golden Gate,
1970, $6.39, illus (L: 5 up) (S: O).

1084 Earth Science Curriculum Project. P.O. Box 1559,
Boulder, CO 80302 (S: Ed); has current projects
having to do with the environment; newsletter is
also available.

1085 Education Product Report, 1971. Washington, DC:
Environmental Education Materials, Vol. 4, Numbers 6 and 7. March-April (S: Ed/DBI); a bibliography of selected materials.

1086 EGLER, Frank. Way of Science: A Philosophy of
Ecology for the Layman. New York: Hafner,
1970, $6.95, illus (S: Et).

1087 EHRLICH, Paul. Eco-Catastrophe. San Francisco: City Lights Books, $0.50 (pap) (S: O).

1088 ELDER, Frederick. Crisis in Eden: A Religious Study of Man and Environment. New York: Abingdon, 1970, $3.95 (S: Et).

1089 ELTON, C. S. Ecology of Invasions by Animals and Plants. New York: Halsted, 1966, $5 (S: Ec).

1090 _____, ed. Ecology of Animals. 3d ed. New York: Halsted, 1966, $2.25 (pap) (S: Ec).

1091 Environmental Education: Education that Cannot Wait. Washington, DC: U.S. Government Printing Office, 1970, $0.30 (S: Ed); defines and gives rationale for environmental education.

1092 Environmental Education for Everyone--A Bibliography of Curriculum Materials for Environmental Studies. Washington, DC: NEA Publication Sales, Stock No. 471-14600, $0.75 (S: Ed/DBI).

1093 ENVIRONMENTAL Information Center. The Environmental Media Guide. New York: The Center, $2.50, 40p (L: HS & up) (S: DBI); lists 500 books and 630 films.

1093a Environmental Research Organizations Directory. Office of Graduate Studies and Research, State University of New York College at Fredonia, Fredonia, NY 14063 (S: DBI).

1094 The Environmentalist: A Guide to Free and Inexpensive Material of Environmental Interest. Available as of spring 1974 from Leonard H. Mooy, 390 Princeton Ave., Santa Barbara, CA 93111 (S: DBI/Ed).

1095 FABUN, Don. Ecology: The Man-Made Planet. New York: Glencoe, 1971, $1.40 (pap) (S: Ec).

1096 FADIMAN, Clifton, and White, Jean, eds. Ecocide and Thoughts Toward Survival. New York: Interbook Inc., 1972, $6.95 (S: O).

1097 FARVAR, M. Taghi and Milton, John P., eds. The Careless Technology: Ecology & International

Development. Garden City, NY: Doubleday, $25,
illus (S: T/A).

1098 FAUSOLD, Martin L. Gifford Pinchot, Bull Moose
Progressive. Syracuse, NY: Syracuse University
Press, 1961; reprinted by Greenwood, 1973,
$12.25, illus (S: B).

1098a FERGUSON, J. G., Pub. Co. Editorial Staff. Career
Opportunities: Ecology, Conservation, and Environ-
mental Control. Chicago: J. G. Ferguson, 1970;
Doubleday, 1971; $6.95, illus (L: 7-12) (S: Cr).

1099 FIRNHABER, R. Paul. Earth Care Manual. Minneapolis, MN: Augsburg, 1971, $1.95 (pap), 110p
(S: O).

1100 FISHER, James, et al. Wildlife in Danger. New
York: Viking, 1969, $12.95 (S: Es).

1101 FORBES, R. J. The Conquest of Nature: Technology
and Its Consequences. New York: Praeger, 1968,
$1.25 (S: T).

1102 FORD, E. B. Ecological Genetics. 3d ed. New
York: Halsted, 1971, $16 (S: Ec).

1103 FORD, Richard F. and Hazen, William E., eds.
Readings in Aquatic Ecology. Philadelphia:
Saunders, 1972, $7 (pap) (S: Ec/A).

1104 FORSTNER, Lorne J. and Todd, John H., eds. Ever-
lasting Universe: Readings on the Ecological Revolution. Lexington, MA: Heath, $4.25 (pap), with
teacher's manual (S: A/O/Ed).

1104a FOSS, Phillip O. Politics and Ecology. Belmont, CA:
Duxbury Press, 1972, $4.95 (pap) (S: Ps).

1105 FRAKES, George and Solberg, Curtis B., eds. Pollution Papers. New York: Appleton, 1971, $7.30
($4.15 pap), illus (S: A/O) (L: Adv HS & up).

1106 FRIENDLY, Natalie. Miraculous Web: The Balance
of Life. Englewood Cliffs, NJ: Prentice-Hall,
$4.95, illus (L: 5-8) (S: Ec).

1107 FRISBEE, Lucy P. John Burroughs: Boy of Field
      and Stream. Indianapolis, IN: Bobbs-Merrill,
      1964, $2.95 ($2.64 'text ed'), illus (L: 3-7)
      (S: B/H).

1108 FULLER, R. Buckminster. Operating Manual for
      Spaceship Earth. New York: Simon & Schuster,
      1970, $1.95 (pap) (also avail, New York: Pocket
      Books, $1.25 pap) (S: O).

1109 FUNDERBURK, Robert Steele. The History of Conser-
      vation Education in the United States. Nashville,
      TN: George Peabody College for Teachers, 1948,
      151p (S: Ed/H); college oriented study.

1110 GILLETTE, Elizabeth, ed. Action for Wilderness.
      San Francisco: Sierra Club, 1972, $3.50 (pap)
      (S: A/W).

1111 GIRL Scouts of the USA. A Council Guide to Eco-
      Action. New York: Girl Scouts, $0.75 (4 for $2)
      (pap) (L: Adult) (S: Ed/Ha).

1112 _____. Eco-Action. New York: Girl Scouts,
      $0.50 (10 for $4) (pap) (L: 7 up) (S: Ha).

1113 GOFMAN, John W. and Tamplin, Arthur R. Poisoned
      Power: The Case Against Nuclear Power Plants.
      Emmaus, PA: Rodale, 1971, $6.95 ($2.95 pap),
      368p (S: N/Eg).

1114 Golden Guide to Environmental Organizations. Racine,
      WI: Western, 1972, $0.95 (pap) (S: DBI).

1115 GOLDMAN, Marshall I. Ecology & Economics: Con-
      trolling Pollution in the 1970's. Englewood Cliffs,
      NJ: Prentice-Hall, 1972, $6.95 ($3.15 pap)
      (S: Ec).

1116 GOLDSTEIN, Jerome, ed. The New Food Chain: An
      Organic Link Between Farm and City. Emmaus,
      PA: Rodale, 1973, $3.95 (pap) (S: U).

1117 GOODMAN, Gordon T., et al., eds. Ecology and the
      Industrial Society. New York: Wiley, 1965, $15
      (S: E).

1118 GRAD, Frank P. , et al. Environmental Control:
      Priorities, Policies, and the Law. New York:
      Columbia University Press, 1971, $9 (S: L/A).

1119 GRAVA, Sigurd. Urban Planning Aspects of Water
      Pollution Control. New York: Columbia University
      Press, 1969 (S: U/Wp); discussion of water pollu-
      tion control measures, the problem of waste dis-
      posal, and the difficulties both impose to the urban
      planner.

1120 GRAY, Oscar S. Cases and Materials on Environ-
      mental Law. 2d ed. Washington, DC: Bureau of
      National Affairs, 1973, $22.50 (S: L).

1121 GRAY, Robert. The Rescue of the World's Vanishing
      Wildlife. New York: W. W. Norton, 1968 (S:
      Es).

1122 GRAY, T. R. and Parkinson, D. Ecology of Soil
      Bacteria. International Symposium on the Ecology
      of Soil Bacteria. Toronto: Toronto University
      Press, 1968, $25 (S: Ec).

1123 GRAYSON, Melvin J. and Shepard, Thomas, Jr.
      The Disaster Lobby: Prophets of Ecological
      Doom. Chicago: Follett, 1973, $7.95, 294p
      (L: HS & up) (S: C): it's a plot concocted by
      the Left working hand-in-hand with the media;
      unimpressive.

1124 GREEN, I. Conservation from A to Z. Mankato, MN:
      Oddo, $3.95 PLB ($1.75 pap), illus (L: 4 up)
      (S: Cn).

1125 GREENWOOD, Ned H. and Edwards, J. M. B. Human
      Environments and Natural Systems: A Conflict of
      Dominion. Belmont, CA: Duxbury Press, 1972,
      $6.95 (pap) (S: O).

1126 GROSSMAN, Adrienne and Beardwood, Valerie. Trails
      of His Own: The Story of John Muir and His Fight
      to Save Our National Parks. New York: McKay,
      1961, $4.50, illus (L: 6-9) (S: B/H).

1127 GROSSMAN, Shelly. Understanding Ecology. New
      York: Grosset & Dunlap, $3.95 (S: Ec).

1128 GUSTAFSON, Axel F., et al. <u>Conservation in the</u>
      <u>United States.</u> 3d ed. Ithaca, NY: Comstock,
      1949, $14.50, illus (S: Cn/H).

1129 GUTNIK, Martin J. <u>Ecology & Pollution--1. Air.</u>
      Chicago: Children's Press, 1973, $4.50 (PLB),
      illus (L: 2-4) (S: Ap/R).

1130 _____. <u>Ecology & Pollution--2. Land.</u> Chicago:
      Children's Press, 1973, $4.50 (PLB), illus (L:
      2-4) (S: Lu/R).

1131 _____. <u>Ecology & Pollution--3. Water.</u> Chicago:
      Children's Press, 1973, $4.50 (PLB), illus (L:
      2-4) (S: Wp/R).

1132 HADDOCK, Robert and Haddock, Sherry. <u>Broken Web.</u>
      Nashville: Southern, 1971, $0.50 (pap) (S: Ec).

1133 HALEY, Gail. <u>Noah's Ark.</u> New York: Atheneum,
      1971, $6.95 (PLB), illus (L: PS-3) (S: R).

1134 HALL, Gus. <u>Ecology: Can We Survive Under Capi-</u>
      <u>talism?</u> New York: International Publishers,
      1972, $1.25 (pap), illus (S: Ps).

1135 HAMBLIN, Lynnette. <u>Pollution: The World Crisis.</u>
      New York: Barnes & Noble, 1971, $4.25 (S: O).

1136 HANBURY-TENISON, Robin. <u>A Question of Survival.</u>
      New York: Scribners, 1973, $9.95 (S: O).

1137 HANSEN, Niles M. <u>The Future of Non-Metropolitan</u>
      <u>America.</u> Lexington, MA: Lexington Books, 1973,
      $13, 256p, illus (S: Lu).

1138 HARRIS, Jacqueline and Steinkemp, Erwin. <u>Ecology:</u>
      <u>Man Explores Life.</u> Columbus, OH: Xerox Edu-
      cational Publications, 1970, $0.40 (pap) (S: Ec).

1139 HARRIS, Melville. <u>Environment Studies</u> (Elem.). Scho-
      lastic Book Services (Publishers), Division of Scholas-
      tic Magazines, 50 W. 44th St., New York, NY 10037.
      1971, $2.65 (pap) (S: Ed/I).

1140 HATCH Association, Inc. <u>Survival Kit: Ecology and</u>
      <u>Social Action.</u> New York: Harper & Row, 1971,

$1.28 text, $1.96 teacher's manual, $50 kit
(S: Ps/Ed) (L: 7-12).

1141 HAY, John. In Defense of Nature. Boston: Little
      Brown, 1970, $2.65 (pap) (S: Pn).

1142 HELD, R. Burnell and Clawson, Marion. Soil Conser-
      vation in Perspective. Baltimore: Johns Hopkins
      University Press, 1965, $11, illus (S: Cn).

1143 HENDERSON, Lawrence J. Fitness of the Environ-
      ment. Gloucester, MA: Peter Smith, $5 (S: O).

1144 HENKIN, Harmon, et al., eds. Environment, the
      Establishment, and the Law. Boston: Houghton
      Mifflin, 1971, $6.95 ($4.75 pap), illus (S: L/A).

1145 HIGHSMITH, Richard, et al. Conservation in the
      United States. Chicago: Rand-McNally, 1962 (S: Cn).

1146 HILLABY, John. Nature and Man. New York: Roy,
      $3.25 (L: 7 up) (S: O).

1147 HOKE, John. The First Book of Solar Energy. New
      York: Watts, 1968, $3.75 (PLB), illus (S: Eg).

1148 HOLDREN, John and Ehrlich, Paul. Global Ecology:
      Readings Toward a Rational Strategy for Man. New
      York: Harcourt Brace Jovanovich, 1971, $4.95
      (pap) (S: O).

1149 HOOD, Donald, ed. Impingement of Man on the Oceans.
      New York: Wiley, 1971, $27.50 (S: Wp).

1150 HOPE, Jack. Parks in Peril. San Francisco: Sierra
      Club, 1972, $3.25 (pap) (S: W).

1151 HORWITZ, Eleanor C. Clearcutting: A View from the
      Top. Washington, DC: Acropolis, 1973, $3.95
      (pap) (S: F).

1152 HOULT, D. P., ed. Oil on the Sea. (Ocean Tech-
      nology Series.) New York: Plenum, 1969, $12.50
      (S: Ol/Wp).

1153 HOYLE, Brian S., ed. Spatial Aspects of Development.
      New York: Wiley, 1973 (S: I/E).

1154 HUMPHREY, Clifford C. and Evans, Robert G. What's
      Ecology? Northbrook, IL: Hubbard Press, 1972,
      $3.95 ($1.50 pap), illus (L: 4-7) (S: Ec).

1155 _____ and _____. What's Ecology? Northbrook,
      IL: Hubbard Press, 1972, $3.95 ($1.50 pap), illus
      (L: 8-12) (S: Ec).

1156 HURLEY, William D. Environmental Legislation.
      Springfield, IL: Thomas, 1971, $6.50 (S: Ps/L).

1157 HUTNICK, Russell and Davis, Grant, eds. Ecology
      and Reclamation of Devastated Land. New York:
      Gordon, 1973, 2 vols (S: Ec/Cn).

1158 HYNES, H. B. Ecology of Running Waters. Toronto:
      University of Toronto Press, 1970, $25 (S: Ec).

1159 Interaction of Man and the Biosphere. Chicago: Rand-
      McNally, 1970 (S: Ed); a JHS science text developed
      to accompany Matter & Energy.

1160 ISE, John. Our National Park Policy: A Critical His-
      tory. Baltimore: Johns Hopkins University Press,
      1961, $17.50 (S: Lu/H).

1161 _____. The United States Forest Policy. (Use and
      Abuse of America's Natural Resource Series.) New
      York: Arno, 1972, reprint of 1920 ed, $17 (also,
      St. Clair Shores, MI: Scholarly Press, 1973,
      $17.50) (S: F/H).

1162 _____. The United States Oil Policy. (Use and
      Abuse of America's Natural Resources Series.)
      New York: Arno, 1972, reprint of 1928 ed, $25
      (S: Ol/H).

1163 IVANY, J. George. Environment: Readings for
      Teachers. Reading, MA: Addison-Wesley, 1972,
      $3.50 (pap) (S: Ed).

1164 IZAAK Walton League of America. Clean Water: It's
      Up to You. Glenview, IL: Izaak Walton League of
      America (S: Wp). Gives background on pollution
      laws, water quality standards, enforcement of
      standards, action individuals can take, lists of
      agencies and organizations concerned with pollution.

1165 JACKSON, Dixie S. Who Needs Nature? New York:
      Wiley, 1973, $3.95 (pap).

1166 JARRETT, Henry, ed. Environmental Quality in a
      Growing Economy. Baltimore: Johns Hopkins
      University Press, 1966 (S: E); good collection.

1167 [no entry]

1168 JOFFE, Joyce. Conservation: Maintaining the Natural
      Balance. Garden City, NY: Doubleday, 1970,
      $6.95 (L: 7-10) (S: Cn).

1169 JOHNSON, C. Natural World: Chaos and Conserva-
      tion. New York: McGraw-Hill, 1972, $5.95
      ($3.95 pap) (S: Cn).

1170 JOHNSON, Huey D., ed. No Deposit-No Return: Man
      and His Environment: A View Toward Survival.
      Reading, MA: Addison-Wesley, 1970, $3.25 (pap)
      (S: A/O).

1171 JONES, Thomas C., ed. Environment of America:
      Present, Future, Past. Garden City, NY: Double-
      day, 1972, $17.50, illus (S: O).

1172 KAILL, W. Michael and Frey, John. Environments in
      Profile: An Aquatic Approach. New York: Har-
      per & Row, 1973, $7.95 (pap), illus (S: Ec).

1173 KAY, David A. and Skolnikoff, Eugene B., eds. World
      Eco-Crisis: International Organizations in Response.
      Madison: University of Wisconsin Press, 1972,
      $12.50 ($2.50 pap), 350p (S: O/I) (L: Adv HS &
      up).

1174 KEOSTNER, E. J. and Dayton Museum of Natural His-
      tory. The Do-It-Yourself Environmental Handbook.
      Boston: Little, Brown, 1972, $1.95 (pap), 76p,
      illus (S: Ha).

1175 KILLEEN, Jacqueline and Ecology Action Educational
      Institute, eds. Ecology at Home. San Francisco:
      101 Products, 1971, $1.95 (pap), illus (S: Ha).

1176 KING, Judson. The Conservation Fight: From Theo-
      dore Roosevelt to the Tennessee Valley Authority.

Washington, DC: Public Affairs Press, 1959
(S: Cn/H). Judson King wrote this book after many
years of championing public control of water resources; his focus is strictly on water conservation.

1177 KLOTZ, John. Ecology Crisis. St. Louis: Concordia,
1971, $2.75 (pap) (S: O).

1178 KNEESE, Allen V., et al. Economics and the Environment: A Materials Balance Approach. Baltimore:
Johns Hopkins University Press, 1971, $2.50 (pap),
illus (S: E/A).

1179 _____, et al., eds. Managing the Environment:
International Economics Cooperation for Pollution
Control. New York: Praeger, 1971, $15 (S:
E/I/A).

1180 _____ and Bower, Blair. Environmental Quality
Analysis: Theory and Method in the Social Sciences.
Baltimore: Johns Hopkins University Press, 1972,
$12, illus (S: O).

1181 KNIGHT, Clifford B. Basic Concepts of Ecology. New
York: Macmillan, 1965, $9.95, 468p, index, illus
(L: Adv HS & up) (S: Ec); fairly technical intro-
ductory text; also useful for the interested layman.

1182 KOFORD, Carl B. The California Condor. Gloucester,
MA: Peter Smith, 1966, $4.50, illus (S: Es).

1183 KOLBAS, Grace H. Ecology: Cycle and Recycle.
New York: Sterling, 1972, $7.95 ($6.89 PLB),
illus (S: Ec).

1184 KORMONDY, Edward J., ed. Readings in Ecology.
Englewood Cliffs, NJ: Prentice-Hall, 1965, $4.95
(pap), illus (S: Ec/A).

1184b LADD, George T. Focus on Environmental Education
in New England: A Compendium of School Programs. Newton, MA: New England School Development Council, 1971 (S: Ed) (L: Adult). Includes
replies to questionnaire about K-12 level environmental education programs in 102 classes throughout New England; entries are detailed according

to purpose, objectives, resources, etc.

1185 LAKE Erie Environmental Studies. <u>Directory of Organ-</u>
      <u>izations Concerned with Environmental Research.</u>
      Fredonia, NY: State University College at Fredonia,
      1970, $2, 150p (L: HS & up) (S: DBI).

1186 LAMBERT, Joyce M. <u>Teaching of Ecology.</u> Philadel-
      phia: F. A. Davis, 1967, $8.50, illus (S: Ed/Ec).

1187 LAWSON, G. W. <u>Ecology and Conservation in Ghana.</u>
      New York: Panther House, 1971, $2.50 (pap)
      (S: Cn/Ec).

1188 LAYCOCK, George. <u>Water Pollution.</u> New York:
      Grossett & Dunlap, 1972, $4.95 ($3.99 PLB),
      illus (L: 4-6) (S: Wp).

1189 LEADLEY-BROWN, Alison. <u>Ecology of Fresh Water.</u>
      Cambridge: Harvard University Press, 1971, $4,
      illus (S: Ec).

1190 LEAVITT, Helen. <u>Superhighway--Superhoax.</u> New
      York: Doubleday, 1970, $6.95 (also avail in pap,
      New York: Ballantine, 1971, $0.95), illus (S:
      U/Lu); critical study of American highways and
      their adverse effect on the urban and rural areas.

1191 LEEN, Nina. <u>And Then There Were None: America's</u>
      <u>Vanishing Wildlife.</u> New York: Holt, Rinehart, &
      Winston, 1973, $8.95, illus (L: 1-7) (S: Es/R).

1192 LEIGH-PEMBERTON, John. <u>Vanishing Wild Animals</u>
      <u>of the World.</u> New York: Watts, 1968, $7.95
      (S: Es).

1193 LEISNER, Robert S. and Kormondy, Edward J.
      <u>Ecology.</u> Dubuque, IA: William C. Brown, 1971,
      $2.50 (pap) (S: Ec).

1194 _____ and _____. <u>Pollution.</u> Rev. ed. Dubuque,
      IA: William C. Brown, 1971, $2.50 (pap) (S:
      O/Wp/Ap).

1195 LEOPOLD, Luna B. and Davis, K. S. <u>Water.</u> New
      York: Time-Life Publications, 1966, $4.95 (S:
      Wp); very good pictorial coverage.

1196 LEWALLEN, John. Ecology of Devastation: Indochina.
      Sante Fe, NM: Gannon, $4.20 (PLB) (also avail in
      pap, Baltimore: Penguin, 1971, $1.95) (S: Ec/I).

1197 LEWIS, Howard R. With Every Breath You Take.
      New York: Crown, 1965, $5, illus (S: Ap).

1198 LEWIS, Marianna O. , ed. The Foundation Directory.
      4th ed. New York: Russell Sage Foundation/
      Columbia University Press, 1971, $15 (L: HS &
      up) (S: DBI).

1199 LIBBY, L. M. , ed. Fifty Environmental Problems of
      Timely Importance. Santa Monica, CA: Rand Cor-
      poration, 1970 (S: Cs); survey of some of the most
      urgent environmental problems, with contemporary
      commentaries on them.

1200 LILLARD, Richard G. Eden in Jeopardy: Man's
      Prodigal Meddling with His Environment: The
      Southern California Experience. New York:
      Knopf, 1966, $6.95 (S: O).

1201 LITTLE, Charles. A Town Is Saved, Not More by the
      Righteous Men in It Than by the Woods and Swamps
      That Surround It. (Landform Series.) New York:
      Scribners, 1973, $19.95, 128p, illus (S: U/Lu).

1202 LONGGOOD, William. Poisons in Your Food. New
      York: Pyramid, 1969, $0.95 (pap) (S: Fp).

1203 LORAINE, John A. and Rumsey, R. D. The Death
      of Tomorrow. Philadelphia: Lippincott, 1972,
      $8.95, 376p (S: O).

1204 LOVE, Glen A. and Love, Rhoda M. Ecological
      Crisis: Readings for Survival. New York: Har-
      court Brace Jovanovich, 1971, $3.95 (S: O).

1205 LOVE, Sam and Obst, David, eds. Ecotage. New
      York: Pocket Books, 1972, $1.25 (pap) (S: O).

1206 LUTZ, Paul and Santmire, H. Paul. Ecological
      Renewal. Philadelphia: Fortress, 1972, $3.95
      (pap) (S: O).

1207 MAASS, Arthur. Muddy Waters: The Army Engineers

and the Nation's Rivers. Cambridge, MA: Harvard University Press, 1951 (S: Wp).

1208   MACAN, T. T. Freshwater Ecology. New York:
John Wiley, 1964 (S: Ec).

1209   McCLELLAN, Grant S. Land Use in the United
States. (Reference Shelf, Vol. 43, No 2.) New
York: Wilson, 1971, $4.50 (L: HS & up) (S: Lu).

1210   _____, ed. Consuming Public. (Reference Shelf,
Vol 40, No 3.) New York: Wilson, 1968, $4.50
(L: HS & up) (S: O).

1211   McCOMBS, Laurence G. and Rosa, Nicholas. Ecology:
Web of Life. Rev. ed. Reading, MA: Addison-
Wesley, 1972, $4 (pap), teacher's manual avail
(L: 7-12) (S: Ec).

1212   McCOY, J. J. To Feed a Nation. New York: Nelson,
1971, $4.95 (L: 7 up) (S: Ag).

1213   _____. Saving Our Wildlife. New York: Macmillan,
1970, $5.95, illus (L: 7-12) (S: Es).

1214   McCUEN, Gary E. and Bender, David L., eds. Ecology Controversy: Opposing Viewpoints. Rev. ed.
Anoka, MN: Greenhaven, 1973, $2.45 (pap) (L:
9-12) (S: Ed/ Ps).

1215   McDONALD, Rita. Guide to Literature on Environmental Sciences. Washington, DC: American
Society for Engineering Education, 1970 (S: DBI).

1216   McLUSKY, Donald S. Ecology of Estuaries. New
York: Hillary, 1972, $6.25 (S: Ec).

1217   McNULTY, Faith. Whooping Crane: The Bird That
Defies Extinction. New York: Dutton, 1966,
$5.95 (S: Es).

1218   McVEAN, D. N. and Lockie, J. D., eds. Ecology
and Land Use in Upland Scotland. Chicago:
Aldine, 1969, $7.50, illus (S: Ec/ Lu).

1219   MALTHUS, Thomas, Huxley, Julian, and Osborn,
Frederick. On Population: Three Essays. New

York: Mentor, 1960, $0.60 (S: P/H).

1220   MASON, William H. and Folkerts, George W. Environ-
       mental Problems: Principles, Readings and Com-
       ments. Dubuque, IA: William Brown, 1973, $5.50
       (pap) (S: O).

1221   MASSINI, Giancarlo. S.O.S. Save Our Earth. New
       York: Grosset & Dunlap, 1972, $3.95 ($3.99 PLB),
       50p, illus (L: 3 up) (S: O).

1222   MENDOZA, George. Goodbye, River, Goodbye.
       Garden City, NY: Doubleday, 1971, $3.95
       (L: 5-12) (S: Wp).

1223   MIGEL, J. Michael, ed. Stream Conservation Hand-
       book. New York: Avon, 1973, $7.95 (S: Wp).

1224   MILGROM, Harry. ABC of Ecology. New York:
       Macmillan, 1972, $4.95 (L: K-2) (S: R/Ec).

1225   MILLS, D. H. An Introduction to Freshwater Ecology.
       New York: Longman (Oliver & Boyd), 1973, $3,
       108p (S: Ec).

1226   MILNE, Lorus and Milne, Margery. Because of a
       Tree. New York: Atheneum, 1963, $3.95 ($4.08
       PLB) (L: 5 up) (S: F).

1227   _____ and _____. Water and Life. New York:
       Atheneum, 1964, $5.75 ($3.25 pap), illus (S: Wp).

1228   Minnesota State Publications Catalog. St. Paul, MN:
       Minnesota State Publications, n.d. (S: Ed). In-
       cludes environmental educational curriculum ma-
       terial; free.

1229   MOLLER, Clifford B. Architectural Environment and
       our Mental Health. New York: Horizon, 1968,
       $5.95 (S: U).

1230   MONTAGU, Ashley. The Endangered Environment.
       Philadelphia: Auerbach, 1972, $9.95 (S: O).

1231   MOORE, J. A. Science for Society: A Bibliography.
       Washington, DC: AAAS Publication, 1971 (S: DBI).

1232 MOSS, F. E. The Water Crisis. New York: Praeger,
      1967, $8.50, illus (S: Wp).

1233 MUIR, John. Gentle Wilderness: The Sierra Nevada.
      (Exhibit Format Series.) San Francisco: Sierra,
      1964, $30, illus (S: Pn/H).

1234 _____. The Mountains of California. Garden City,
      NY: Doubleday, 1961, reprint of 1913 ed, $1.45
      (pap) (S: Pn/H).

1235 _____. My First Summer in the Sierra. Dunwoody,
      GA: Berg, 1972, $12.50 (PLB), illus (S: Pn/H/B).

1236 _____. Our National Parks. New York: AMS
      Press, 1970, reprint of 1901 ed, $11.50 (also
      avail, St. Clair Shores, MI: Scholarly Press,
      $7.95), illus (S: Pn/H).

1237 _____. South of Yosemite: Selected Writings of
      John Muir, ed. by Frederick R. Gunsky. Garden
      City, NY: Doubleday, 1968, $7.50, illus (S:
      Pn/H).

1238 _____. Story of My Boyhood and Youth. Madison:
      University of Wisconsin Press, 1965, $2.50, illus
      (S: Pn/H/B).

1239 _____. Thousand Mile Walk to the Gulf. Dunwoody,
      GA: Berg, 1969, $12.50 (PLB) (S: Pn/H/B).

1240 _____. Trails of Wonder, ed. by Peter Seymour.
      Kansas City, MO: Hallmark, 1972, $2.50, illus
      (S: Pn/H).

1241 _____. Travels in Alaska. New York: AMS Press,
      1971, reprint of 1915 ed, $9.50 (S: Pn/H).

1242 _____. The Wonders of America's Wilderness in
      the Words of John Muir, ed. by Kent Dannen and
      Country Beautiful. Beautiful Country Corporation,
      24198 West Bluemound Rd., Waukesha, WI 53186.
      1973, $12.95, 160p, illus (S: Pn/H).

1243 _____. The Yosemite. Garden City, NY: Doubleday,
      1962, reprint of 1912 ed, $1.25 (pap) (S: Pn/H).

1244 MUNZER, Martha and the Conservation Foundation.
Planning Our Town. New York: Knopf, 1964,
$4.99 (PLB), illus (L: 7 up) (S: U).

1245 MURPHY, M. Blakely, ed. Conservation of Oil and
Gas: A Legal History, 1948. (Use and Abuse of
America's Natural Resources Series.) New York:
Arno, 1972, reprint of 1949 ed, $33 (S: Ol).

1246 MYERS, C. Environmental Crisis: Will We Survive?
Englewood Cliffs, NJ: Prentice-Hall, 1972, $4.95
($1.84 pap) (S: O).

1247 NATIONAL Audubon Society. Directory of Nature
Centers and Related Environmental Education
Facilities. The Society, Nature Center Planning
Division, 950 Third Avenue, New York, NY 10022
(S: Ed/DBI).

1248 NATIONAL Education Association. Environment and
Population: A Sourcebook for Teachers. Washington, DC: NEA, 1972, $5.25 ($3.75 pap) (S: Ed/P/O).

1249 _____. Man and His Environment: An Introduction
to Using Environmental Studies Areas. Washington,
DC: NEA, 1970, $1.75 (pap), 14-min color film
strip with record narration and script, $17 (S: Ed).

1250 NATIONAL Foundation for Environmental Control.
Directory of Environmental Information Sources.
The Foundation, 151 Tremont Street, Boston, MA
02111, n.d. (S: DBI).

1251 NATIONAL School Public Relations Association. Environment and the Schools. Arlington, VA: The
Association, 1971, $4.75 (S: Ed).

1252 NATURAL Science for Youth Foundation. Directory--
Natural Science Centers for Youth. The Foundation,
763 Silvermine Rd., New Canaan, CT 06840, 1972/
73, $4./professionals and libraries; $5./general
public (S: DBI).

1253 NAUMOV, N. P. Ecology of Animals, ed. by Norman
D. Levine; tr. from Russian by Frederick K.
Plous, Jr. Urbana: University of Illinois, 1972,
$17.50 (S: Ec).

1254   NAVARRA, John Gabriel. Our Noisy World: The
       Problems of Noise Pollution. Garden City, NY:
       Doubleday, 1969, $4.95 (L: 6-9) (S: Np).

1255   NICHOLSON, Max. The Big Change: After the En-
       vironmental Revolution. New York: McGraw-Hill,
       1973, $8.96, 300p (S: O).

1256   NIKOLSKY, G. V. Ecology of Fishes, tr. by L.
       Birkett. New York: Academic, 1963, $17 (S: Ec).

1257   NIXON, Edgar G., ed. Franklin D. Roosevelt and
       Conservation 1911-1945, New York: Arno, 1972,
       reprint of 1957 ed, $58, 2 vols (S: B/H/Ps).

1258   NOVICK, Sheldon and Cottrell, Dorothy, eds. Our
       World in Peril: An Environmental Review. New
       York: Fawcett, 1971, $1.50 (pap), illus (S: O).

1259   ODUM, Eugene P. Ecology. New York: Holt, Rine-
       hart & Winston, 1963, $4.25 (S: Ec/Ed); was long
       the foremost ecology text and the touchstone against
       which subsequent ones were measured.

1260   ODUM, Howard T. Environment, Power, and Society.
       New York: Wiley, 1971, $10.95 ($5.95 pap) (S:
       Eg).

1261   [no entry]

1262   OLMSTED, Frederick Law, Jr. and Kimball, Theodore,
       eds. Frederick Law Olmsted--Landscape Architect,
       1822-1903. New York: Putnam, 1928 (S: B/H/Lu).

1263   OLSEN, Spang Ib. Smoke, tr. from Danish by Vir-
       ginia A. Jensen. New York: Coward McCann,
       1972, $4.95, illus (L: K-3) (S: R/Ap).

1264   OPIE, John, ed. Americans and Environment: The
       Controversy Over Ecology. Lexington, MA: Heath,
       1971, $2.50 (pap) (S: O).

1265   OSBORN, Fairfield. Limits to the Earth. Westport,
       CT: Greenwood, 1971, reprint of 1953 ed, $10.50
       (S: O).

1266   _____. Our Crowded Planet. Garden City, NY:

Doubleday, $4.95 (S: P).

1267 OWEN, D. F. Man's Environmental Predicament:
      Human Ecology in Tropical Africa. New York:
      Oxford University Press, 1973, $6.50, 220p
      (S: Ec/I).

1268 OWINGS, Loren C. Environmental Values 1860-1970:
      An Information Guide. Detroit: Gale, n.d., $15
      (S: Et/H).

1269 PADDOCK, Paul and Paddock, William. Famine 1975:
      America's Decision, Who Will Survive? Boston:
      Little, Brown, 1968, $6.95 ($2.65 pap) (S: P).

1270 PARSON, R. L. Conserving American Resources.
      2d ed. Englewood Cliffs, NJ: Prentice-Hall,
      1964, $11.80 (S: Cn).

1271 PARSON, Ruben A. Conserving American Resources.
      3d ed. Englewood Cliffs, NJ: Prentice-Hall,
      1972, $11.95 (S: Cn).

1272 PAULSEN, David F. and Denhardt, Robert B., eds.
      Pollution & Public Policy: A Book of Readings.
      New York: Dodd Mead, 1973, $4.95 (pap), 250p
      (L: College) (S: A/Ps); an excellent anthology for
      advanced government students.

1273 People and Their Environment, by the Conservation
      Curriculum Improvement Project, South Carolina
      Department of Education, Columbia, SC. Chicago:
      J. G. Ferguson, 1969, $34./set or $4.25 for each
      of the 8 vols (S: Ed/Ps/Ha). A set of teacher guides
      providing environmental questions to be raised with
      children in classes K-12; workbooks for the secondary
      level include wider subject areas such as life science,
      social studies, and home economics.

1274 PERERA, Thomas and Perera, Gretchen. Louder &
      Louder: The Dangers of Noise Pollution. New
      York: Watts, 1973, $4.95 (PLB), illus (L: 4-6)
      (S: Np).

1275 PERLOFF, H. S., ed. The Quality of the Urban En-
      vironment; Essays on New Resources in an Urban
      Age. Baltimore: Johns Hopkins University Press,

1969, $6.50 (pap), illus (S: A/O).

1276 PETERSON, Robin and Phillips, William. Ecology and
      the Marketplace. New York: MSS Information,
      1972, $13 (S: Ec).

1277 PINE, Tillie S. and Levine, Joseph. Air All Around
      Us. New York: McGraw-Hill, 1960, $3.95
      ($3.83 PLB), illus (L: 2-5) (S: Ap).

1278 PINKETT, Harold T. Gifford Pinchot: Private and
      Public Forester. Urbana: University of Illinois
      Press, 1970, $6.95 (L: HS & up) (S: B); a biog-
      raphy of America's first forester, the father of
      conservation.

1279 PITTS, James N., Jr. and Metcalf, Robert L. Ad-
      vances in Environmental Science & Technology, in
      4 vols. New York: Wiley, 1969-1973; vol 1
      $17.95, vol 2 $19.95, vols 3-4, price not set
      (S: DBI).

1280 PLATT, Rutherford. Open Land in Urban Illinois:
      Roles of the Citizen Advocate. Dekalb: Northern
      Illinois University Press, 1971, $4 (pap) (S: Lu/Ps).

1281 PLOWDEN, David. Hand of Man on America. New
      York: Smithsonian, 1971, $12.50 (also avail in
      pap, Riverside, CT: Chatham Press, 1973, $5.95),
      illus (S: O).

1282 Pollution Control Directory. American Chemical So-
      ciety, 1155 16th St. N.W., Washington, DC 20036
      n.d. (S: DBI).

1283 POSTMAN, Neil and Weingarten, Charles. Teaching
      as a Subversive Activity. New York: Delacorte,
      1969 (also avail in pap, Dell, 1971) (S: Ed).

1284 POTTER, Van Resalaer. Bioethics: Bridge to the
      Future. Englewood Cliffs, NJ: Prentice-Hall,
      1971, $6.95 ($4.50 pap), illus (S: Et).

1285 PRATT, A. L., ed. Environmental Education in the
      Community College. Washington, DC: American
      Association of Junior Colleges, n.d., $4 (S: Ed);
      a collection of articles with special reference to
      careers.

1286 PRINGLE, Laurence. From Pond to Prairie: The
      Changing World of a Pond and Its Life. New York:
      Macmillan, 1972, $4.95, illus (L: 4-6) (S: Ec).

1287 _____. Pests and People: The Search for Sensible
      Pest Control. New York: Macmillan, 1972, $4.95,
      illus (L: 7 up) (S: Pc).

1288 _____. This Is a River: Exploring an Ecosystem.
      New York: Macmillan, 1972, $4.95, illus (L:
      4 up) (S: Ec).

1289 _____, et al. Highlights Ecology Handbook. Colum-
      bus, OH: Highlights, 1973, $1 (pap) (L: 2-6)
      (S: Ec).

1290 Programs in Environmental Education, by the National
      Science Teachers Association, Washington, DC:
      NEA Publication Sales (Stock No. 471-14394), 1970,
      $1.50 (S: Ed).

1291 The Quest for Environmental Quality. Washington, DC:
      U.S. Government Printing Office, 1971, $0.35
      (S: DBI); an annotated bibliography of federal and
      state action.

1292 RAMSAY, William and Anderson, Claude. Managing
      the Environment: An Economic Primer. New
      York: Basic, 1972, $8, 302p, index (S: Ec).

1293 RANWELL, D. S. Ecology of Salt Marshes and Sand
      Dunes. New York: Halsted, 1973, $14.50, illus
      (S: Ec).

1294 REID, George K. Ecology of Inland Waters and
      Estuaries. New York: Van Nostrand Reinhold,
      1961, $10.50, illus (S: Ec).

1295 REVELLE, Charles and Revelle, Penelope. Source-
      book on the Environment: The Scientific Per-
      spective. Boston: Houghton-Mifflin, 1973, $5.95
      (pap) (S: O).

1296 REVELLE, Roger, et al., eds. Survival Equation:
      Man, Resources, & His Environment. Boston:
      Houghton Mifflin, 1971, $5.75 (pap), illus
      (S: Ed).

144   Conservation/Ecology

1297 RIEDMAN, Sarah R. and Witham, Ross. Turtles:
      Extinction or Survival? New York: Abelard, 1973,
      $8.95, illus (L: 5 up) (S: Es).

1298 RITTER, Paul. Educreation: Education for Creation,
      Growth, and Change. Elmsford, NY: Pergamon
      Press, 1966, $7.50 ($5.50 pap) (S: Ed).

1299 ROBINS, Eric. Ebony Ark: Black Africa's Battle to
      Save Its Wildlife. New York: Taplinger, 1970,
      $6.50 (S: Es/I).

1300 ROBINSON, R. K. Ecology of Fungi. New York:
      Crane-Russack, 1967, $4.75 (S: Ec).

1301 ROELOFS, Robert, et al. Environment and Society:
      A Book of Readings on Environmental Policy,
      Attitudes, and Values. Englewood Cliffs, NJ:
      Prentice-Hall, 1973, $11.95 ($5.95 pap) (S: A/O).

1302 ROLAN, Robert G. Laboratory and Field Investigations
      in General Ecology. New York: Macmillan, 1973,
      $5.95, illus (S: Ec/Ed).

1303 ROLOFF, Joan G. and Wylder, Robert C. There Is
      No Away: Readings and Language Activities in
      Ecology. New York: Glencoe, 1971, $5.95 (pap)
      (S: Ec/En/Ed) (L: HS & up).

1304 RONDIERE, Pierre. Purity or Pollution: The
      Struggle for Water. New York: Watts, 1971,
      $4.95 (PLB) (L: 7 up) (S: Wp).

1305 RUBLOWSKY, John. Nature in the City. New York:
      Basic, 1967, $5.95 (L: 9 up) (S: U).

1306 SALMOND, John A. The Civilian Conservation Corps,
      1933-1942: A New Deal Case Study. Durham,
      NC: Duke University Press, 1967, $7.50 (S:
      Cs/H).

1307 SANDBERG, Inger. Where Does All That Smoke Come
      From? New York: Delacorte, 1972, $4.95 ($4.58
      PLB), illus (L: PS-3) (S: Ap/R).

1308 SANTMIRE, H. Paul. Brother Earth. Camden, NJ:
      Thomas Nelson, 1970, $4.95 (S: Et); reconciliation

of religious views of God, man, and nature.

1309 SARNOFF, Paul. The New York Times Encyclopedic
      Dictionary of the Environment. New York: Quad-
      rangle, 1972, $10 (also avail in pap, New York:
      Avon, 1973, $3.95) (S: DBI).

1310 SAVAGE, Henry, Jr. Lost Heritage. New York:
      Morrow, 1970 (S: W/H). A look at the primeval
      parts of the American continent before it was
      settled. Seen through the eyes of the 19th-and
      18th-century naturalists with a final essay from the
      vantage of the 20th.

1311 SAX, Karl. Standing Room Only: The World's Ex-
      ploding Population. Gloucester, MA: Peter Smith,
      1960, $4.25 (also avail in pap, Boston: Beacon,
      $1.75) (S: P).

1312 SCHILDHAUER, Carole. Environmental Information
      Sources: A Selected Annotated Bibliography. New
      York: Special Libraries Assoc., 1972, $3.80
      (pap) (S: DBI).

1313 SCHROEDER, Henry A. Pollutions, Profits, and
      Progress. Brattleboro, VT: Greene, 1971,
      $4.95 (S: E).

1314 SCIENTIFIC American. Man and the Ecosphere:
      Readings from Scientific American, Introduction
      by Paul Ehrlich. San Francisco: W. H. Freeman,
      1971, $5.75 (pap) (S: Ec/A).

1315 SCHWARTZ, Eugene. Overkill: Technology and the
      Myth of Efficiency. New York: Quadrangle, 1971,
      $8.95 (also avail in pap, New York: Ballantine,
      1972, $1.65), illus, graphs (S: T).

1316 SCHWARTZ, William, ed. Voices for the Wilderness.
      New York: Ballantine, 1969, $1.25 (S: W/A);
      key papers from the Sierra Club Wilderness Con-
      ferences.

1317 SCOBY, Donald R., ed. Environmental Ethics: Studies
      of Man's Self Destruction. Minneapolis: Burgess,
      1971, $4.50 (pap) (S: Et).

1318 SCOTT, David L. The Economics of Environmental
      Pollution: The Case of the Electric Power Industry.
      Lexington, MA: Lexington Books, 1973, $10 (S:
      Eg/E).

1319 SEARS, Paul B. Life & Environment. Educational
      Programs Improvement Corp. , P.O. Box 3406,
      8383 S. Boulder Rd. , Boulder, CO 80303, 1973
      (S: Ed/O).

1320 _____. This Is Our World. Norman: University
      of Oklahoma Press, 1971, $5.95 ($2.95 pap), illus
      (S: O).

1321 _____. Where There Is Life. New York: Dell,
      1970, $0.75 (pap) (S: O).

1322 SHEPARD, Daniel, and Shepard, Jean. Earthwatch:
      Notes on a Restless Planet. Garden City, NY:
      Doubleday, 1973, $8.95 (S: O).

1323 SHEPARD, Paul. Man in the Landscape. New York:
      Knopf, 1967 (S: H); an extremely good history of
      the perception of nature that has shaped and in-
      fluenced American attitude.

1324 _____ and McKinley, Daniel, eds. Environmental
      Essays on the Planet As a Home. Boston:
      Houghton Mifflin, 1971, $4.75 (pap), illus (S: A/O).

1325 SHERRELL, Richard E. Ecology: Crisis and New
      Vision. Richmond, VA: John Knox, 1971, $3.95
      (pap) (S: Ec/Et).

1326 SHERROD, H. Floyd. Environment Law Review, 1969,
      1970, 1971, 1972. New York: Boardman, $29.50
      (S: L).

1327 SHOMON, Joseph J. Open Land for Urban America:
      Acquisition, Safekeeping, and Use. Baltimore, MD:
      Johns Hopkins, 1971, $7.50 ($2.50 pap), 176p,
      index, illus (S: Lu/U); written by the Nature
      Center Planning Division of the Audubon Society.

1327a SHUTTLESWORTH, Dorothy E. A Sense of Wonder:
      Selections from Great Writers of Nature. Garden
      City, NY: Doubleday, 1963, 252p, illus (L: JHS &

up) (S: A). Selections from such noted writers
as Darwin, Einstein, Thoreau, and Rachel Carson;
included are suggestions for further reading.

1328 SIERRA Club. Space for Survival: How to Stop the
Bulldozer in Your Own Back Yard. New York:
Pocket Books, $1.25 (S: U/Lu).

1329 SIMON, Noel M. and Girondet, Paul. Last Survivors.
New York: World, 1970, $19.95 (S: Es); natural
history of 48 animals in danger of extinction.

1330 SITTIG, Marshal. Pollutant Removal Handbook. Park
Ridge, NJ: Noyes, 1973, $36, 528p, illus (S:
Ap/Wp).

1331 SLOAN, Irving. Environment and the Law. Dobbs
Ferry, NY: Oceana, 1971, $4 (S: L).

1332 SLUSSER, Gerald and Slusser, Dorothy M. Technology,
the God That Failed: The Environmental Catas-
trophe. Philadelphia: Westminster, 1971, $2.95
(S: T).

1333 SMITH, Robert L. Ecology and Field Biology. New
York: Harper & Row, 1966, $15 (S: E).

1334 _____, ed. Ecology of Man: An Ecosystem Approach. New York: Harper & Row, 1972, $6.95
(pap) illus (S: Ec/Ed); teaching notes also avail.

1335 SMITHSONIAN Institution. The Fitness of Man's Environment. Washington, DC: The Institution,
1967, $6.50 (S: O/A); papers by world authorities
on the quality of man's environment.

1336 SOUTHWICK, Charles H. Ecology and the Quality of
Our Environment. New York: Van Nostrand Reinhold, 1972, $6.95 ($4.95 pap) (S: Ec).

1337 Special Reports Ecology. New York: Special Reports,
1973 (S: DBI).

1338 SPROULL, Wayne T. Air Pollution and Its Control.
Jericho, NY: Exposition Press, 1972, $6, illus
(S: Ap).

148   Conservation/Ecology

1339 SPROUT, Harold and Sprout, Margaret. Ecological
      Perspective on Human Affairs, with Special Refer-
      ence to International Politics. Princeton, NJ:
      Princeton University Press, 1965, $10 (S: I).

1340 SQUIRES, C. B. Heroes of Conservation. New York:
      Fleet Press, 1973, $5, illus (L: 5 up) (S: B).

1341 STACKS, John F. Stripping: The Surface Mining of
      America. San Francisco: Sierra, 1972, $2.95
      (pap), illus (S: S).

1342 STAMP, L. Dudley. Man and The Land. New York:
      W. Collins, 1955, $6.50, illus (L: Lu).

1343 _____. Nature Conservation in Britain. New
      York: W. Collins, $7.50 (S: Cn/I).

1344 STAPP, William B. Environmental Education: An
      Information Guide. Detroit: Gale, $15 (S: Ed/
      DBI).

1345 STEGNER, Wallace. Beyond the Hundredth Meridian:
      John Wesley Powell and the Second Opening of the
      West. Boston: Houghton Mifflin, 1954, $2.65
      (pap) (S: B/H).

1346 STEPHEN, David and Lockie, James. Nature's Way.
      New York: McGraw-Hill, 1969, $4.95 ($4.72
      PLB) (L: 5 up) (S: Ec).

1347 STEVENS, Leonard A. Clean Water: Nature's Way
      to Stop Pollution. New York: Dutton, 1973, $7.95
      (S: Wp).

1348 _____. How a Law Is Made: The Story of a Bill
      Against Air Pollution. New York: Crowell, 1970,
      $3.95 (L: 5-9) (S: L/Ps).

1349 STEWARD, Leland and Clarke, Wentworth. Pollution.
      New York: John Day, 1971, $2.95 (pap), illus
      (L: 9-12) (S: Wp/Ap).

1350 STILL, Henry. In Quest of Quiet: Meeting the Menace
      of Noise Pollution. Harrisburg, PA: Stackpole,
      1970, $6.95 (S: Np).

1351 STONE, Christopher D. Should Trees Have Standing?
      Toward Legal Rights for Natural Objects. Los
      Altos, CA: W. Kaufman, 1973, $6 ($3 pap), 100p
      (S: L).

1352 STONE, Harris A. and Collins, Stephan. Populations:
      Experiments in Ecology. New York: Watts, 1972,
      $4.95 (PLB) (L: 5 up) (S: Ec/P).

1353 STORER, John H. Man in the Web of Life. New
      York: Signet, 1968 (also avail in pap, New York:
      New American Library, $0.95) (S: O).

1354 STROBBE, Maurice A., ed. Understanding Environ-
      mental Pollution. St. Louis: Mosby, 1971, $6.40
      (pap), illus (S: Wp/Ap).

1355 STRONG, Douglas H. The Conservationists. New ed.
      Reading, MA: Addison-Wesley, 1971, $2.16 (pap)
      (L: 9-12) (S: Cn/B).

1356 SUTTON, Ann and Sutton, Myron. Guarding the
      Treasured Lands: The Story of the National Park
      Service. Philadelphia: Lippincott, 1965, $3.95,
      illus (L: 7-9) (S: H/W).

1357 SUTTON, David and Harmon, Paul. Ecology. (Self-
      Teaching Guides Series.) New York: Wiley, 1973,
      $3.95 (pap) (S: Ec/Ed).

1358 SWIFT, Ernest F. A Conservation Saga. Washington,
      DC: National Wildlife Federation, 1967, $3 (S:
      Cn/H); partly historical reminiscence by one of
      the central figures in wildlife conservation.

1359 TAYLOR, Ron. Subdividing the Wilderness. Sierra
      Club Bulletin, January 1971, 4-9 (S: W); land
      developers and their operations.

1360 TEALE, Edwin W., ed. The Wilderness World of
      John Muir. Boston: Houghton Mifflin, 1954,
      $7.95 (S: B/W).

1361 TEALE, John and Teale, Mildred. Life and Death of
      the Salt Marsh. Boston: Little Brown, 1969,
      $7.95 (also avail in pap, New York: Ballantine,
      1969, $1.25), 274p.

1362   TEMPE, Gertrude G. and Moore, David F. Education
        for Survival: Ecology in Science and Social Studies.
        Morristown, NJ: New Jersey Conservation Founda-
        tion, 1972, 4 vols: grade 4, 1971, $4; grades 1,
        2, and 3, 1970, $6; grade 5, 1972, $6; grade 6,
        1972, $5; all illus (S: Ed).

1363   THOMAS, E. Harold. Conservation of Ground Water:
        A Survey of the Present Ground Water Situation in
        the United States. Westport, CT: Greenwood, $17
        (S: Cn/Wp).

1364   THOMAS, W. L., Jr., ed. Man's Role in Changing
        the Face of the Earth. Chicago: University of
        Chicago Press, 1956 (S: Lu).

1365   TROOST, Cornelius and Altman, Harold, eds. En-
        vironmental Education: A Sourcebook. New York:
        Wiley, 1972, $11.95 ($8.95 pap) (S: Ed).

1366   TURK, Amos, et al. Ecology, Pollution, and Environ-
        ment. Philadelphia: Saunders, 1972, $3.95 (pap),
        illus (S: O).

1367   UDALL, Steward L. 1976 Agenda for Tomorrow.
        New York: Harcourt, 1968, $3.75 (S: O).

1368   UNESCO. Ecology of the Subarctic Regions. New
        York: Unipub, 1970, $19, illus (S: Ec/I).

1369   U.S. Department of Commerce. The Automobile and
        Air Pollution: A Program for Progress, Part 1.
        (1967 Report on Panel on Electrically Powered
        Vehicles.) Washington, DC: U.S. Government
        Printing Office, 1967, $0.60 (S: Ap, T).

1370   VAN DERSAL, William R. The American Land, Its
        History and Its Uses. New York: Oxford Univer-
        sity Press, 1943 (S: Lu/H); a simplified, but ex-
        cellent, environmental history.

1371   _____. Wildlife for America. Rev. ed. New
        York: Walck, 1970, $6.50 (L: 7-9) (S: Es).

1372   _____ and Graham, Edward H. Water for America:
        The Story of Water Conservation. New York:
        Walck, 1956, $5, illus (L: 7-9) (S: Cn/Wp).

1373 VAN HISE, C. R. Conservation of Our Natural Re-
      sources. Millwood, NY: Kraus Reprint Co.,
      1973, reprint of 1930 ed, $20 (S: Cn).

1374 VAN SICKLE, Dirck. The Ecological Citizen: Good
      Earth Keeping in America. New York: Harper &
      Row, 1971, $1.25 (pap), 295p (S: Ha).

1375 VOGT, William. Road to Survival. New York:
      William Sloan Assoc., 1948 (S: O).

1376 VOSBURGH, John. Land We Live On (orig title:
      Land Management). New York: Coward, 1971,
      $4.49 (PLB), illus (L: 6-9) (S: Lu).

1377 WADDINGTON, C. H., ed. Biology and the History
      of the Future. Chicago: Aldine Atherton, 1973,
      $2.95.

1378 WALLWORK, J. A. Ecology of Soil Animals. New
      York: McGraw-Hill, 1971, $10.50 (S: Ec).

1379 WANG, J. Y. and Balter, Raymond. A Survey of
      Environmental Science Organizations. San Fran-
      cisco: Ecology Center Press, 1970, $5.50 (S:
      DBI).

1380 WARD, M. A., ed. Man and His Environment. New
      York: Pergamon Press, 1970, $12 (S: Wp/Ap/Wt);
      vol I, "Water, Air, and Solid Waste Pollution."

1381 WATKINS, William J. and Snyder, Eugene V. Eco-
      death. Garden City, NY: Doubleday, 1972, $5.95.

1382 WATSON, Geoffrey G. Fun with Ecology. New York:
      Winchester, 1971, $2.95 (L: 5-9) (S: Ec).

1383 WATSON, Jane W. Our World Tomorrow. Los
      Angeles: Western, 1973, $5.95 ($6.95 PLB)
      (S: O) (L: Adv HS & up)

1384 WATT, Kenneth E. Ecology and Resource Manage-
      ment: A Quantitative Approach. New York:
      McGraw-Hill, 1967, $14.50 (S: Ec/Cn).

1385 _____. Principles of Environmental Science. New
      York: McGraw-Hill, 1973, $10.95, illus (S: Ec).

1386 WEAVER, Elbert C. , ed. Scientific Experiments in
      Environmental Pollution. New York: Holt, Rine-
      hart and Winston, 1968 (S: Ap/Wp).

1387 WEBB, L. J. , et al. Last of Lands: Conservation in
      Australia. New York: Warne, 1971, $15, illus
      (S: Cn/I).

1388 WEISBERG, Barry, ed. Ecocide in Indochina. New
      York: Harper & Row (Canfield Press), 1970,
      $3.95 (pap) (S: I).

1389 WELCH, Macaela and La Monte, Francesca. Vanishing
      Wilderness. New York: Liveright, $6.95, illus
      (S: W).

1390 WENGERT, Norman. Administration of Natural Re-
      sources: The American Experience. New York:
      Asia, n. d. , $2.25 (S: Cn/H).

1391 WERNER, Ben, Jr. Ecology for Earthlings. Setauket,
      NY: Edmond, 1973, $3.95, illus (L: 3 up) (S: Ec).

1392 WESTBROOK, Perry D. John Burroughs. New York:
      Twayne, 1973, $5.50 (S: B/H).

1393 WESTON, Harold. Freedom in the Wilds: A Saga of
      the Adirondacks. St Huberts, NY: Adirondack
      Trail Society, 1972, $12.50 ($4.95 pap), illus
      (S: W).

1394 WHEELER, David L. Human Habitat: Contemporary
      Readings. New York: Van Nostrand Reinhold,
      1971, $6.95 ($3.50 pap) (S: O).

1395 Who's Who in Ecology. New York: Special Reports,
      1973 (S: DBI).

1396 WHYTE, W. H. , Jr. The Last Landscape. Garden
      City, NY: Doubleday, 1968, $7.95 ($2.50 pap),
      illus (S: Lu).

1397 _____. Securing Space for Urban America: Con-
      servation Easements. Washington, DC: Urban
      Land Institute, 1959, $4 (pap) (S: Lu).

1398 WILBUR, Ray L. and DuPuy, William. Conservation

in the Department of the Interior. Freeport, NY:
Books for Libraries, 1972, reprint of 1932 ed,
$38.50 (S: Cn/H).

1399 WILEY, Farida, ed. John Burroughs's America.
Old Greenwich, CT: Devin, 1951, $7.50, illus
(L: 9 up) (S: H/B).

1400 _____, ed. Theodore Roosevelt's America. Old
Greenwich, CT: Devin, 1955, $7.50, illus (S:
H/B).

1401 WILLIAMS, George H. and Glacken, Clarence. Traces
on the Rhodian Shore: Nature and Culture in
Western Thought from Ancient Times to the End of
the Eighteenth Century. Berkeley: University of
California Press, 1967 (S: W/Et); comprehensive.

1402 _____ and _____. Wilderness and Paradise in
Christian Thought. New York: Harper, 1962
(S: W/Et); comprehensive account of American
experience with nature.

1403 WOLFF, Garwood R. & Company. Environmental Information Sources Handbook. New York: Simon &
Schuster (Monarch), $25 (S: DBI).

1404 WOODBURN, John H. Whole Earth Energy Crisis.
New ed. New York: Putnam, 1973, $4.89 (PLB),
illus (L: 6 up) (S: Eg).

1405 WOODS, Barbara, ed. Eco-Solutions: A Casebook for
Environmental Crisis. Cambridge, MA: Schenk-
man, 1972, $10.95, illus (S: O/Cs).

1406 WORSTER, Donald E., ed. American Environmentalism: The Formative Period 1860-1915. New
York: Wiley, 1973, $7.50 ($4.50 pap) (S: O/H).

1407 WRIGHT, Robert H. What Good Is a Weed? Ecology
in Action. West Caldwell, NJ: Lothrop, 1972,
$4.95 ($4.59 PLB) (L: 4-7) (S: Ec).

1408 ZON, Raphael and Cooper, William, eds. Conservation of
Renewable Natural Resources. Pennsylvania University Bicentenniel Conference. Port Washington,
NY: Taylor Pub. Co. (Kennikat), reprint of 1941
ed, 1973, $7.50 (S: Cn).

1409   ZURHORST, Charles.   The Conservation Fraud.   New
       York: Cowles,   1970 (S: C).

Section III

PERIODICAL ARTICLES OF INTEREST TO EDUCATORS

Articles in this section are alphabetized by author (where one was cited), or when unknown, by publication. The listing includes the title of the article, the publication in which it is included, the date, volume number (when indicated), and the page on which the article begins. No level is indicated as all articles are directed towards professionals in the field of education. Articles on broad environmental topics are not included. These can readily be obtained from the Readers' Guide to Periodical Literature and other indexes.

2001 Abel, Dana L. "Environmental Education." Bioscience, 1970, vol 20, p1015.

2002 Abraham, G. K. "Oversimplification? Pollution Problems." Forecast for Home Economics, 1970, vol 16, pF.

2003 Adams, U. A. "Education for Survival." School Management, 1970, vol 14, p10.

2004 Agricultural Education. "Environmental-Related Research in Agricultural Education," 1971, vol 43, p229.

2005 _____. "Environmental Science Education in Ohio." 1971, vol 43, p244.

2006 American Biology Teacher. "Teachers and Students Write a Curriculum on Water Pollution." vol 33, p22.

2007 American Education. "Support for Environmental Education." January 1972, p31.

2008 American Forests. "Chair for Loyola; W. S.

Rosecrans Chair of Conservation and Water Resources." March 1972, p27.

2009 American Vocational Journal. "Agri-business and Its Potential for Environmental Education." 1971, vol 46, p24.

2010 _____. "Ecological Programs in Vocational Education." 1971, vol 46, p20.

2011 _____. "Teaching for Consumer Conscience in Business Education." vol 46, p22.

2012 Ames, E. A. "Schools and the Environment." Theory Into Practice, 1970, vol 9, p175.

2013 Archibald, David and Gundlack, Paul. "Environmental Education: An Integrated Approach." Environmental Education, 1970, vol 1, p75.

2014 Art Education. "Art, Artists, and Environmental Awareness." 1970, vol 23, p53.

2015 _____. "Environmental Citizenship: Where to Begin?" 1970, vol 23, p33.

2016 _____. "Toward Real Public Involvement in Environmental Decision Making." 1970, vol 23, p30.

2017 Arth, A. A., et al. "Environmental Awareness, the Way of Survival." Educational Leadership, 1970, vol 28, p274.

2018 Bain, H. P. "Education for Survival." Art Education, 1970, vol 23, p14.

2019 Balzer, L. "Environmental Education in the K-12 Span." American Biology Teacher, 1971, vol 33, p220.

2020 Barnhart, L. "Outdoor Recreation and Environmental Attitudes." Parks and Recreation, April 1973, p48.

2021 Bates, M. "Human Environment." Theory into Practice, 1970, vol 9, p146.

2022 Beatty, V. L. "Growing Citizens as Well as Plants;
      Teaching Chicago Public School Children about
      Nature." Horticulture, November 1973, p38.

2023 Brehman, T. R., et al. "Environmental Activities
      and Problem Solving." Science Teacher, 1971,
      vol 38, p55.

2024 Brennan, Matthew J. "Making Tomorrow Now."
      Education Digest, February 1971, p13.

2025 Bulger, Paul G. "Youth Education in Conservation:
      A Vital Force." Conservationist, August 1971,
      p33.

2026 Camping Magazine. "Forest Rangers Can Spark
      Ecology Programs." September 1971, p15.

2027 Carlson, R. E. "Ecological Programs Can Create
      Camper Consciousness," Camping Magazine,
      June 1973, p8.

2028 Christiansen, M. A. "What to Do till the World Ends."
      Clearing House, February 1972, p342.

2029 Cottrell, ed. "Overview: Education." Environment,
      January 1973, p20; March 1973, p5; April 1973,
      p5.

2030 Cravens, Jay H. "Feeling Our Way to a Good En-
      vironment." American Education, October, 1971,
      p25.

2031 Crowley, Claude D. "Closing the Environmental Edu-
      cation Gap." Today's Education, April, 1972,
      p24.

2032 Damio, W. "Ecology Bookology." Media and Methods,
      1971, vol 7, p26.

2033 Derr, Richard L. "Adaptive Strategies of Urban
      Schools." Intellect, November, 1972, p88.

2034 Driscoll, M. "Kids Meet the Wilderness; Student
      Environmental Learning Facility, Huntington
      Beach, California." McCall's, October, 1972,
      p. 70.

158   Conservation/Ecology

2035   Duffy, William J. "Training the Somebodies; An En-
       vironmental Training Center." American Education,
       March, 1972, p20.

2036   Dwyer, R. L. "School Camping Programs: Ecology
       in the Outdoor Classroom." Social Education,
       1971, vol 35, p74.

2037   Educational Product Report. "Lack of Material,
       Jealousy Hamper Environmental Courses." 1971,
       vol 4, p5.

2038   _____. "Update: Environmental Studies--Critical
       Reviews of Two Major Curricula." 1971, vol 4,
       p35.

2039   Engleson, D. E. "Status of Conservation Courses in
       Wisconsin High Schools." Science Teacher, 1970,
       vol 37, p33.

2040   Entorf, J. F. "Becoming Aware of Waste: Teaching
       Unit on Recycling." School Shop, 1971, vol 30,
       p78.

2041   Environmental Science Center. "A List of Available
       Curriculum Materials." Environmental Science
       Center, 5400 Glenwood Avenue, Golden Valley, MN
       55422.

2042   Evans, B. "Traditional Conservation Education Is
       Inadequate." Compact, 1971, vol 5, p18.

2043   Fleck, H. "Facing the Environmental Crisis." Fore-
       cast for Home Economics, 1970, vol 16, pF.

2044   Fong, M. K. "Survival Training." Compact, 1971,
       vol 5, p31.

2045   Frutkin, Ren. "School for Life Now: Redington Pond
       School." Harper's, January 1973, p97.

2046   Fuller, D. M. "Junk Environment Project." Art
       Education, 1970, vol 23, p16.

2047   Glass, B. "Human Multitude: How Many Is Enough?"
       American Biology Teacher, 1971, vol 33, p265.

2048 Glenn, H. T. "Learn and Teach the New Pollution-
      Control Methodology." School Shop, 1971, vol 30,
      p71.

2049 Godfrey, Arthur. "We Have a Long Way to Go: And
      Time Is Running Out." Address, July 13, 1971.
      Conservationist, October, 1971, p8.

2050 Good Housekeeping. "Fun Gifts that Teach About the
      Environment." December 1972, p185.

2051 Grubough, R., et al. "Environmental Management and
      Vocational Agricultural." Agricultural Education,
      1971, vol 43, p222.

2052 Gustafson, J. A. "Conservation Education, Today and
      Tomorrow." Science Education, 1969, vol 53,
      p187.

2053 Hardy, C. A. "Environmental Education: An Action
      Proposal." Contemporary Education, 1971, vol 42,
      p276.

2054 Harrison, Charles H. "E. E. Needs You!" Scholastic
      Teacher Junior/Senior High School Teacher's Edi-
      tion, October 1971, p13.

2055 Hebert, R. "Ecology: A Shared Journey." Personnel
      and Guidance Journal, 1971, vol 49, p737.

2056 Hill, W. "Relating Geography to Environmental Educa-
      tion." Journal of Geography, 1970, vol 69, p485.

2057 Hoke, J. "Environmental Programs of National Capital
      Parks." Parks and Recreation, June 1973, p35.

2058 Horn, B. Ray. "Saturday Is for the Environment;
      Program Drawn Up in Michigan." American Edu-
      cation, October 1973, p9.

2059 Howarth, C., Jr. "Challenge to Environmental Educa-
      tion." Art Education, 1970, vol 23, p36.

2060 Keller, Martha A. "Outdoor Education Comes of Age;
      Learning about Life from Life; Maine Environ-
      mental Project." Parents, September 1973, p38.

2061   Kormondy, E. J.   "Environmental Education: The
       Whole Man Revisited."   American Biology Teacher,
       1971, vol 33, p15.

2062   Krall, R.   "Mudhole Ecology."   American Biology
       Teacher, 1970, vol 32, p351.

2063   Krupsky, C. H.   "Stop Our Pollution: Projects and Ac-
       tivities."   School and Community, 1971, vol 57, p32.

2064   Lanier, V.   "Ecology: Cop-Out or Foul-Up?"   Arts
       and Activities, 1970, vol 68, p46.

2065   Lear, John.   "Ecologic of Nursery Rhymes."   Saturday
       Review, November 6, 1971, p73.

2066   Lindsay, Sally.   "APEX: It's a Computer Simulation
       Game."   Saturday Review, May 13, 1972, p55.

2067   Louviere, Vernon.   "Dow Spurs a Factual Approach to
       Pollution."   Nation's Business, August, 1971, p16.

2068   McCammon, L. C.   "Man Greatest Challenge, the
       Quest for Environmental Quality."   Journal of
       School Health, 1970, vol 40, p284.

2069   McGowan, A.   "Experiment in Environmental Educa-
       tion."   Physics Teacher, 1971, vol 9, p141.

2070   Maley, D.   "Environmental Education: Solving the
       Problems."   Man/Science/Technology, 1971,
       vol 30, p146.

2071   Manson, G. A. , et al.   "Perspectives on Man and
       His Environment."   Journal of Geography, 1970,
       vol 69, p279.

2072   Marland, Sidney Percy, Jr.   "Environmental Education
       Cannot Wait"; with editorial comment.   American
       Education, May 1971, p6.

2073   Martin, E.   "Student Volunteers in the National Parks
       and Forests."   National Parks and Conservation,
       February 1973, p24.

2074   Marvinney, S.   "Age of Homespun; SUNY Field
       Program."   Conservationist, December 1973, p34.

2075 Math Teacher. "Mathematics Educators Must Help
      Face the Environmental Pollution Challenge." 1970,
      vol 64, p33.

2076 Meadows, B. J. "Denver School Dramatizes Population-
      Pollution." American Biology Teacher, 1970, vol
      32, p281.

2077 Mergen, F., et al. "What's Going on at Yale"; with
      editorial comment. (School of Forestry and Environ-
      mental Studies) American Forests, July 1973, p23.

2078 Mings, R. C. "Some Suggestions for Reorienting Con-
      servation Education." Social Studies, 1971, vol
      62, p160.

2079 Murphy, J. "Exercise in Winter Ecology." Science
      Teacher, 1970, vol 37, p59.

2080 Needham, D. "Pollution Is a Teaching and Action
      Program." Grade Teacher, 1970, vol 88, p24.

2081 Norton, T. W. "Atmosphere as a Science Classroom
      Resource." Physics Teacher, 1971, vol 9, p265.

2082 O'Neill, Edward A. "Children's Crusade in the Virgin
      Islands." American Education, July 1972, p22.

2083 Overcash, J. R. "Environmental Study in the City--
      Boston." Science Teacher, 1971, vol 38, p18.

2084 Publishers Weekly. "New Sierra Books to Feature
      People." March 6, 1972, p47.

2085 Reidel, C. H. "The University: An Environmental Per-
      spective." Speech delivered by Carl H. Reidel, Di-
      rector, The Environmental Program, Univ. of Ver-
      mont, before the convocation of the Univ. of Vermont,
      Burlington, Sept. 6, 1972. Vital Speeches of the Day,
      November 1, 1972, p45.

2086 Roberts, A. D. and Dyrli, Odvard Egil. "Environmental
      Education." Clearing House, April 1971, p451.

2087 Rogers, L. "Conservation 70's: A Concept for En-
      vironmental Action." Science Education, 1971,
      vol 55, p57.

162 Conservation/Ecology

2088 Roth, R. "Environmental Management Education: Where From Here." Theory into Practice, 1970, vol 9, p187.

2089 Roth, Robert E. "Fundamental Concepts for Environmental Management Education" (K-16). Environmental Education, 1970, vol 1, p65.

2090 Rumpf, E. L. "Ecological Challenge: Response at the National Level: USOE Takes First Steps." American Vocational Journal, 1971, vol 46, p20.

2091 Sager, M. C. "Ecological Balance of the Planet Earth." Social Education, 1971, vol 35, p47.

2092 Scherff, G. E. "Exploring Industrial Pollution Control." School Shop, 1971, vol 30, p77.

2093 Schlich, Victor A. "Environmental Encounters: Yarmouth, Me." American Education, August 1971, p23.

2094 Scholastic Teacher Junior/Senior High Teacher's Edition. "Teacher's Survival Guide to Environmental Education Resources." October 1971, p32. Includes guides to multimedia, booklets, pamphlets, etc., and paperback resources.

2095 School Shop. "Industrial Education and the Environment." 1971, vol 30, p63.

2096 Schrank, J. J. "What Good Are Pelicans? A Guide to Teaching Materials in Ecology." Media and Methods, 1970, vol 6, p32.

2097 Science News. "Getting Down to Earth in Environmental Education; Anacostia Program." July 8, 1972, p21.

2098 Sehgal, P. P. "Basis for Action in the Environmental Crisis." American Biology Teacher, 1970, vol 32, p480.

2099 Senior Scholastic. "Can a Bunch of Kids Fight City Hall? Students at Hinton High Tried and ...?" October 11, 1973, p6.

2100   Senior Scholastic (teacher ed.). "Where the Action Is:
       What Young People Have Done; with Discussion."
       April, 1971, p3.

2101   _____. "It's a Natural." March 15, 1971, p12.
       U. S. Youth Conservation Corps

2102   Serrin, Judith. "Earth Day Year Around; Ecology
       Center, Inc., of Ann Arbor." American Education,
       January 1972, p26.

2103   Silber, Robert L. "Where Do We Begin?" Chemistry,
       December 1971, p2.

2104   Smalley, L. "Is Industrial Arts Relevant Without
       Talking about Pollution Control?" Industrial Arts
       and Vocational Education, 1970, vol 59, p38.

2105   Smith, A. and Smith, C. M. "Aesthetics and Environ-
       mental Education." Journal of Aesthetic Education,
       1970, vol 4, p125.

2106   Social Education. January 1971. Entire issue devoted
       to environmental education.

2107   Sonnenfeld, J. "Geopolitical Environment as a Per-
       ceptual Environment." Journal of Geography,
       1970, vol 69, p415.

2108   Stahr, Elvis J. "Camp: The Ideal Place for Teaching
       Environmental Urgencies." Camping Magazine,
       March 1971, p20.

2109   Stokes, R. L. "Art Education Fights Pollution."
       School and Community, 1971, vol 57, p26.

2110   Stotler, Donald. "Environmental Education as Libera-
       tion." Education Digest, May 1972, p38.

2111   Swan, James. "The Challenge of Environmental Edu-
       cation." Journal of Phi Delta Kappa, 1969, vol
       51, p26.

2112   Tanner, R. P. "Future: Alternatives for Man's En-
       vironment." Man/Science/Technology, 1971, vol
       30, p149.

164   Conservation/Ecology

2113 Theory into Practice. "Toward a More Humane En-
      vironment: A Symposium." vol 9, p145.

2114 Today's Education. "Update: Report of the NEA Task
      Force on Environmental Education." September
      1971, p33.

2115 _____. "What Schools Can Do about Pollution: A
      Symposium." vol 59, p14.

2116 Trohanis, P. "Environmental-Ecological Education via
      Simultaneously Projected Multiple Images with
      Sound." Audio-Visual Instruction, 1971, vol 16,
      p19.

2117 Trueblood, Ted. "Scouts Can Help: Project SOAR."
      Field & Stream, February 1971, p16.

2118 Van Matre, Steve. "Your Camp Ecology Program."
      Camping Magazine, June 1971, p8.

2119 Viran, V. E., et al. "Environmental Education--Infor-
      mation, Ideas, and Activities." The Instructor,
      1971, vol 80, p51.

2120 Wagar, J. Alan. "Challenge of Environmental Educa-
      tion." Education Digest, February 1971, p9.

2121 Winkel, G. H., et al. "Ecology of Cities." Science
      Teacher, 1971, vol 38, p16.

2122 Wood, W. "Ecological Drums Along the Cuyahoga;
      Students Fight Pollution in Ohio's Cuyahoga River
      Watershed Region." American Education, January
      1973, p15.

2123 Worrell, A. C. "Natural Resources Policy in a
      Changing World." American Forests, July 1973,
      p35.

Section IV

RELEVANT PERIODICALS: A CHECKLIST

Included in this section are periodicals that enjoy a fairly
large circulation. Some are free, but generally there is a
subscription price which we have noted. In the few cases
where we were unable to get data on circulation, subscription price, or publication frequency, but the publication
seemed particularly interesting, we have listed it with the
information we were able to get. For additional periodicals
put out by private organizations and government agencies see
end of Section V, U.S. Government Publications, and Section
VII, Private Organizations.

AEOE Newsletter
The Association for Environmental and Outdoor Education,
2428 Walnut Blvd, Walnut Creek, CA 94596

Access
Ecology Forum, Suite 303 E, 200 Park Ave., New York, NY
10017
    26 times/yr, $110/yr

Adirondac
Adirondack Mountain Club, Inc., R.D. 1, Ridge Road, Glens
Falls, NY 12801
    bimonthly, $3/yr (free to conservation groups and
    libraries), circ 3500

Air and Water News
McGraw-Hill, 330 W. 42d St., New York, NY 10036
    weekly, $120/yr

Air Currents
Citizens for Clean Air, 40 W. 57th St., New York, NY
10019
    quarterly, free, circ 8000

Alabama Conservation
Department of Conservation and Natural Resources, 711 High
St. , Montgomery, AL 36104
    bimonthly, free to qualified people, circ 16,000

Alaska Conservation Review
Alaska Conservation Society, Box 5-A2, College, AK   99701
quarterly, $3/yr, circ 1000

All Clear
All Clear Publishing, Inc. , 299 Forest Ave. , Paramus, NJ
07652
    10 times/yr, $10/yr

The American Biology Teacher
National Association of Biology Teachers, 1420 N. St. , N. W. ,
Washington, DC   20005
    monthly (school year), $10/yr, circ 15,200

American Forests
American Forestry Association, 1319 16th St. N. W. ,
Washington, DC   20036
    monthly, $7. 50/yr, circ 75,000

Annual World Population Data Sheet
Population Reference Bureau, Inc. , 1755 Massachusetts Ave.
N. W. , Washington, DC   20036

Appalachia
Appalachian Mountain Club, 5 Joy St. , Boston, MA   02108
    semi-annual, $3. 50/yr, circ 11,000

Atlantic Naturalist
Audubon Naturalist Society of the Central Atlantic States, Inc. ,
8940 Jones Mill Rd, Washington, DC   20015
    quarterly, $5/yr, circ 1900

Audubon
National Audubon Society, 950 Third Ave. , New York, NY
10022
    bimonthly, $8. 50 ($7. 50 institutions)/yr, circ 50,000

Awareness
Paul E. Goff, Apt. 209, 4031 Royer Rd. , Toledo, OH   43623
    monthly, $3/yr

Big Rock Candy Mountain

Relevant Periodicals Checklist 167

Portola Institute, Inc., 115 Merrill St., Menlo Park, CA
94025
    bimonthly, $8/yr

Bimonthly Calendar of Environmental Events
Washington Ecology Center, Rm. 612, 2000 P St. N.W.,
Washington, DC 20006

Bulletin ... see under name of issuing agency, society, etc.

CF Newsletter
Conservation Foundation, 1717 Massachusetts Ave. N.W.,
Washington, DC 20036
    monthly, $6/yr

Catalyst
333 E. 46th St., New York, NY 10017
    $5/yr

Catalyst for Environmental Quality
274 Madison Ave., New York, NY 10016
    $5/yr

Central Atlantic Environment News
Central Atlantic Environment Service, 1717 Massachusetts
Ave. N.W., Washington, DC 20036

Clean Air and Water News
Commerce Clearing House, Inc., 4025 West Peterson Ave.,
Chicago, IL 60646
    weekly, $80/yr

Compost Science--Journal of Waste Recycling
Rodale Press, Inc., 33 E. Minor St., Emmaus, PA 18049
    quarterly, $4 (free to municipal officials, engineers, and
    industrial officials)

Conservation Law Notes
Conservation Law Foundation of New England, Inc., 506
Statler Office Bldg, Boston, MA 02116

The Conservationist
New York State Department of Environmental Conservation,
50 Wolf Rd., Albany, NY 12201
    bimonthly, $2/yr, circ 150,000

Cry California

California Tomorrow, 681 Market St. , San Francisco, CA
94105
   quarterly, $12 ($9 libraries)/yr, circ 7200

Current Publication in Population/Family Planning
Population Council, 245 Park Ave. , New York, NY   10017
   bimonthly, circ 8000

Defenders of Wildlife News
Defenders of Wildlife, 1346 Connecticut Ave. N.W. , Washington, DC   20036
   quarterly, $5/yr, circ 15,000

Delaware Conservationist
Department of Natural Resources and Environmental Control,
Edward Tathall Bldg. , Legislative Ave. and D St. , Dover,
DE   19901
   quarterly, free, circ 6300

Earthtimes
Straight Arrow Publishers, 625 Third St. , San Francisco, CA
94107
   monthly, $5/yr

Ecolog
Logical Ecology, Inc. , Box 184, Oyster Bay, NY   11771
   weekly, $200/yr

Ecological Monographs
Duke University Press, Box 6697, College Sta. , Durham, NC
27708
   quarterly, $6/yr, circ 1200

Ecological Society of America Bulletin
Ecological Society of America, 24 Wildwood Dr. , Oak Ridge,
TN   37830
   quarterly, $4/yr, circ 3100

Ecologist
Darby House, Blenchingley Rd. , Merstham, Redhill, Curry,
England.
   monthly, $8/yr, circ 45,000

Ecology
Ecological Society of America, Duke University Press,
Box 6617, Durham, NC   27708
   quarterly, $24/yr, circ 8000

Ecology Action: The Journal of Cultural Transformation
Ecology Action Educational Institution, 737 N. Franklin St.,
Modesto, CA   95352
   quarterly, $10($5 institutions)/yr, circ 2000

Ecology Law Quarterly
Boalt Hall, School of Law, University of California, Berkeley,
CA   94720.

Ecology News Letter
Total Energy Pub. Co., 522 Briar Oak Lane, San Antonio,
TX   78216
   bimonthly, $45/yr

Ecology Today
Ecological Dimensions, Inc., Box 180, West Mystic, CT
06388
   bimonthly, $6/yr

Eco-News: A Young People's Environmental Newsletter
Environmental Action Coalition, Inc., 235 E. 49th St.,
New York, NY   10017

Econotes
Western Regional Environmental Education Council, 721
Capitol Mall, Sacramento, CA   95814.

Ecosphere
Forum International, International Ecosystems University,
2905 Benvenue Ave., Berkeley, CA   94705.

Eco-Tips
Concern, Inc., 2233 Wisconsin Ave. N.W., Washington, DC
20007.

Environment
Scientists' Institute for Public Information, 30 E. 68th St.,
New York, NY   10021.
   10 times/yr, $10/yr, circ 25,000

Environment Action Bulletin
Rodale Press, Inc., 33 E. Minor St., Emmaus, PA   18049.

Environment Information Access
Ecology Forum Inc., Suite 303 E, 200 Park Ave., New
York, NY   10017.
   biweekly, $100/yr

The Environment Monthly
420 Lexington Ave., New York, NY 10017

Environment Report
Frends Publishing, Inc., National Press Bldg, Washington,
DC 20004
    bimonthly, $60/yr

Environment Reporter
Bureau of National Affairs, Inc., 1231 25th St. N.W.,
Washington, DC 20037
    weekly, $296/yr

Environmental Action
Environmental Action, Inc., Rm. 731, 1346 Connecticut Ave.
N.W., Washington, DC 20036
    biweekly, $7.50/yr, circ 5000 (controlled)

Environmental Action Guide
National Association of Conservation Districts, 1025 Vermont
Ave. N.W., Washington, DC 20005

Environmental Education
Dembar Educational Research Services, Ind., P.O. Box
1605, Madison, WI 53701
    quarterly, $7.50/yr

The Environmental Law Reporter
Environmental Law Institute, Suite 614, 1346 Connecticut
Ave. N.W., Washington, DC 20036
    monthly, $50/yr

Environmental Law Review
Sage Hill Publishers, Inc., Clark Boardman Co., Ltd.,
435 Hudson St., New York, NY 10014

Environmental Quality Magazine
10658 Burbank Blvd., North Hollywood, CA 91061
    quarterly, $10/yr, circ 105,160

Environmental Quality Report
Girard Associates, Inc., 25 Broad St., New York, NY
    biweekly, $50/yr

Environmental Science and Technology
American Chemical Society, 1155 16th St. N.W., Washington,
DC 20036

monthly, $9 ($6 members)/yr, circ 30,000

Forest History
Forest History Society, Inc., P.O. Box 1581, Santa Cruz,
CA 95060
quarterly, $7.50/yr, circ 1400

Grus Americana
Whooping Crane Conservation Association, Inc., Box 485A,
R.R. 1, Kula, Main, HI 96790
quarterly, $3(free to members)

IUCN Bulletin
International Union for Conservation of Nature and Natural
Resources, 1110 Morges, Switzerland.
monthly, $5/yr, circ 2500

IMPACT Newsletter
Oregon Student Public Interest Research Group, 408 S.W.
Second Ave., Portland, OR 97204

International Journal of Environmental Studies
Gordon & Breach Science Publishers, Ltd., Box 1305, Long
Island City, NY 11101
quarterly, $41($14.50 individuals)/yr

International Wildlife
National Wildlife Federation, 534 N. Broadway, Milwaukee,
WI 53202
bimonthly, $6.50(non-members)/yr, circ 125,000

Izaak Walton Magazine
Izaak Walton League of America, 1326 Waukegan Rd, Glen-
view, IL 60025
monthly, $2.50/yr, circ 55,000

The Journal of Environmental Education
Dembar Educational Research Services, Inc. [DERS], Box
1605, Madison, WI 53701

Journal of Soil and Water Conservation
Soil Conservation Society of America, 7515 N.E. Ankeny Rd,
Ankeny, IA 50021
bimonthly, for members, circ 13,600

Journal of the Air Pollution Control Association
Air Pollution Control Assoc., 4400 Fifth Ave., Pittsburgh,
PA 15213

Journal of the Water Pollution Control Federation
Water Pollution Control Federation, 3900 Wisconsin Ave.
N.W., Washington, DC 20016

Journal of Wildlife Management
Wildlife Society, Suite S-176, 3900 Wisconsin Ave. N.W.,
Washington, DC 20016
    quarterly, $15/yr, circ 65,000

Kids for Ecology: Entertainment and Information by Kids for
Kids
Kids for Ecology, P.O. Box P-7126, Philadelphia, PA 19117
    $4/yr

The Living Wilderness
Wilderness Society, 729 15th St. N.W., Washington, DC
20005
    quarterly, $7.50($4 libraries)/yr, circ 70,000

Maine Times
Main Street, Topsham, ME   04086
    weekly, $7/yr

Michigan Out-of-Doors
Michigan United Conservation Clubs, Box 2235, Lansing, MI
48911
    monthly, $1/yr, circ 50,000

Minnesota Out-of-Doors
Minnesota Conservation Federation, 4313 Shady Oak Road,
Hopkins, MN 55343
    monthly, $1/yr, circ 12,500

The Minnesota Volunteer
Natural Resources, 301 Centennial Bldg, 658 Cedar St.,
St. Paul, MN 55155
    bimonthly, priority to Minnesota residents, teachers, and
    libraries, circ 65,000

Missouri Conservationist
Department of Conservation, P.O. Box 180, Jefferson City,
MO 65101
    monthly, $1/yr(out of state; free in Missouri), circ
    177,000

Mother Earth News
Box 38, Madison, OH   44057

monthly, $6/yr, circ 10,000

National Parks and Conservation Magazine
National Parks and Conservation Assoc., 1701 18th St. N.W.,
Washington, DC 20009
monthly, $10/yr(free to members)

National Wildlife Magazine
National Wildlife Federation, 534 N. Broadway, Milwaukee,
WI 53202
bimonthly, $5/yr, circ 340,000

Natural History
American Museum of Natural History, Central Park West
at 79th St., New York, NY 10024
10 times/yr, $8/yr, circ 285,000

Omen
Omen Press Inc., P.O. Box 12457, Tucson, Arizona 85711
9 times/yr, $8/yr

Organic Gardening & Farming
Rodale Press, Inc., 33 Minor St., Emmaus, PA 18049
monthly, $5.85/yr, circ 400,000

Our Daily Planet
Mayor's Council on the Environment, Rm. 228, 51 Chambers
St., New York, NY 10007
monthly, $3.50/yr, circ 3000

Outdoor Oklahoma
Department of Wildlife Conservation, 1801 N. Lincoln, P.O.
Box 53465, Oklahoma City, OK 73105
monthly (exc Aug), $2/yr(free to libraries, schools in
state), circ 25,000

Parks and Recreation Magazine
National Recreation and Park Assoc., 1601 N. Kent St.,
Arlington, VA 22209
monthly, $7.50, circ 30,000

Pennsylvania Forests
Pennsylvania Forestry Assoc., 5221 E. Simpson St.,
Mechanicsburg, PA 17055
quarterly, $3/yr

Pollution Abstracts

P.O. Box 2369, La Jolla, CA.
    bimonthly, $70/yr

Population Bulletin
Population Reference Bureau, Inc., 1755 Massachusetts Ave.
N.W., Washington, DC 20036
    monthly, $8($5 teachers and libraries)/yr, circ 9000

Ranger Rick's Nature Magazine
National Wildlife Federation, 1412 16th St. N.W., Washington,
DC 20036
    monthly(exc June, Sept), $6/yr, circ 400,000

Roots
Ecology Action East, Box 244, Cooper Sta., New York, NY
10003
    2 times/yr, $5/5 issues

Sierra Club Bulletin
Sierra Club, 1050 Mills Tower, San Francisco, CA 94104
    monthly, $5/yr, circ 54,000

Smithsonian
Smithsonian Institution, 1000 Jefferson Dr. S.W., Washington,
DC 20560

Tennessee Conservationist
Department of Conservation, 2611 West End Ave., Nashville,
TN 37203
    monthly, free, circ 25,000

Texas Parks and Wildlife Magazine
Parks and Wildlife Department, John H. Reagan Bldg,
Austin, TX 78701
    monthly, $2/yr, circ 53,000

Underwater Naturalist
American Littoral Soc., Sandy Hook, Highlands, NJ 07732
    quarterly, $7.50($15 institutions)/yr

Washington Environmental Protection Report
Callahan Publications, Box 3751, Washington, DC 20007
    bimonthly, $100/yr

Water Resources Bulletin
American Water Resources Assoc., 206 E. University Ave.,
Urbana, IL 61801

quarterly, $6/yr, circ 1500

World Ecology 2000: Econsystems and Environmental Management
Nautilus Press, 1056 National Press Bldg, Washington, DC 20004.

monthly, $125/yr

Section V

U.S. GOVERNMENT AGENCIES/PUBLICATIONS

Congress--Senate

Committee on Agriculture and Forestry
Rm. 324, Old Senate Office Building, Washington, DC   20510
(202) 225-2035

Committee on Appropriations
Rm. 1235, New Senate Office Building, Washington, DC
20510
(202) 225-3471
    Subcommittee: Agriculture, Environmental and
    Consumer Protection.

Committee on Commerce
Rm. 5202, New Senate Office Building, Washington, DC
20510
(202) 225-5115
    Subcommittee on Environment.

Committee on Interior and Insular Affairs
Rm. 3106, New Senate Office Building, Washington, DC
20510
(202) 225-4971

Committee on Public Works
Rm. 4204, New Senate Office Building, Washington, DC
20510
(202) 225-6176
    Subcommittees: Air and Water Pollution; Economic De-
    velopment; Environmental Science and Technology; Roads.

Congress--House of Representatives

Committee on Agriculture
Rm. 1301, Longworth House Office Building, Washington, DC
20515
(202) 225-2171

Committee on Appropriations
Rm. H-218, Capitol Building, Washington, DC   20515
(202) 225-2771
   Subcommittee on Environmental and Consumer Protection.

Committee on Interior and Insular Affairs
Rm. 1324, Longworth House Office Building, Washington, DC
20515
(202) 225-2761
   Subcommittees: Environment, Irrigation and Reclamation,
   Mines and Mining; National Parks and Recreation; Public
   Lands.

Committee on Interstate and Foreign Commerce
Rm. 2125, Rayburn House Office Building, Washington, DC
20515
(202) 225-2927
   Subcommittees: Communications and Power; Public Health
   and Environment; Transportation and Aeronautics.

Committee on Merchant Marine and Fisheries
Rm. 1334, Longworth House Office Building, Washington, DC
20515
(202) 225-4047

Executive Departments

Department of Agriculture
14th St. and Jefferson Dr. S.W., Washington, DC   20250
(202) 447-5247, Director of Information

   Agricultural Research Service
   Washington, DC   20250
   (202) 655-4000

   Forest Service
   Washington, DC   20250
   (202) 447-3957

   Soil Conservation Service
   Washington, DC   20250
   (202) 655-4000

Department of Commerce
Commerce Building, 14th St. between Constitution Ave. and
E St. N.W., Washington, DC   20230
(202) 967-5035, Director of Public Affairs

National Industrial Pollution Control Council
Washington, DC 20230
(202) 967-4513, Public Affairs Officer

National Oceanic and Atmospheric Administration
Washington, DC 20230
(202) 967-5181, Office of Ecology and Environmental
Conservation

Department of Defense
Department of the Army, The Pentagon, Washington, DC
20310
   U.S. Army Corps of Engineers
   Office of the Chief of Engineers, Forestal Building,
   Washington, DC 20314

Department of Health, Education, and Welfares
330 Independence Ave. S.W., Washington, DC 20201
(202) 962-2245, Information Center
  Deputy Assistant Secretary for Population Affairs
  (202) 962-3822

   Food and Drug Administration
   5600 Fishers Lane, Rockville, MD 20852
   (301) 443-3380, Commissioner's Office

   Office of Education
   Washington, DC 20202
     Director, Office of Environmental Education
     (202) 962-7807

Department of the Interior
Interior Building, C St., between 18th and 19th sts. N.W.
Washington, DC 20240
(202) 343-1100, Information

   Bureau of Land Management
   Washington, DC 20240
   (202) 343-1100

   Bureau of Mines
   Washington, DC 20240
   (202) 343-1100
     Mineral Resources and Environmental Development

   Bureau of Outdoor Recreation
   Washington, DC 20240
   (202) 343-1100

Bureau of Reclamation
Washington, DC 20240
(202) 343-4662

Bureau of Sport Fisheries and Wildlife
Washington, DC 20240
(202) 343-5634, Office of Conservation Education

Regional Conservation Education Coordinators (Department
of the Interior):

Pacific Region (Hawaii, California, Idaho, Montana,
Nevada, Oregon, Washington)
1500 Plaza Building, 1500 N.E. Irving St., Portland,
OR 97208
(503) 234-3361, ext. 4050

Southwest Region (Arizona, Colorado, Kansas, New
Mexico, Oklahoma, Texas, Utah, Wyoming)
Federal Building, U.S. Post Office and Court House,
500 Gold Ave. S.W., Albuquerque, NM 87103
(505) 766-2321

North Central Region (Illinois, Indiana, Iowa, Minnesota, Missouri, Nebraska, North Dakota, South
Dakota, Ohio, and Wisconsin)
Federal Building, Fort Snelling, Twin Cities, MN
55111
(612) 725-3500

Southeast Region (Alabama, Arkansas, Florida,
Georgia, Kentucky, Louisiana, Mississippi, North
Carolina, South Carolina, Tennessee, and Virginia)
17 Executive Park Dr., Atlanta, GA 30329
(404) 526-4671

Northeast Region (Connecticut, Delaware, Maine,
Massachusetts, New Hampshire, New Jersey, New
York, Pennsylvania, Rhode Island, Vermont, West
Virginia)
U.S. Post Office and Courthouse, Boston, MA 02109
(617) 223-2961

Alaska Area
813 D St., Anchorage, AK 99501
(907) 265-4864

Denver Region

10597 W. Sixth Ave. , Denver, CO 80215
(303) 234-2209

National Park Service
Interior Building, Washington, DC 20240
(202) 343-1100, Information

Department of State
Washington, DC 20520
Special Assistant for Fisheries and Wildlife
(202) 632-2335
Special Assistant for Environmental Affairs and Director,
Office of Environmental Affairs
(202) 632-7964

Department of Transportation
400 7th St. S.W. , Washington, DC 20590
(202) 426-4000

Federal Highway Administration
400 7th St. S.W. , Washington, DC 20590
(202) 426-0539

Independent Agencies

Atomic Energy Commission
Washington, DC 20545
(301) 973-1000
Director, Division of Biomedical and Environmental
Research
(301) 973-3208

Council on Environmental Quality and Citizen's Advisory
Committee on Environmental Quality
722 Jackson Place N.W. , Washington, DC 20006
(202) 382-5948

Environmental Protection Agency
U.S. Waterside Mall, Washington, DC 20460
(202) 755-2673

Regional Administrators (Environmental Protection
Agency):

Region I
Rm. 2303, John F. Kennedy Federal Building,

Boston, MA 02203
(617) 223-7223

Region II
Rm. 908, 26 Federal Plaza, New York, NY 10007
(212) 264-2515

Region III
Curtis Building, 6th and Walnut sts., Philadelphia,
PA 19106
(215) 597-9370

Region IV
1421 Peachtree St. N.E., Atlanta, GA 30309
(404) 526-3004

Region V
One North Wacker Drive, Chicago, IL 60606
(312) 353-4800

Region VI
1600 Patterson, Dallas, TX 75201
(214) 749-1151

Region VII
Rm. 249, 1735 Baltimore Ave., Kansas City, MO
64108
(816) 374-5495

Region VIII
Rm. 900, Lincoln Tower Building, 1860 Lincoln St.,
Denver, CO 80203
(303) 837-4905

Region IX
100 California St., San Francisco, CA 94111
(415) 556-6695

Region X
1200 Sixth Ave., Seattle, WA 98108
(206) 442-1203

Federal Power Commission
441 G St. N.W., Washington, DC 20426
(202) 386-6102, Director of Public Information

National Water Commission

800 N. Quincy St. , Arlington, VA   22203
(703) 557-1960

Smithsonian Institution
1000 Jefferson Dr. S.W. , Washington, DC   20560
(202) 628-4422

Tennessee Valley Authority
New Sprankle Building, Knoxville, TN   37902
(615) 637-0101

Water Resources Council
Suite 800, 2120 L St. N.W. , Washington, DC   20037
(202) 254-6303

Federal Working Group on Pest Management
5600 Fishers Lane, Rockville, MD   20852
(301) 443-3230

Publications

The Government Printing Office offers many informative publications on ecology, conservation, and related subjects. A
listing is available free of charge from:

                The Superintendent of Documents
                Government Printing Office
                Washington, DC   20402

Prices of individual publications vary but range generally from
under a dollar to approximately four dollars. A master list
is issued annually; supplementary, shorter lists, bimonthly.
For library use, the Monthly Catalogue of U.S. Government
Publications, a comprehensive listing of current publications
of all departments, is available by subscription for $6 a
year. Many government publications reflect institutional
rather than ecological interests, however, and should be used
with a grain of environmental enlightenment. But if the prej-
udice is recognized, even those less ecologically sensitive
publications can be useful. A subject list of available governmental publications follows. The numbers identify the Government's code and should be included along with the subject
title with requests.

10.   Laws, Rules, and Regulations.

11. Home Economics. Foods and cooking.
15. Geology.
21. Fish and Wildlife.
25. Transportation, Highways, Roads, and Postal Service.
28. Finance. National economy, accounting, insurance, Securities.
31. Education.
33A. Occupations. Professions and job descriptions.
35. National Parks. Historic Sites, National Monuments.
36. Government Periodicals and Subscription Services.
38. Animal Industry. Farm animals, poultry, and dairying.
41. Insects. Worms and insects harmful to man, animals, and plants.
42. Irrigation, Drainage, and Water Power.
43. Forestry. Managing and using forest and range land, including timber and lumber, ranges and grazing, American woods.
44. Plants. Culture, grading, marketing, and storage of fruits, vegetables, grass, and grain.
46. Soils and Fertilizers. Soil surveys, erosion, conservation.
48. Weather, Astronomy, and Meterorology.
50. American History.
51. Health and Hygiene. Drugs and sanitation.
51A. Diseases. Contagious and infectious diseases, sickness, and vital statistics.
53. Maps. Engineering, surveying.
54. Political Science. Government, crime, District of Columbia.
55. Smithsonian Institution. National Museum, and Indians.
58. Mines. Explosives, fuel, gasoline, gas, petroleum, minerals.
59. Interstate Commerce.
62. Commerce. Business, patents, trademarks, and foreign trade.
64. Scientific Tests, Standards. Mathematics, physics.
65. Foreign Relations of the United States. Publications relating to foreign countries.
68. Farm Management. Foreign agriculture, rural electrification, agricultural marketing.
70. Census. Statistics of agriculture, business, governments, housing, manufactures, minerals, population, and maps.
71. Children's Bureau, and other publications relating to children and youth.
72. Homes. Construction, maintenance, community development.

184   Conservation/Ecology

78. <u>Social Security</u>. Industrial hazards, health and hygiene,
    safety for workers, pensions, workmen's compensation
    and insurance.
79A. <u>Space, Missiles, the Moon, NASA, and Satellites</u>.
    Space education, exploration, research, and technology.
81. <u>Posters and Charts</u>.
83. <u>Library of Congress</u>.
84. <u>Atomic Energy and Civil Defense</u>.
86. <u>Consumer Information</u>. Family finances, appliances,
    recreation, gardening, health and safety, food, house
    and home, child care, and clothing and fabrics.
87. <u>States and Territories of the United States and Their
    Resources</u>.

Section VI

OTHER PUBLIC AGENCIES

International, National,
and Interstate Commissions

ATLANTIC STATES MARINE FISHERIES COMMISSION
1717 Massachusetts Ave. N.W., Washington, DC 20036
(202) 387-5330

DELAWARE RIVER BASIN COMMISSION
25 State Police Rd., Box 360, Trenton, NJ 08603
(609) 883-9500

FORUM INTERNATIONAL: International Ecosystems
University
2905 Benvenue Ave., Berkeley, CA 94705
(415) 642-1954
Publication: Ecosphere

GREAT LAKES BASIN COMMISSION
P.O. Box 999, Ann Arbor, MI 48106
(313) 763-3590
Publication: The Communicator

GREAT LAKES COMMISSION
514 I.S.T. Bldg., 2200 Bonisteel Blvd., Ann Arbor, MI
48105
(313) 665-9135
Publications: Great Lakes Newsletter; Great Lakes Research
Checklist

GREAT LAKES FISHERY COMMISSION
1451 Green Rd., P.O. Box 640, Ann Arbor, MI 48107
(313) 662-3209

INTERNATIONAL COMMISSION FOR THE NORTHWEST
ATLANTIC FISHERIES
P.O. Box 638, Dartmouth, Nova Scotia, Canada
(902) 466-7587

185

186   Conservation/Ecology

INTERNATIONAL COMMISSION ON NATIONAL PARKS
P. O. Box 19347, Washington, DC   20036; IUCN Headquarters:
1110 Morges, Switzerland
Washington Phone: (202) 667-3352

INTERNATIONAL NORTH PACIFIC FISHERIES COMMISSION
6640 N. W. Marine Dr. , Vancouver 8, BC, Canada
(604) 224-0722

INTERNATIONAL WHALING COMMISSION
Great Westminster House, Horseferry Rd. , London, S. W. 1,
England
(01) 834-8511, ext. 405

INTERSTATE COMMISSION ON THE POTOMAC RIVER BASIN
Suite 407, Global Bldg. , 1025 Vermont Ave. N. W. , Washington, DC   20005
(202) 393-1978

NEW ENGLAND INTERSTATE WATER POLLUTION CONTROL
COMMISSION
607 Boylston St. , Boston, MA   02116
(617) 261-3758
Publication: Aqua News

NEW ENGLAND RIVER BASINS COMMISSION
55 Court St. , Boston, MA   02108
(617) 223-6244

OHIO RIVER VALLEY WATER SANITATION COMMISSION
414 Walnut St. , Cincinnati, OH   45202
(513) 421-1151

PACIFIC MARINE FISHERIES COMMISSION
342 State Office Bldg. , 1400 S. W. Fifth Ave. , Portland, OR
97201
(503) 229-5840

PACIFIC NORTHWEST RIVER BASINS COMMISSION
One Columbia River, Vancouver, WA   98660
(206) 694-2581
Publication: PNWRBC Newsletter

UPPER COLORADO RIVER COMMISSION
355 S. Fourth St. , Salt Lake City, UT   84111
(801) 364-5629

Governmental and Quasi-Governmental
Agencies, by State

ALABAMA

Department of Conservation and Natural Resources
64 North Union St. , Montgomery, AL 36104
(205) 269-7221

The Alabama Conservancy
2408 Seventh Ave. S. , Birmingham, AL 35233
(205) 251-3107

ALASKA

Department of Environmental Conservation
Pouch O, Juneau, AK 99801
(907) 586-6721

Department of Natural Resources
Pouch M, Goldstein Bldg. , Juneau AK 99801
(907) 586-6352

Alaska Conservation Society
Box 80192, College, AK 99701
(907) 479-6372

Alaska Environmental Institute, Inc.
Rm 3, 913 W. Sixth Ave. , Anchorage, AK 99501
(907) 274-2341/3052

ARIZONA

Game and Fish Department
2222 W. Greenway, Phoenix, AZ 85023
(602) 942-3000

Land Department
400 State Office Bldg. , Phoenix, AZ 85007
(602) 271-4621

Outdoor Recreation Coordinating Commission
2222 W. Greenway, Phoenix, AZ 85023
(602) 943-3000

Arizona Conservation Council
7302 N. Tenth St. , Phoenix, AZ 85020

ARKANSAS

Department of Pollution Control and Ecology
P.O. Box 9583, 8001 National Dr. , Little Rock, AR
72209

CALIFORNIA

The Resources Agency
1416 Ninth St., Sacramento, CA 95814
(916) 445-5656

Council for Planning and Conservation
Box 228, Beverly Hills, CA 90213
(213) 276 2685

Ecology Center
2179 Allston Way, Berkeley, CA 94704
(415) 548-2220

Planning and Conservation League
909 12th St., Sacramento, CA 95814
(916) 444-8726

Student Environmental Confederation
RM 915, 926 J St., Sacramento, CA 95814
(916) 444-6168

COLORADO

Department of Natural Resources
1845 Sherman, Denver, CO 80203
(303) 892-3311

Colorado Open Space Council
1742 Pearl St., Denver, CO 80203
(303) 573-9241

CONNECTICUT

Department of Environmental Protection
State Office Bldg, 165 Capitol Ave., Hartford, CT
06115

DELAWARE

Department of Natural Resources and Environmental
Control
Edward Tathall Bldg., Legislative Ave. and D St.,
Dover, DE 19901

Delaware Conservation Education Association
Box 45, Dover, DE 19901

DISTRICT OF COLUMBIA

Department of Environmental Service
1875 Connecticut Ave. N.W., Washington, DC 20009

Public Agencies   189

Washington Ecology Center
Rm 612, 2000 P St. N.W., Washington, DC 20006
(202) 833-1778

FLORDIA

Department of Pollution Control
315 S. Calhoun St., Tallahassee, FL 32301
(904) 224-9151

Department of Natural Resources
Larson Bldg., Gaines St. at Monroe, Tallahassee, FL
32304
(904) 224-7141

Environmental Information Center of the Florida
Conservation Foundation, Inc.
935 Orange Ave., Winter Park, FL 32789
(305) 644-5377

GEORGIA

Department of Natural Resources
270 Washington St. S.W., Atlanta, GA 30334

Save America's Vital Environment
P.O. Box 52652, Atlanta, GA 30305
(404) 237-5693

HAWAII

Department of Land and Natural Resources
Box 621, Honolulu, HI 96809
(808) 548-6550

Life of the Land
404 Pilkoi St., Honolulu, HI 96814
(808) 521-1300

The Outdoor Circle
200 North Vineyard Blvd., Honolulu, HI 96817
(808) 533-6774

IDAHO

Department of Environmental Protection and Health
Statehouse, Boise, ID 83707

Idaho Environmental Council
P.O. Box 3371, University Sta., Moscow, ID 83843
(208) 882-3511, ext. 6417

ILLINOIS

Department of Conservation
State Office Bldg., Springfield, IL   62706
(217) 525-6302

Environmental Protection Agency
2200 Churchill Rd., Springfield, IL   62706
(217) 525-3397

Illinois Wildlife Federation
Box 116, 13005 South Western Ave., Blue Island, IL
60406

INDIANA

Department of Natural Resources
608 State Office Bldg., Indianapolis, IN   46204

Stream Pollution Control Board
1330 W. Michigan St., Indianapolis, IN   46206
(317) 633-4420

Indiana Conservation Council, Inc.
2128 E. 46th St., Indianapolis, IN   46205
(317) 293-1533

IOWA

Department of Environmental Quality
Lucas State Office Bldg., Des Moines, IA   50319
(515) 281-3045

State Conservation Commission
State Office Bldg., 300 4th St., Des Moines, IA   50319
(515) 281-5145

Iowa Conservation Education Council, Inc.
823 Federal Bldg., Des Moines, IA   50309

KANSAS

Forestry, Fish and Game Commission
Box 1028, Pratt, KS   67124
(316) 672-6473

State Department of Health
535 Kansas Ave., Topeka, KS   66603

Kansas Wildlife Federation, Inc.
R.R. #1, Wamego, KS   66547
(913) 456-2500

KENTUCKY

Department of Natural Resources
5th Floor, Capital Plaza Tower, Frankfort, KY 40601
(502) 564-3350

Department of Public Information
New Capitol Annex, Frankfort, KY 40601

Water Pollution Control Commission
State Dept. of Health, 275 E. Main St. , Frankfort, KY
40601
(502) 564-3401

Action for Clean Air, Inc.
Box 8242, Sta. E, Louisville, KY 40208
(502) 637-1948

Kentucky Audubon Council
1020 E. 20th St. , Owensboro, KY 42301
(502) 685-1849

LOUISIANA

State Department of Conservation
P.O. Box 44275, Capitol Sta. , Baton Rouge, LA 70804
(504) 389-5161

Louisiana Wildlife Federation
Box 16089, Louisiana State Univ. , Baton Rouge, LA
70803
(504) 357-8795

MAINE

Department of Natural Resources
State Office Bldg. , Augusta, ME 04330
(207) 289-3821

Natural Resources Council of Maine
20 Willow St. , Augusta, ME 04330
(207) 622-3101

MARYLAND

Department of Natural Resources
Rowe Blvd. and Taylor Ave. , Annapolis, MD 21401
(301) 267-5681

State Department of Health and Mental Hygiene
Environmental Health Admin. , 610 N. Howard St. ,
Baltimore, MD 21201
(301) 383-2740

192   Conservation/Ecology

Conservation Education Council of Maryland
Chairman: James A. Ruckert, 705 Stirling Rd.,
Silver Spring, MD 20901

MASSACHUSETTS

Office of Conservation Education
Dept. of Educ., 182 Tremont St., Boston, MA 02111
(617) 727-5742

Department of Natural Resources
Leverett Saltonstall Bldg., 100 Cambridge St.,
Boston, MA 02202
(617) 727-3163

Executive Office of Environmental Affairs
18 Tremont St., Boston, MA 02108
(617) 727-7700

Massachusetts Association of Conservation Commissions
506 Statler Office Bldg., Park Square, Boston, MA
02116
(617) 542-1584

Massachusetts Audubon Society, Inc.
South Great Rd., Lincoln, MA 01773
(617) 259-9500

Massachusetts Forest and Park Association
One Court St., Boston, MA 02108
(617) 742-2553

MICHIGAN

Department of Natural Resources
Mason Bldg., Lansing, MI 48926
(517) 373-1220

Water Resources Commission
Mason Bldg., Lansing, MI 48926
(517) 373-3560

Michigan United Conservation Clubs
Box 2235, Lansing, MI 48911
(517) 371-1041

Michigan Natural Resources Council
Dept. of Natural Resources, Mason Bldg., Lansing,
MI 48926

MINNESOTA

Department of Natural Resources

301 Centennial Bldg. 658 Cedar St. , St. Paul, MN
55155
(612) 296-3336

Pollution Control Agency
717 Delaware St. , SE, Minneapolis, MN 55440
(612) 296-5591

Clean Air, Clean Water-Unlimited
Box 311, South St. Paul, MN 55075

Friends of the Wilderness
3515 E. Fourth St. , Duluth, MN 55804

Minnesota Association for Conservation Education
5400 Glenwood Ave. , Golden Valley, MN 55422

Minnesota Environmental Control Citizens Association
26 E. Exchange St. , St. Paul, MN 55101
(612) 222-2998

MISSISSIPPI

Air and Water Pollution Control Commission
P.O. Box 827, Jackson, MS 39205
(601) 354-6783

Mississippi Wildlife Federation
P.O. Box 1814, Jackson, MS 39205
(601) 353-6922

MISSOURI

Department of Conservation
P.O. Box 180, Jefferson City, MO 65101
(314) 751-4115

Clean Water Commission
Dept. of Public Health and Welfare, Rm 102, Capitol
Bldg. , P.O. Box 154, Jefferson City, MO 65101
(314) 635-9117

Conservation Federation of Missouri
312 E. Capitol Ave. , Jefferson City, MO 65101
(314) 635-7188

Missouri Prairie Foundation
P.O. Box 200, Columbia, MO 62201
(314) 449-3761

MONTANA

Department of Natural Resources and Conservation

Sam W. Mitchell Bldg. , Helena, MT   59601
(406) 449-3647

State Department of Health
Helena, MT   59601
(406) 449-2544

Montana Conservation Council, Inc.
Box 175, Missoula, MT   58901

NEBRASKA

Department of Environmental Control
Box 4844, State House Sta. , Lincoln, NE   68509

Nebraska Natural Resources Commission
Box 94725, State House Sta. , Lincoln, NE   68509
(402) 471-2081

Nebraska Wildlife Federation
c/o V. J. Skutt, 3301 Dodge St. , Omaha, NE   68131
(404) 342-7450

NEVADA

Environmental Protection Commission
State Health Div. , 201 S. Fall St. , Carson City, NV
89701
(701) 882-7458

Department of Conservation and Natural Resources
Nye Bldg. , Carson City, NV   89701
(702) 882-7482

Nevada Wildlife Federation, Inc.
Box 49, Sparks, NV   89431
(702) 358-7668

NEW HAMPSHIRE

Council of Resources and Environment
State House Annex, Concord, NH   03301
(603) 271-2155

Department of Resources and Economic Development
State House Annex, Concord, NH   03301

Water Supply and Pollution Control Commission
Prescott Park, 105 Loudon Rd. , Concord, NH   03301
(603) 271-3502

Land Use Foundation of New Hampshire
7 S. State St. , Concord, NH   03301
(603) 224-7615

New Hampshire Natural Resources Council, Inc.
5 S. State St., Concord, NH   03301
(603) 224-1896

Seacoast Anti-Pollution League
Rt. 84, Hampton Falls, NH   03844
(603) 742-1097

Society for the Protection of New Hampshire Forests
5 South State Street, Concord, NH   03301
(603) 224-9945

SPACE: Statewide Program of Action to Conserve Our
Environment
Box 757, Concord, NH   03301
(603) 679-8731

NEW JERSEY

Department of Environmental Protection
Labor and Industry Bldg., Box 1390, Trenton, NJ
08625
(609) 292-2886

Association of New Jersey Conservation Commissions
Box 157, Mendham, NJ   07945
(201) 539-7547

Atlantic County Citizens Council on Environment, Inc.
137 S. Main St., Pleasantville, NJ   08232
(609) 823-1733

North Jersey Conservation Foundation
300 Mendham Rd., Morristown, NJ   07960
(201) 539-7540

NEW MEXICO

Environmental Improvement Agency
P.O. Box 2348, Santa Fe, NM   87501
(505) 827-2473

New Mexico Conservation Coordinating Council
P.O. Box 142, Albuquerque, NM   87103

NEW YORK

Bureau of Environmental Protection
Department of Law, State of New York, 80 Centre St.,
New York, NY   10013
(212) 488-3475

New York State Department of Environmental Conservation

50 Wolf Rd. , Albany, NY   12201
(518) 457-3446

Environmental Action Coalition, Inc.
235 E. 49th St. , New York, NY   19917
(212) 486-9550

Consumer Action Now, Inc. [CAN]
30 E. 68th St. , New York, NY   10021
(212) 628-2295

NORTH CAROLINA

Department of Conservation and Development
P.O. Box 27687, Raleigh, NC   27611
(919) 829-4177

Department of Natural and Economic Resources
P.O. Box 27687, Raleigh, NC   27611
(919) 829-4984

Conservation Council of North Carolina
Box 1207, Chapel Hill, NC   27514
(919) 942-1122

NORTH DAKOTA

Department of Health
Bismarck, ND   58501
(701) 224-2371, 2386, 2374, 2382

State Outdoor Recreation Agency
900 East Blvd. , Bismarck, ND   58501
(701) 224-2430

North Dakota Wildlife Federation
Box 1694, Suite 9, 200 W. Main, Bismarck, ND   58501
(701) 223-8741

OHIO

Department of Health
P.O. Box 118, Columbus, OH   43216
(614) 469-2253

Department of Natural Resources
907 Ohio Departments Bldg. , Columbus, OH   43215
(614) 469-3770

Conservation and Outdoor Education Association
Dr. John Thomson, Chairman, Dept. of Geography,
Miami University, Oxford, OH

OKLAHOMA

Department of Wildlife Conservation
1801 N. Lincoln, P.O. Box 53465, Oklahoma City, OK
73105
(405) 521-3851

State Department of Health
3400 North Eastern, Oklahoma City, OK   73105
(405) 427-6561

Oklahoma Conservation Commission
Rm 114, State Capitol, Oklahoma City, OK   73105
(405) 521-2384

Oklahoma Wildlife Federation
Box 1262, Norman, OK   73069

OREGON

Department of Environmental Quality
1234 S.W. Morrison, Portland, OR   97205
(503) 229-5696

Oregon Environmental Council
2637 S.W. Water Ave., Portland, OR   97201
(503) 222-1963

Oregon Student Public Interest Research Group
408 S.W. Second Ave., Portland, OR   97204
(503) 222-9641

PENNSYLVANIA

Department of Environmental Resources
Public Relations, Rm 522, South Office Bldg.,
Harrisburg, PA   17120
(717) 787-1323

Environmental Planning and Information Center of
  Pennsylvania, Inc.
313 S. 16th St., Philadelphia, PA   19102
(215) 732-1958

Pennsylvania Citizen's Advisory Council
521 South Office Bldg., Harrisburg, PA   17120

Pennsylvania Environmental Council, Inc.
313 S. 16th St., Philadelphia, PA   19102
(215) 735-0966

PUERTO RICO

Department of Public Works, Area of Natural Resources

P.O. Box 8218, San Juan, PR
(809) 725-6550

The Natural History Society of Puerto Rico, Inc.
Box 1393, Hato Ray, PR   00919

RHODE ISLAND

Department of Health
Davis St., Providence, RI   02903
(401) 277-2234

Department of Natural Resources
83 Park St., Providence, RI   02903
(401) 277-2776

Environmental Council of Rhode Island, Inc.
40 Bowen St., Providence, RI   02903
(401) 521-1670

SOUTH CAROLINA

Pollution Control Authority
Box 11628, 1321 Lady St., Columbia SC   29211
(803) 758-2915

State Land Resources Conservation Commission
2414 Bull St., Columbia, SC   29201
(803) 758-2824

South Carolina Wildlife Federation
Lone Star Rd., Elloree, SC   29047
(803) 897-2550

SOUTH DAKOTA

Committee on Water Pollution
State Department of Health
Pierre, SD   57501
(605) 244-3351

Conservation Commission
State Capitol, Pierre, SD   57501
(605) 224-3258

South Dakota Wildlife Federation
1217 S. Lake Ave., Sioux Falls, SD   57105
(605) 332-2583

TENNESSEE

Department of Conservation
2611 West End Ave., Nashville, TN   37203
(615) 741-2301

Tennessee Conservation League, Inc.
Suite 221, 2010 Church St., Nashville, TN   37203
(615) 327-9492

Tennessee Citizens for Wilderness Planning
130 Tabor Rd., Oak Ridge, TN   37830
(615) 482-2153

Tennessee Environmental Council
Botanic Hall, Tennessee Botanical Gardens, Chee Rd.,
Nashville, TN   37205
(615) 356-3306

TEXAS

Parks and Wildlife Department
John H. Reagan Bldg., Austin, TX   78701
(512) 474-2087

Water Quality Board
314 W. 11th St., Austin, TX   78701 (mail: P.O. Box
13245, Capitol Sta., Austin   78711)
(512) 475-2651

Texas Advisory Committee on Conservation Education
H. J. Knight, Superintendent, Livingston Independent
School District, Box 971, Livingston, TX   77351

Texas Conservation Council, Inc.
Secretary: Mrs. A. V. Emmott, 730 E. Friar Tuck
Lane, Houston, TX   77024
(713) 686-4165

UTAH

State Department of Natural Resources
225 State Capitol, Salt Lake City, UT   84114
(801) 328-5357

State Division of Health
44 Medical Dr., Salt Lake City, UT   84113
(801) 328-6111

Utah Wildlife and Outdoor Recreation Federation
1008 Walker Bank Bldg., Salt Lake City, UT   84111
(801) 485-8361

VERMONT

Agency of Environmental Conservation
Montpelier, VT   05602
(802) 828-3357

State Natural Resources Conservation Council
State Office Bldg. , Montpelier, VT   05602
(802) 828-3351

Vermont Natural Resources Council
26 State St. , Montpelier, VT   05602
(802) 229-9496

Conservation Society of Southern Vermont
Townshend, VT   05353
(802) 365-7754

VIRGINIA

Department of Conservation and Economic Development
1100 State Office Bldg. , Richmond, VA   23219
(703) 770-2121

Resource-Use Education Council
Chairman: Franklin D. Kizer, Supervisor of Science,
State Dept. of Educ. , 1322-28 E. Grace St. , Richmond,
VA   23216
(703) 770-2672

Conservation Council of Virginia, Inc.
200 W. Grace St. , Richmond, VA   23203

Northern Virginia Conservation Council
P.O. Box 304, Annandale, VA   22003

WASHINGTON

Department of Ecology
Box 829, Olympia, WA   98504
(206) 753-2800

Department of Natural Resources
Olympia, WA   98504
(206) 753-5327

Washington Environmental Council, Inc.
President: Joan Thomas, Rm 4, 107 S. Main St. ,
Seattle, WA   98104
(206) 623-1483

WEST VIRGINIA

Department of Natural Resources
1800 Washington St. E. , Charleston, WV   25305
(304) 348-2754

West Virginia Wildlife Federation
Box 275, Paden City, WV   26159

Public Agencies   201

WISCONSIN

    Department of Natural Resources
    Box 450, Madison, WI 53701
    (608) 266-2121

    Wisconsin Environmental Education Council
    Lowell Hall, 610 Langdon St., Madison, WI 53706
    (608) 263-3327

    Citizens Natural Resources Association of Wisconsin,
    Inc.
    President: George C. Becker, 2617 Prais St., Stevens
    Point, WI 54481
    (715) 344-2401

WYOMING

    Department of Economic Planning and Development
    720 W. 18th St., Cheyenne, WY 82001
    (307) 777-7284

    Department of Health and Social Services
    Div. of Health and Medical Services, State Office
    Bldg., Cheyenne, WY 82001
    (307) 777-7275

    Wyoming Wildlife Federation
    Box 1406, Casper, WY 82601
    (307) 234-5212

                    Canadian Government Agencies/
                         Citizen Groups

Government Agencies

CANADIAN COUNCIL OF RESOURCE MINISTERS
1170 Beaver Hall Sq., Montreal 111, Que. (514) 283-4052
Publications: Resources Bulletin; Man and Resources
Newsletter; References.

CANADIAN WILDLIFE SERVICE
400 Laurier Ave., West, Ottawa, ON KIA OH4.

DEPARTMENT OF THE ENVIRONMENT, ON KIA OH3.

DEPARTMENT OF INDIAN AFFAIRS AND NORTHERN
    DEVELOPMENT
400 Laurier Ave. W., Ottawa, ON KIA OH4.

Citizen Groups

ATLANTIC SALMON ASSOCIATION
Suite 409, 1405 Peel St. , Montreal 110, Que.
(514) 282-0007. Publication: Atlantic Salmon Journal

CANADIAN INSTITUTE OF FORESTRY
P.O. Box 5000, Macdonald College, Quebec.
Publication: Forestry Chronicle.

CANADIAN NATURE FEDERATION
46 Elgin St. , OH AWA, Ont. K1P5K6   (613) 233-3486.

CANADIAN WILDLIFE FEDERATION
1419 Carling Ave. , Ottawa, ON KIZ 7L7.
Publication: Wildlife News.

CANADIAN WOLF DEFENDERS
Box 3480, Edmonton 41, AB T5L 4J3.
Publication: Newsletter.

DUCKS UNLIMITED
1495 Pembina Highway, Winnipeg, MB R3T 2E2 (204) 474-1476.

INTERNATIONAL COUNCIL FOR BIRD PRESERVATION
c/o Canadian Nature Federation, 46 Elgin St. , Ottawa, ON
KIP 5K6.

NATIONAL AND PROVINCIAL PARKS ASSOCIATION OF
  CANADA
Suite 18, 43 Victoria St. , Toronto 1, ON.

THE NATURE CONSERVANCY OF CANADA
Suite 611, 2200 Yonge St. , Toronto M4S 2E1
(416) 486-1011.

Other Agencies and Citizen Groups, by Province or Territory

ALBERTA

        Alberta Fish and Game Association
        212-8631 109th St. , Edmonton, AB T6G 1E8.
        Publication: Defending All Outdoors.

        Alberta Wilderness Association
        Box 6398 Sta. D, Calgary, AB T2P 2E1.

        Department of Lands and Forests

Natural Resources Bldg., Edmonton T5K 2E1, AB.

Ducks Unlimited (Canada--Alberta Operation)
218 Alberta Block, 10526 Jasper Ave., Edmonton, AB
T5J 1Z7.

FEDERATION OF ALBERTA NATURALISTS
Box 1472, Edmonton T5J 2N5.   Publications:
Alberta Naturalist;   Newsletter.

BRITISH COLUMBIA

British Columbia Waterfowl Society
5191 Robertson Rd. R.R. J. Delta (604) 946-6980.
Publication: Marshnote.

British Columbia Wildlife Federation
3020 Sumner Ave., Burnaby 2, BC.   Publication:
BCWF Newsletter.

Department of Recreation and Conservation
Parliament Bldgs., Victoria, BC.   Publication:
Wildlife Review.

Ducks Unlimited (Canada--British Columbia Operation)
240-777 Broughton St., Victoria, BC

Federation of British Columbia Naturalists
P.O. Box 34246, Sta. D, Vancouver, BC.
Publication: Newsletter.

MANITOBA

Department of Mines, Resources and Environmental
   Management
Winnipeg, MB R3C OV8.   Environmental Management
Div: Asst. Deputy Minister: Dr. W. G. Bowen, 309
Norquay Bldg., Winnipeg, R3C OP8.

Ducks Unlimited (Canada--Manitoba Operation)
1495 Pembina Highway, Winnipeg, MB R3T 2E2.

Manitoba Naturalists Society
214-190 Rupert Ave., Winnipeg R3B ON2, MB.
Publication: Manitoba Nature.

Manitoba Wildlife Federation
1870 Notre Dame Ave., Winnipeg, MB R3E 3E6.
Publication: Wildlife Crusader.

NEW BRUNSWICK

Department of Natural Resources
Centennial Bldg., Fredericton, NB.

New Brunswick Wildlife Federation
49 Richmond Ave. , Moncton, NB.

NEWFOUNDLAND

Department of Mines, Agriculture and Resources
Confederation Bldg. , St. John's, Newfoundland.

Newfoundland Labrador Wildlife Federation
c/o G. Behr, President, Box 1087, St. John's,
Newfoundland.

NORTHWEST TERRITORIES

Department of Industry and Development
Government of the N. W. T. , Yellowknife, N. W. T.

NOVA SCOTIA

Department of Lands and Forests
Halifax, NS.

Nova Scotia Forestry Association
6070 Quinpool Rd. , Halifax, NS.

Nova Scotia Wildlife Federation
P. O. Box 654, Halifax, NS.

ONTARIO

Algonquin Wildlands League
Box 114, Sta. Q, Toronto 7, ON.   Publications:
Wildland News; Wilderness Now; Why Wilderness.

Conservation Authorities Branch
Dept. of the Environment, 5th Fl. , 880 Bay St. ,
Toronto 5, ON.   St

Conservation Council of Ontario, The
Suite 604, Board of Trade Bldg. , 11 Adelaide St. W. ,
Toronto 1, ON.   Publication: The Bulletin.

Ministry of Natural Resources
Parliament Bldgs. , Toronto 5, ON.

Federation of Ontario Naturalists
1262 Don Mills Rd. , Don Mills, ON.   Publications:
The Ontario Naturalist; The Young Naturalist;
FON Newsletter.

Ontario Forestry Association
150 Consumers Rd. , Willowdale, ON.   Publication:
Ontario Forests.

PRINCE EDWARD ISLAND

Department of Environment & Tourism
P.O. Box 2000, Charlottetown, P. Ed. I.

Prince Edward Island Fish and Game Association
c/o Jack McAndrew, Secretary, 22 West St.,
Charlottetown, P. Ed. I.

QUEBEC

Department of Tourism, Fish and Game
Parliament Bldgs. (Complex G), Quebec City, Quebec.

The Provancher Society for Natural History of Canada--
La Société Provancher d'Histoire Naturelle du Canada
1160 Bourlamaque St., Quebec City 6, Quebec.

Province of Quebec Society for the Protection of Birds,
Inc.
c/o J. D. Delafield, President, 3496 Westmore Ave.,
Montreal 262, Quebec.

Quebec Forestry Association, Inc.--Association
Forestière Quebeçoise, Inc.
Suite 210, 915 St. Cyrille, West, Quebec City, Quebec.
Publication: Forest-Conservation (monthly).

Quebec Wildlife Conservation Association
Rm 1260, 1245 Sherbrooke St. W, Montreal 109, Que.

Quebec Wildlife Federation
6424 St. Denis St., Montreal 326, Quebec.

SASKATCHEWAN

Department of Natural Resources
Government Administration Bldg., Regina, Saskatchewan.

Ducks Unlimited (Canada--Saskatchewan Operation)
1651 11th Ave., Regina, Saskatchewan.

Saskatchewan Natural History Society
Box 1321, Regina, Saskatchewan. Publication: The
Blue Jay; Newsletter.

Saskatchewan Wildlife Federation
1122 Temperance St., Saskatoon, Saskatchewan.

YUKON TERRITORY

Environment Canada, Fisheries Service
1100A First Ave., Whitehorse, Yukon Territory.

Section VII

ORGANIZATIONS: INTERSTATE, NATIONAL, AND
INTERNATIONAL

AFRICAN WILDLIFE LEADERSHIP FOUNDATION, INC.
1717 Massachusetts Ave. N. W. , Washington, DC   20036
(202) 265-8394
Provides wildlife management training in US and
abroad for Africans; finances and operates conservation education centers in Africa;   maintains a staff
in Nairobi which includes a wildlife management expert, scientific officer, educator, and visual aids expert; finances and executes ecological research programs and Game Ranching programs;   assists development of national parks in Africa.
Publication: African Wildlife News.

AIR POLLUTION CONTROL ASSOCIATION
4400 Fifth Ave. , Pittsburgh, PA   15213
(412) 621-1100
Nonprofit technical association whose activities are
directed to the collection and dissemination of information about air pollution and its control.   Sponsors
annual observance of Cleaner Air Week which is held
the last week in October.
Publication: Journal of the Air Pollution Control
Association.

ALLIANCE FOR ENVIRONMENTAL EDUCATION, INC.
c/o Dr. Kenneth Dowling, Dept. of Public Instruction,
126 Langdon St. , Madison, WI   53702
(608) 266-3319
Twenty four organizations whose objective is to enhance both formal school and informal public education activities at all levels in order to produce individuals and a society that are informed, concerned,
and motivated to commit themselves and their resources to the protection of environmental quality.
Publications: Alliance Exchange (Newsletter);

Instant Exchange (Bulletin).

AMERICA THE BEAUTIFUL FUND
219 Shoreham Bldg. , Washington, DC 20005
(202) 638-1649
> Gives recognition, technical support and small grants
> to private citizens and community groups to initiate
> new local action projects improving the quality of the
> environment, including design, land preservation and
> planning, arts, historical and cultural preservation,
> and communications.
> Publication: Old Glory.

AMERICAN ASSOCIATION FOR CONSERVATION INFORMATION
c/o Malcolm Johnson, President, Missouri Dept. of Conservation, P.O. Box 180, Jefferson City, MO 65101
(314) 751-4115
> Facilitates free exchange of ideas, materials, tech-
> niques, experiences, and procedures bearing on con-
> servation information and education; establishes media
> furthering such exchange; promotes public under-
> standing of basic conservation principles; informs
> states, territories, and provinces of the desirability
> of conservation education programs (if they do not
> already have them), and assists in setting up conser-
> vation education, information, and public relations
> programs.

AMERICAN ASSOCIATION FOR THE ADVANCEMENT OF
SCIENCE
1515 Massachusetts Ave. N.W. , Washington, DC 20005
(202) 467-4400
> Works to further the work of scientists and coopera-
> tion among them; to improve the effectiveness of
> science in the promotion of human welfare; and to
> increase public understanding of the importance and
> worth of the methods of science in human progress.
> Conducts a variety of interdisciplinary programs in
> environmental subjects, publishes proceedings of
> symposiums on the environment, and sells audio-
> tapes and cassettes on environmental topics.
> Publication: Science.

AMERICAN ASSOCIATION FOR HEALTH, PHYSICAL
EDUCATION AND RECREATION
1201 16th St. N.W. , Washington, DC 20036
(202) 833-5530
> A voluntary professional organization for educators

in the fields of physical education, sports and athletics, dance, health and safety, recreation, and outdoor and environmental education. Publications: Journal of Health-Physical Education-Recreation; School Health Review; Research Quarterly; Update.

AMERICAN ASSOCIATION OF UNIVERSITY WOMEN
2401 Virginia Ave. N. W. , Washington, DC   20037
(202) 785-7700
Engages in study/action programs on the environment, working with its branches and state chairmen to provide program materials on environmental topics. Publishes a variety of materials of interest to the general public.

AMERICAN ASSOCIATION OF ZOOLOGICAL PARKS AND AQUARIUMS
Oglebay Park, Wheeling, WV   26003
(304) 242-2160
Promotes the welfare of zoological parks and aquariums and their advancement as public educational institutions, as scientific and medical research centers, as natural science and wildlife exhibitions and conservation agencies, and as cultural and recreational establishments dedicated to the enrichment of human and natural resources. Conservation of wildlife and the preservation and propagation of endangered and rare species are among their more important programs. Publication: AAZPA Newsletter-Monthly

AMERICAN CETACEAN SOCIETY
4725 Lincoln Blvd. , Marina del Rey, CA   90291
(213) 823-7311
Dedicated to extending man's knowledge of the sea and the animals inhabiting it, especially the Cetacea: whales, dolphins, and porpoises. Encourages a policy of conservation and protection of Cetacea and other marine mammals, and the natural environments supporting them. Publication: The Whalewatcher.

AMERICAN COMMITTEE FOR INTERNATIONAL WILDLIFE PROTECTION, INC.
c/o The Wildlife Society, 3900 Wisconsin Ave. N. W. ,
Washington, DC   20016
(202) 363-2435

Assists and promotes interest of U. S. organizations
in international conservation activities; specially concerned with international conservation treaties, endangered species fauna and flora habitats, national
parks and reserves, and ecological research.

AMERICAN CONSERVATION ASSOCIATION, INC.
30 Rockefeller Plaza, New York, NY 10020
(212) 247-8141
   Nonmembership, nonprofit, educational and scientific
   organization formed to advance knowledge and understanding of conservation and to preserve and develop
   natural resources for public use.

AMERICAN FARM BUREAU FEDERATION
225 Ouhy Ave., Park Ridge, IL 60068
(312) 696-2020
425 13th St. N.W., Washington, DC 20004
(202) 638-6315
   A free, independent, non-governmental, voluntary
   organization of farm and ranch families united for the
   purpose of analyzing their problems and formulating
   action to achieve educational improvement, economic
   opportunity, and social advancement and, thereby, to
   promote the national well-being.
   Publications: The American Farmer; American
   Farm Bureau Official News Letter.

AMERICAN FISHERIES SOCIETY
Fourth Floor Suite, 1319 18th St. N.W., Washington, DC
20036
(202) 872-8282
   Promotes the conservation, development, and wise
   utilization of fisheries, both recreational and commercial.
   Publication: Transactions of the American Fisheries
   Society.

AMERICAN FOREST INSTITUTE
1619 Massachusetts Ave. N.W., Washington, DC 20036
(202) 667-7807
   The nation's forest industries support this nonprofit,
   nonpolitical, conservation education organization in
   order to broaden and improve security of the forest
   products industry through encouraging intensive management of commercial forest lands and private for-
   estlands and the practice of such methods as the Tree

Farm concept.
Publications: Tree Farm News (quarterly); Green
America (quarterly).

THE AMERICAN FORESTRY ASSOCIATION
1319 18th St. N. W. , Washington, DC 20036
(202) 467-5810
Seeks the advancement of intelligent management and
use of forests, soil, water, wildlife, as well as all
other natural resources, and to create an enlightened
public appreciation of these resources and their role
in the social and economic life of the Nation.
Publication: American Forests.

AMERICAN GEOGRAPHICAL SOCIETY
Broadway at 156th St. , New York, NY 10032
(212) 234-8100
Central clearinghouse of geographical information
which tries to advance the science of geography by
originating, collecting, coordinating, and disseminating knowledge of geography through research and car-
tographic programs, periodical and special publications, and map and library holdings.
Publications: Geographical Review; Focus; Current
Geographical Publications; Soviet Geography.

AMERICAN LITTORAL SOCIETY
Sandy Hook, Highlands, NJ 07732
(201) 872-0200
Fosters the public's interest in aquatic life and its
awareness of the need for conservation action in
estuaries as well as encouraging underwater study of
aquatic life by collecting, compiling, and publishing
records of members in solving problems of scientific
study, identification, and description.
Publication: Underwater Naturalist.

AMERICAN LUNG ASSOCIATION
1740 Broadway, New York, NY 10019
(212) 245-8000
(Formerly known as the National Tuberculosis and
Respiratory Disease Association) A voluntary agency
that is concerned with the prevention and the control
of lung disease and aggravating factors, including air
pollution. Works with other groups for effective air
pollution control.
Publication: Air Conservation Newsletter; Bulletin;

American Review of Respiratory Disease.

THE AMERICAN MUSEUM OF NATURAL HISTORY
Central Park West at 79th St., New York, NY   10024
(212) 873-1300
> Along with conducting basic research in systematic
> zoology, anthropology, animal behavior, etc., pub-
> lishes scientific and popular material designed to in-
> struct the public in natural sciences, ecological re-
> lationships, evolution of earth and life, and the de-
> velopment of human cultures.
> Publications: Natural History; Bulletin of the
> American Museum of Natural History; American
> Museum Novitates; Anthropological Papers; Cata-
> logue of Foraminifera; Catalogue of Ostracoda;
> Micropaleontology; The Bibliography and Index of
> Micropaleontology; The Catalogue of Polycystine
> Radiolaria; Index of Smaller Foraminifera; Index
> of Larger Foraminifera; Curator.

AMERICAN NATURE STUDY SOCIETY
R. D. 1, Homer, NY   13077
(607) 749-3655
> Promotes environmental education and avocation by
> conducting meetings and field trips, producing and
> distributing publications, and contributing to publica-
> tions of other agencies; cooperates with organiza-
> tions with similar interests by encouraging its mem-
> bers to contribute consultant services; and assists in
> training nature lay leaders.
> Publications: Nature Study; A Journal of Environ-
> mental Education and Interpretation.

AMERICAN PEDESTRIAN ASSOCIATION
170 Broadway, Suite 201, New York, NY   10038
> Independent, nonprofit pedestrian group that works
> for spatial, conservational, planning, safety and
> urban needs for pedestrians.

AMERICAN PETROLEUM INSTITUTE
1801 K St. N.W., Washington, DC   20006
(202) 833-5600
> This is the major, national, nonprofit trade associa-
> tion of the petroleum industry. Is concerned with
> developing business and technological skills through
> coordination with the government in matters of national
> concern, including energy usage and environmental

212   Conservation/Ecology

quality.
Publication: Petroleum Today.

AMERICAN RIVERS CONSERVATION COUNCIL
324 C St. S.E., Washington, DC 20005
(202) 547-6500
    The goal of this national organization is the preser-
    vation of America's remaining free-flowing rivers.
    Works on legislation aimed at the protection of wild
    and scenic rivers (federal and state level), and pro-
    vides assistance to groups and individuals concerned
    with river conservation.

AMERICAN SCENIC AND HISTORIC PRESERVATION SOCIETY
Federal Hall Memorial, Wall and Nassau Sts., New York,
NY 10005
(212) 344-3830

THE AMERICAN SOCIETY OF LANDSCAPE ARCHITECTS
1750 Old Meadow Rd., McLean, VA 22101
(703) 893-3140
    Society dedicated to the advancement of the profession
    and to serving the public. The official accrediting
    agency for courses in educational institutions leading
    to degrees in Landscape Architecture.

AMERICAN WATER RESOURCES ASSOCIATION
206 E. University Ave., Urbana, IL 61801
(217) 367-9695
    Nonprofit scientific organization dedicated to the ad-
    vancement of water resources research, planning,
    development, and management; the establishment of
    a common meeting ground for engineers, and physical,
    biological and social scientists concerned with water
    resources; the collection, organization, and dissem-
    ination of information in the field of water resources
    science and technology.
    Publications: Hydata; Water Resources Bulletin;
    Water Resources Abstracts.

APPALACHIAN HIGHLANDS ASSOCIATION, INC.
1428 Route 23, Wayne, NJ 07470
(201) 694-0800

APPALACHIAN MOUNTAIN CLUB
5 Joy St., Boston, MA 02108
(617) 523-0636

Sponsors a program of recreational services in the
northeastern mountains, including trail and shelter
maintenance in eight states, publishing guidebooks
and maps, operation of a public hut system, and
various activities and educational programs.
Publications: Appalachia; Appalachia Bulletin.

APPALACHIAN TRAIL CONFERENCE
P.O. Box 236, Harpers Ferry, WV   25425
(304) 535-6331
Coordinates maintenance, preservation, and general
welfare of the Appalachian Trail as well as preparing
and distributing trail guidebooks and other user information.
Publication: Appalachian Trailway News.

ARBOR DAY FOUNDATION
Arbor Lodge 100, Nebraska City, NB   68410
(402) 477-1972
A nonprofit corporation which is overseen by a national board of trustees selected from conservation
and business leaders throughout the United States.
It was organized to encourage the media to tell the
story of trees as an important resource.

ARCTIC INSTITUTE OF NORTH AMERICA, INC.
3458 Redpath St., Montreal 109, Quebec, Canada
(514) 937-4607
A research organization dedicated to the acquisition,
interpretation, and dissemination of knowledge about
the polar regions.
Publications: Arctic Journal; The Arctic Bibliography; Information North.

ASPEN INSTITUTE FOR HUMANISTIC STUDIES
717 Fifth Ave., New York, NY   10022
P.O. Box 219, Aspen, CO   81611
Conducts and encourages a broad range of inquiries
into the direct and indirect impact of major environmental problems on policy formulation, decision-
making, institutional structures, and the role of social goals, priorities and value systems.   Sponsors
an annual international summer workshop on environ-
ment-related problems at Aspen, CO.

ASSOCIATION FOR ENVIRONMENTAL AND OUTDOOR
EDUCATION

2428 Walnut Blvd. , Walnut Creek, CA 94596
(415) 935-5983
   Goal is the awakening of a wide and intelligent interest in environmental and outdoor education; the
   acquisition, development, and dissemination of accurate information on environmental and outdoor education; and the encouragement, sponsorship, and
   conducting of workshops and other meetings concerned
   with environmental and outdoor education.
   Publication: AEOE Newsletter.

ASSOCIATION FOR VOLUNTARY STERILIZATION, INC.
14 W. 40th St. , New York, NY 10018
(212) 524-2344
   Makes known through education, research, and service the vital role voluntary contraceptive sterilization plays in population control in the United States
   and abroad.
   Publication: AVS News.

THE ASSOCIATION FOR THE PROTECTION OF THE
ADIRONDACKS
P. O. Box 951, Schenectady, NY 12309
(518) no listing
   Protects the natural character of the New York State
   forest preserve lands as water sheds and regulating
   forests that serve as a home for wildlife and as
   wilderness recreation areas.

ASSOCIATION OF AMERICAN GEOGRAPHERS
1710 16th St. N.W. , Washington, DC 20009
(202) 234-1450
   Furthers the field of geography and encourages its
   use in education, government, and business.
   Publications: The Annals; The Professional
   Geographer; AAG Newsletter.

ASSOCIATION OF CONSERVATION ENGINEERS
c/o Allen I. Lewis, P.E. , President, Fish & Game Engineer, NH Fish & Game Dept. , Div. of Engineering,
Maintenance & Construction, 34 Bridge St. , Concord, NH
03301
(603) 271-2224
   Goal is to encourage and broaden the educational,
   social, and economic interests of engineering practices; to promote recognition of the importance of
   sound engineering practices in fish, wildlife, and

Organizations   215

recreation development; to enable each member to
take advantage of experiences of other states.

ASSOCIATION OF INTERPRETIVE NATURALISTS, INC.
International Business Office, 6700 Needwood, Rd. , Derwood,
MD 20855
(301) 948-8844
    A professional organization concerned with resources
    conservation and management, and the interpretation
    of the natural environment as a service to the public.
    Publication: AIN Quarterly Newsletter.

AUDUBON NATURALIST SOCIETY OF THE CENTRAL
ATLANTIC STATES, INC.
8940 Jones Mill Rd. , Washington, DC 20015
(301) 652-9188
    Dedicated to conservation activities, environmental
    education, and public understanding of natural his-
    tory and the importance of saving and renewing
    natural resources.
    Publication: Atlantic Naturalist.

BASS ANGLERS FOR CLEAN WATER
P.O. Box 3044, Montgomery, AL 36109
(205) 272-9530
    Nonprofit sister corporation of the Bass Anglers
    Sportsman Society. Fights polluters and generates
    public awareness of the general pollution problem.
    Publication: BACW Newsletter.

BOONE AND CROCKETT CLUB
c/o Carnegie Museum, 4400 Forbes Ave. , Pittsburgh, PA
15213
(412) 622-3131
    One of America's oldest conservation clubs. Works
    for preservation of wildlife, especially big game, and
    furthers legislation, supports existing laws, and edu-
    cates the public about the importance of proper game
    preservation.

BOUNTY INFORMATION SERVICE
Stephens College Post Office, Columbia, MO 65201
(314) 442-0509
    Promotes the removal of bounties in North America
    by publishing Bounty News and studies of the bounty
    system, and by coordinating activities and legal aspects.
    Publication: Bounty News.

BOYSCOUTS OF AMERICA
National Council, North Brunswick, NJ   08902
(201) 249-6000
    Supplements and enlarges established modern educa-
    tional facilities for activities in the out-of-doors, as
    well as attempting to better develop physical strength
    and endurance, self-reliance, and powers of initiative
    and resourcefulness, all for the purpose of establish-
    ing through the boys of today the highest type of citi-
    zen.

THE BROOKS BIRD CLUB, INC.
707 Warwood Ave., Wheeling, WV   26003
    Nonprofit organization to encourage the study and
    conservation of birds and other phases of natural
    history.
    Publication: The Redstart.

THE BROTHERHOOD OF THE JUNGLE COCK, INC.
4th Floor, 10 E. Fayette St., Baltimore, MD   21202
    Seeks to teach youth the true meaning of conserva-
    tion, primarily the preservation of American game
    fishes. Places great emphasis on adult responsibility
    of personal instruction along those lines.

CALIFORNIA TOMORROW
681 Market St., San Francisco, CA   94105
(415) 391-7544
    Publication: Cry California.

CAMPAIGN AGAINST POLLUTION
600 W. Fullerton, Chicago, IL   60614
(312) no listing

THE CAMP FIRE CLUB OF AMERICA
230 Camp Fire Rd., Chappaqua, NY   10514
(212) 944-5478
    Objective to preserve forests and woodland, protect
    and conserve the wildlife of our country, sponsor and
    support measures to the end that present and future
    generations may continue to enjoy advantages and
    venefits of life in the great outdoors.
    Publication: The Backlog.

CAMP FIRE GIRLS, INC.
1740 Broadway, New York, NY   10019
(212) 581-0500

For girls from six through high school and boys in
high school, provides enjoyable and educational experiences for young people in small groups to help
them grow as self-reliant, sensitive, and responsible individuals. Activities involve outdoors and
home-oriented experiences, ecology, community
service, social and personal concerns, creative arts,
travel, etc.
Publication: Camp Fire Leadership.

CARIBBEAN CONSERVATION ASSOCIATION
P.O. Box 4187, St. Thomas, Virgin Islands 00801
(809) 775-3225
Encourages the creation of national and other conservation organizations in each island and country,
and helps to foster in the people of the Caribbean a
greater awareness of the value of their natural and
cultural resources.

CAYMAN ISLANDS CONSERVATION ASSOCIATION
Box 800, Grand Cayman, British West Indies (9-3493)
President/Editor: Ms. Nancy Sefton, Box 800,
Grand Cayman, BWI.

CENTER FOR SCIENCE IN THE PUBLIC INTEREST
1779 Church St. N.W., Washington, DC 20036
(202) 332-6000
Group of public interest scientists. Staff conducts
investigations into consumer and environmental problems, issues reports, and initiates legal actions.
Conducts a summer intern program, training college
students in the methods and philosophy of public interest work, and matches scientists and economists
to citizens' groups needing technical assistance.
Publications: CSPI quarterly newsletter and reports.

CENTER FOR STUDY OF RESPONSIVE LAW
P.O. Box 19367, Washington, DC 20036
(202) 833-3400
(Ralph Nader).

CENTRAL ATLANTIC ENVIRONMENT SERVICE
1717 Massachusetts Ave. N.W., Washington, DC 20036
(202) 265-1587
Nonprofit public service organization committed to
providing full and accurate information on environmental issues and disseminating this information to

citizens and civic, business, and government leaders
in the service region of Virginia, Maryland, Delaware,
and the District of Columbia.
Publication: Central Atlantic Environment News.

CITIZENS COMMITTEE ON NATURAL RESOURCES
1346 Connecticut Ave. N.W., Washington, DC   20036
(202) 785-1261
Influences legislation in behalf of conservation;   seeks
to inform public of matters before Congress and to
alert Congress to the thinking of conservation leaders
and organizations.

CITIZENS FOR CLEAN AIR
502 Park Ave., New York, NY   10022
(212) 943-2400
Promotes public educational programs concerning
various effects of air pollution.

CITIZENS FOR ENVIRONMENTAL IMPROVEMENT
333 North 14th St., Lincoln, NE   68508
(402) no listing

CITIZENS LEAGUE AGAINST THE SONIC BOOM
19 Appleton St., Cambridge, MA   02138
(617) no listing

CLEAN AIR COORDINATING COMMITTEE
1440 W. Washington Blvd., Chicago, IL   60607
(312) 243-2000

COMMISSION ON CRITICAL CHOICES FOR AMERICA
Suite 2218, 1270 Ave. of the Americas, New York, NY
10020
(212) 977-9320
Bi-partisan national commission of prominent Americans whose purpose is to ascertain critical problems
confronting the nation and to examine alternative
choices for meeting them, thus helping chart the future of America.

COMMON CAUSE
2030 M St. N.W., Washington, DC   20036
(202) 833-1200
Works for environmental protection through efforts in
clean water legislation, preservation of the National
Environmental Policy Act of 1969, conservation of

energy and increased support for research and development of nonnuclear, nonfossil fuel sources of energy.

CONCERN, INC.
2233 Wisconsin Ave. N. W. , Washington, DC   20007
(202) 965-0066
 Nonprofit organization which educates the American
 consumer to exercise selective buying practices in
 the market and otherwise to demonstrate concern for
 the environment.
 Publication: Eco-Tips.

CONNECTICUT RIVER WATERSHED COUNCIL, INC.
125 Combs Rd. , Easthampton, MA   01027
(413) 584-0057
 Nonprofit organization whose objectives are conservation, pollution abatement, adequate water supplies,
 flood control, recreation, and wildlife preservation
 throughout the 11, 260 square-mile river basin in
 Vermont, New Hampshire, Massachusetts, and Connecticut.
 Publication: The Valley Newsletter.

THE CONSERVATION AND RESEARCH FOUNDATION, INC.
c/o Richard H. Goodwin, Box 1445, Connecticut College,
New London, CT   06320
(203) 442-5391, ext. 306
 Promotes the conservation of renewable natural resources, encourages study and research in the biological sciences, and seeks to deepen understanding
 of the intricate relationship between man and the environment that supports him.

CONSERVATION ASSOCIATES
1500 Mills Tower, 220 Bush St. , San Francisco, CA   94104
(415) no listing

CONSERVATION EDUCATION ASSOCIATION
c/o Jane Westenberger, President, Environmental Education
Branch, Forest Service, USDA, Div. of I. & E. , South
Agricultural Bldg. , Washington, DC   20250
(202) 447-6605
 Encourages local, state, and national conservation
 education programs by disseminating news, ideas,
 and suggestions on conservation education through
 annual conferences and reports, a newsletter, other
 publications, special projects, and cooperation with

organizations and agencies active in this field.

THE CONSERVATION FOUNDATION
1717 Massachusetts Ave. N.W., Washington, DC   20036
(202) 265-8882
>   Conducts research, education and information programs
>   to develop knowledge, improve techniques, and stimu-
>   late public and private decision-making and action to
>   improve the environment.   Places special emphasis on
>   land use and energy issues.
>   Publication: Conservation Foundation Letter (monthly).

CONSERVATION LAW FOUNDATION OF NEW ENGLAND, INC.
506 Statler Office Bldg., Boston, MA   02116
(617) 542-1354
>   Nonprofit organization.   Clearinghouse for legal con-
>   servation organizations, citizen groups, and individuals
>   in New England.   Promotes the use of law, including
>   law suits, legal research, publications and forums,
>   for the wise use and conservation of natural resources.
>   Publication: Monthly Newsletter.

THE CONSERVATION LAW SOCIETY OF AMERICA
c/o Robert W. Jasperson, Executive Secretary and General
Counsel, 1500 Mills Tower, 220 Bush St., San Francisco,
CA   94104
(415) 981-7800
>   Provides services of a legal staff on a fee basis to
>   research the laws, decisions, and other precedents
>   relating to conservation problems;   advises conserva-
>   tion groups, and represents groups in court when ne-
>   cessary.

CONSERVATION LIBRARY OF THE DENVER PUBLIC
LIBRARY
1357 Broadway, Denver, CO   80203
(303) 573-5152, ext. 254
>   Provides research and information services on the
>   conservation of natural resources--current problems
>   and historical perspective--through books, periodicals,
>   pamphlets, government publications, pictures, tapes,
>   and manuscripts.   Summaries, state-of-the-art re-
>   ports, literature searches, extensive research by ar-
>   rangement.
>   Publications: Selected New Readings in Conservation;
>   Newsletter of Library Reference Service;   Federal Aid
>   in Fish and Wildlife Restoration;   Habitat Management

Organizations   221

Series for Endangered Species.

CONSERVATION SERVICES, INC.
S. Great Rd., Lincoln, MA   01773
(617) 259-9500
  Nongovernmental, nonprofit agency, publishing maga-
  zines, newsletters, and environmental brochures for
  New England conservation organizations and developing
  television, radio, and audio-visual materials that can
  be used in any area east of the 100th meridian.

COOPER ORNITHOLOGICAL SOCIETY
c/o William H. Behle, Dept. of Biology, University of Utah,
Salt Lake City, UT   84112
  Observation and cooperative study of birds; the spread
  of interest in bird study; the conservation of birds
  and wildlife in general.
  Publications: The Condor; Pacific Coast Avifauna.

COUNCIL ON ECONOMIC PRIORITIES
84 Fifth Ave., New York, NY   10011
(212) 691-8550
  Nonprofit organization committed to research and the
  dissemination of unbiased, detailed information of the
  practices and policies of U.S. corporations as they affect five socially vital areas: environmental quality,
  fair employment, military production, overseas trade
  and investment, and political decision making. Operates on the belief that the practices of corporations
  have a profound impact on the quality of American life.
  By providing specific quantitative comparisons of companies, it seeks to give the American public a chance
  to evaluate the impact of corporate policy on society
  and to work to assure social responsibility on the part
  of U.S. industry.
  Publication: Economic Priorities Report (bi-monthly).

COUNCIL ON ENVIRONMENTAL QUALITY
722 Jackson Place N.W., Washington, DC   20006
(202) 382-1415
  Established in 1970 to assist and advise the President
  in the preparation of the Environmental Quality Report;
  to gather information about trends and quality of the
  environment; to review and appraise activities of the
  federal government; to develop and recommend national
  policies to the Administration; to prepare studies and
  reports with respect to matters of policy and legislation

as the President may request.

COUNCIL ON POPULATION AND ENVIRONMENT, INC.
100 E. Ohio St., Chicago, IL 60611
(312) 787-1114
    Brings together diverse interests to examine trade-
    offs between ecology, the economy, and social justice.
    More than 200 citizens' organizations, corporations,
    and governmental agencies are taking part in the
    Chicago Pilot Project on Urban Concerns, with focus
    on effective citizen participation, access to informa-
    tion, and innovative processes for problem identifica-
    tion and wholistic planning.

J. N. (DING) DARLING FOUNDATION, INC.
c/o Central National Bank and Trust Co., Des Moines, IA
50304
(515) 243-8181
    Committed to initiate, coordinate, guide and expedite
    programs, research, and education that will bring
    about conservation and sound management of our
    country's natural resources of water, woods, and
    soil; restoration and preservation of historical sites.
    Creates and assists in wildlife management plans,
    seeks to improve and assure outdoor recreational op-
    portunities for present and future generations.

DAVIS CONSERVATION LIBRARY
404 E. Main, P.O. Box 776, League City, TX 77573
(713) 332-3402
    Collects, catalogs and loans materials pertinent to the
    social, economic, and political aspects of the conser-
    vation movement in America.

DEFENDERS OF WILDLIFE
2000 N St. N.W., Washington, DC 20036
(202) 223-1993
    National nonprofit educational organization dedicated to
    the preservation of all forms of wildlife. Promotes,
    through education and research, protection and humane
    treatment of all mammals, birds, fish, and other wild-
    life and the elimination of painful methods of trapping,
    capturing, and killing wildlife.
    Publication: Defenders of Wildlife News.

DESERT BIGHORN COUNCIL
1500 N. Decatur Blvd., Las Vegas, NV 89109

(702) no listing
International organization to promote the advancement
of knowledge concerning the desert bighorn sheep and
the long-range welfare of these animals in Mexico and
the U. S.

THE DESERT PROTECTIVE COUNCIL, INC.
P. O. Box 33, Banning, CA   92220
Committed to the safeguard by wise use those desert
areas that are of unique scenic, scientific, historical,
spiritual, and recreational value; to educate children
and adults to better understanding of the desert so
that it may be preserved.
Publication: quarterly Newsletter, El Paisano.

DUCKS UNLIMITED, INC.
P. O. Box 66300, Chicago, IL   60666
(312) 299-3334
Nonprofit, nonpolitical membership corporation committed to perpetuate wild ducks and other wild waterfowl on the North American continent, principally by
development, preservation, restoration, management,
and the maintenance of wetland areas on the Canadian
primary breeding grounds.   Also establishes, promotes,
aids, and contributes to conservation, restoration, and
management of waterfowl habitats.
Publication: Ducks Unlimited Magazine.

EAGLE VALLEY ENVIRONMENTALISTS, INC.
P. O. Box 152, Apple River, IL   61001
(815) 594-2305
Nonprofit corporation which was organized for the purpose of preservation and restoration of the natural environment, including its flora, fauna, and physical conditions; the development of an awareness of the natural environment; and education of the general public
as to the needs for natural areas and what benefits
are to be derived from its preservation.
Publication: Eagle Valley News.

EARTH AWARENESS FOUNDATION
1740 Nasa Blvd. , Suite 209, Houston, TX   77058
(713) 333-3101
Nonprofit, educational organization organized to bring
about attitudinal changes within the general public
which will result in healthier environments for all
citizens and thus more productive lives for them.

Publication: Earth, I Care newsletter.

EASTERN FEDERATION OF MINERALOGICAL AND LAPIDARY
SOCIETIES, INC.
c/o David E. Jensen, 199 E. Brook Rd., Pittsford, NY
14534
(716) 585-1659
  Committed to the education of the general public in
  the earth sciences and to teach the conservation of
  natural mineral resources.
Publication: Eastern Federation newsletter.

ECOLOGICAL SOCIETY OF AMERICA
c/o Dr. Frederick E. Smith, President, Graduate School of
Design, Harvard University, Cambridge, MA 02138
(617) 495-1000
  Promotes the study of organisms in relation to their
  natural environment and facilitates exchange of ideas
  among people interested in ecology.
Publications: Ecology; Ecological Monographs;
Bulletin of the Ecological Society of America.

ECOLOGY CENTER COMMUNICATIONS COUNCIL
P.O. Box 21072, Washington, D.C. 20009
(202) no listing
  Sponsors research, liaison and referral services for
  community-based centers in the United States and in
  Canada; aids citizens to establish local centers.
  Publishes a newsletter.

ECOLOGY FORUM, INC.
Suite 303 E, 200 Park Ave., New York, NY 10017
(212) 972-0523

ENVIRONMENTAL ACTION COALITION
235 E. 49th St., New York, NY 10017
(212) 486-9550
  Began the first cooperative recycling program in the
  United States and is soon to distribute nationally a
  film on recycling. Distributes teaching packets on
  environmental subjects and publishes a newsletter for
  children in grades 4-6.
Publication: Eco-News.

ENVIRONMENTAL ACTION FOUNDATION, INC.
Rm 732, DuPont Circle Bldg., Washington, DC 20036
(202) 833-1845

A public foundation formed to develop and conduct a broad educational and research program. Basically a research group, it is currently emphasizing problems of energy, solid waste management, and utility rate inequities. Provides information on environmental issues and acts as a resource for committed citizens and organizations.

ENVIRONMENTAL ACTION, INC.
Rm 731, 1346 Connecticut Ave. N.W., Washington, DC 20036
(202) 833-1845
Outgrowth of the Environmental Teach-In. Lobbies for legal, political, and social change on a broad range of environmentally-oriented subjects and issues. Publication: bi-monthly magazine with articles presenting legal, political, and social views on ecological issues.

ENVIRONMENTAL DEFENSE FUND, INC.
162 Old Town Rd., East Setauket, NY 11733
(516) 751-5191
National tax-exempt, nonprofit organization of lawyers and scientists which serves as the legal action arm for scientists. Takes cases dealing with such issues as Power and Energy, Land Use, Water Resources, Pesticides, Highways, Wildlife, and Environmental Health. Presents alternatives to environmentally destructive programs. Publication: EDF Newsletter.

ENVIRONMENTAL INFORMATION CENTER, INC.
124 E. 39th St., New York, NY 10016
(212) 685-0845
Service organization whose objective is to facilitate access to and quick retrieval of environmental information. Publication: Environmental Index.

THE ENVIRONMENTAL LAW INSTITUTE
Suite 614, 1346 Connecticut Ave. N.W., Washington, DC 20036
(202) 659-8037
Conducts analytic and investigative research and publishes material furthering the development of sound environmental law. Engages, also, in related educational activities.

Publications: The Environmental Law Reporter;
Effluent Charges on Air and Water Pollution; NEPA
in the Courts, A Legal Analysis of the National Environmental Policy Act.

ENVIRONMENTAL POLICY CENTER
324 C St. S.E., Washington, DC 20008
(202) 547-6500
Attempts to influence decisions of Congress and the
Administrative branch about national environmental
issues. Specializes in energy, water resources, and
land use problems. Develops, also, needed information which can inform public and thereby prompt its
participation in environmental decisions. Serves as
a Washington base for local and regional citizens'
groups.

ENVIRONMENTAL LOBBY, INC.
2233 Wisconsin Ave. N.W., Washington, DC 20007
(202) no listing
Works to initiate and promote legislation affecting the
environment, especially relating to consumer products.
Sends out an "Alert" mailing to members on pending
Congressional legislation.

ENVIRONMENTAL RESEARCH INSTITUTE
Box 156, Moose, WY 83012
(307) no listing
Nonprofit professional organization of scientists who
are committed to the exploration of the cause-and-
effect relationships of man and his environment. Conducts activities in research, education, and conservation. Emphasis is on ecological and interdisciplinary
approach.

ESP: ENDANGERED SPECIES PRODUCTIONS
84 Berkeley St., Boston, MA 02116
(617) 423-2238
Has available for school bookings (grades K through 6
and grades 7 through 12), 50-minute live theatre entertainment which is described as "accurate, informative, up-to-the-moment, flashy and fun mixed-media
about endangered species." For rates and information,
contact Phoebe Wray, Director.

FAUNA PRESERVATION SOCIETY
c/o Zoological Society of London, Regents Park, London,

NW1 4RY, England
01-586 0872
Publication: Oryx.

FEDERATION OF FLY FISHERMEN
12071 Chianti Dr. , Los Alamitos, CA   90720
(213) 431-2820
    Promotes methods of fishing most consistent with
    preserving and conserving fishing waters and game
    fish.
    Publication: Flyfisher.

FEDERATION OF WESTERN OUTDOOR CLUBS
c/o Robert Wenkam, President, 4534 1/2 University Way
N. E. , Seattle, WA   98105
    Organization comprised of 42 clubs who have banded
    together for mutual service and to promote the proper
    use, enjoyment, and protection of America's wilder-
    ness and outdoor recreation resources.
    Publications: Western Conservation Briefs; Western
    Outdoors Annual.

FONTANA CONSERVATION ROUNDUP
Fontana Dam, NC   28733
(704) 498-2211
    Primarily concerned with issues pertinent to the seven
    surrounding states, though many of their interests are
    of national importance as well.

FOREST HISTORY SOCIETY, INC.
P. O. Box 1581, Santa Cruz, CA   95060
(408) 426-3770
    An affiliate of the University of California whose pur-
    pose is to preserve the history of North America's
    forests, forestry, conservation, and wood-using indus-
    tries by collecting source materials and encouraging
    historical research and writing on these subjects.
    Publication: Forest History.

FORESTA INSTITUTE FOR OCEAN AND MOUNTAIN STUDIES
6205 Franktown Rd. , Carson City, NV   89701
(702) 882-6361
    Nonprofit, scientific, educational, and research insti-
    tute which conducts training programs in the analysis
    of environmental quality and in the teaching of an ap-
    preciation of the complex nature of natural ecosystems.
    Special emphasis on endangered species, fauna and

flora habitats, parks and reserves, ecological research (national and international), and consulting services in Environmental Education, Natural Area Acquisition, Water and Land Management, Regional Planning and Equal Opportunity Education.

FRIENDS OF AFRICA IN AMERICA
330 S. Broadway, Tarrytown, NY   10591
(914) 631-5168
Nonprofit educational organization which promotes
understanding of wildlife and its support, mainly in
the area of East Africa.

FRIENDS OF ANIMALS, INC.
11 W. 60th St., New York, NY   10023
(212) 247-8077
International humane conservation organization, committed to regaining ecological balance of the environment through the preservation of wildlife territory and
the elimination of brutality to animals by human be-
ings.
Publication: Actionline.

FRIENDS OF THE EARTH
620 C St. S. E., Washington, DC   20003
(202) 543-4312
30 E. 42nd St., New York, NY   10017
529 Commercial St., San Francisco, CA   94111
International organization dedicated to the preservation, restoration, and rational use of the earth. It is
affiliated with other Friends of the Earth organizations
in France, Germany, the United Kingdom, Switzerland,
Sweden, The Netherlands, and is establishing organizations in Canada, Italy, Australia, Kenya, and
Japan.
Publication: Not Man Apart.

FRIENDS OF NATURE, INC.
Brooksville, ME
c/o Russell Johnson, President, Petersham, MA   01366
(617) 724-3368
Nonprofit conservation society whose objective is to
preserve the balance of nature for the mutual benefit
of man, plants, and animals.

FRIENDS OF THE SEA OTTER
Big Sur, CA   93920

(408) 667-2254
> Dedicated to the preservation of the sea otter.
> Publication: The Otter Raft.

THE GARDEN CLUBS OF AMERICA
598 Madison Ave. , New York, NY 10022
(212) 753-8287
> National nonprofit organization dedicated to the conser-
> vation of natural resources, the protection of the en-
> vironment, control of pollution, historic preservation,
> and wise land use. Publishes and distributes "The
> World Around You," an educational packet.

GET OIL OUT
111 E. De La Guerra, Santa Barbara, CA 92101
(805) 965-1519

GENERAL FEDERATION OF WOMEN'S CLUBS
1734 N St. N.W. , Washington, DC 20036
(202) 347-3168
> Brings together women's clubs and similar organiza-
> tions throughout the world for the benefit and promo-
> tion of common fields of interest, among them conser-
> vation education (headed by Mrs. James A. Scarbro)
> and environmental responsibility (headed by Mrs. Paul
> Keller, 710 Sunset Drive, Smithfield, NC 27577).

GIRL SCOUTS OF THE UNITED STATES OF AMERICA
830 Third Ave. , New York, NY 10022
(212) 751-6900
> Includes within its wide variety of programs and in-
> terests projects in environmental action.
> Publications: Girl Scout Leader; American Girl;
> The Brownie Reader.

HAWK MOUNTAIN SANCTUARY ASSOCIATION
R. D. 2, Kempton, PA 19529
(215) 756-3431
> Purpose is to establish and maintain preserves for the
> conservation and protection of wildlife as well as to
> provide means for educating the general public con-
> cerning wildlife and the need to protect and preserve
> it.

INTERCOLLEGIATE OUTING CLUB ASSOCIATION
c/o Ellis Lader, 3410-G Paul Ave. , Bronx, NY 10468
(212) 589-5144

A nonpolitical organization which sponsors intercollegiate activities designed to educate participants in safe techniques for enjoying the wilderness and to encourage public appreciation of the outdoors and the importance of conserving the nation's natural resources.

INTERNATIONAL ASSOCIATION OF GAME, FISH AND CONSERVATION COMMISSIONERS
1709 New York Ave. N. W. , Washington, DC 20006
(202) 872-8866, 8867
Included are each state or territory of the United States, each Province of Canada, the Commonwealth of Puerto Rico, the U. S. Government, the Dominion Government of Canada, and each Government of countries of the Western Hemisphere, and individual Associate members whose aim is conservation, protection, and proper management of wildlife and other natural resources are members.
Publications: Annual Proceedings; Newsletter.

THE INTERNATIONAL ATLANTIC SALMON FOUNDATION
P. O. Box 429, St. Andrews, N. B. , Canada
(506) 529-3818
425 Park Ave. , New York, NY 10022
Nonprofit research and educational organization whose aim is the conservation and wise management of the Atlantic salmon and its habitat. Also directs as well as supports vital programs in areas of education, public information, research, and international cooperation between likeminded groups.
Publications: IASF Newsletter; Special Publication Series.

INTERNATIONAL COUNCIL FOR BIRD PRESERVATION
c/o Roland C. Clement, National Audubon Society, 950 Third Ave. , New York, NY 10022
(212) 832-3200
U. S. Section, Canadian Section, and Pan American Section which includes representatives of leading scientific and conservation societies in Argentina, Bolivia, Brazil, Canada, Chile, Colombia, Costa Rica, Cuba, Guatemala, Ecuador, Mexico, Panama, Paraguay, Peru, Surinam, the United States, and Venezuela.

INTERNATIONAL INSTITUTE FOR ENVIRONMENTAL AFFAIRS

United Nations Plaza, 345 E. 46th St., New York, NY 10017
(202) 687-4606
> Independent, nonprofit, non-governmental organization
> which acts as a clearing house and catalyst for action
> in environmental matters. Provides multidisciplinary,
> international perspective on efforts to improve the en-
> vironment.
> Publication: World Environmental Newsletter.

INTERNATIONAL UNION FOR CONSERVATION OF NATURE
AND NATURAL RESOURCES
1110 Morges, Switzerland
021, 71-4401
> Independent international organization whose member-
> ship includes governments, governmental departments,
> international organizations, and private institutions.
> Seeks to support and promote action to preserve na-
> ture and natural resources in as many parts of the
> world as is possible for their intrinsic cultural and
> scientific value as well for the long-term economic
> and social welfare of mankind.
> Publications: IUCN Bulletin; IUCN Yearbook; IUCN
> Publication, new series; IUCN Supplementary Paper;
> IUCN Monographs, Occasional Papers and Environ-
> mental Policy and Law Papers; Red Data Book (list
> of endangered species in 5 volumes).

INTERNATIONAL WHALING COMMISSION
Great Westminster House, Horsefeny Rd., London, SW1,
England
> Organization of whaling countries and other countries
> concerned with whales. Coordinates and sets quotas
> for the annual whale kill.
> Publication: annual report.

INTERNATIONAL WILD WATERFOWL ASSOCIATION
Box 1075, Jamestown, ND 58401
(701) no listing
> Object is the protection, conservation, and reproduc-
> tion of all wild waterfowl species in danger of even-
> tual extinction. Encourages breeding of well known
> and rare species that are in captivity.

THE IZAAK WALTON LEAGUE OF AMERICA
Suite 806, 1800 N. Kent St., Arlington, VA 22209
(703) 528-1818
> Works to promote means and opportunities to educate

the general public to conserve, maintain, protect and
restore natural resources of the United States such as
soil, forest, and water. Promotes, also, the enjoyment and wholesome use of these resources.
Publication: Outdoor America.

JACKSON HOLE PRESERVE, INC.
30 Rockefeller Plaza, New York, NY 10020
(212) 247-8141
Nonprofit, charitable, and educational organization
whose objective is to conserve areas of outstanding
primitive grandeur and natural beauty. Seeks, also,
to provide facilities for their use and enjoyment by
the general public.

JOHN MUIR INSTITUTE FOR ENVIRONMENTAL STUDIES,
INC.
2118-C Vine St., Berkeley, CA 94709
(415) 548-0525
Tax-deductible, membership organization for environmental education and research.

KEEP AMERICA BEAUTIFUL, INC.
99 Park Ave., New York, NY 10016
(212) 682-4564
Nonprofit, public service organization established to
promote environmental improvement by, among other
ways, combatting litter as the first step toward solving the general environmental problem. Conducts
programs of public education to stimulate individual
responsibility for keeping the overall ecosystems clean,
safe, and healthful.

LAKE ERIE CLEANUP COMMITTEE, INC.
3003 11th St., Monroe, MI 48161
(313) no listing
Works to stop the pollution of Lake Erie and all fresh
water lakes and streams by educating the public of the
need for greater pollution controls.

LAKE MICHIGAN FEDERATION
53 W. Jackson Blvd., Chicago, IL 60604
(312) 427-5121
Coalition of citizen organizations from Wisconsin,
Illinois, Indiana, and Michigan committed to the protection of Lake Michigan.
Publications: Monthly Newsletter; Information Reports.

Organizations

Organizations 233

LEAGUE OF CONSERVATION VOTERS
324 C St. S. E. , Washington, DC 20003
(202) 547-7200
Nonpartisan, national political campaign committee
dedicated to the promotion of the election of public
officials who will work for a healthy environment.
Among its activities, it evaluates environmental records of Congressmen, Senators, and Presidential can-
didates and researches and publishes Congressional
voting records on the more important environmental
legislation.
Publications: How Your Congressman Voted on Critical Environmental Issues ($1); How Your Senators
Voted on Critical Environmental Issues ($1).

LEAGUE OF WOMEN VOTERS OF THE U. S.
1730 M St. N. W. , Washington, DC 20036
(202) 296-1700
Nonpartisan organization of members from all 50
states, the District of Columbia, Puerto Rico, and
the Virgin Islands that works to promote political responsibility through informed participation of citizens
in their government. The principal issues for political action in the environmentally related fields include
water and air quality and solid waste management.
Associated with the organization is the League of
Women Voters Education Fund which carries out educational projects, publishes materials, and arranges
conferences.
Publication: The National Voter.

MASSACHUSETTS AUDUBON SOCIETY, INC.
S. Great Rd. , Lincoln, MA 01773
(617) 259-9500
Sponsors conservation, education, and research programs. Overall goal is to educate the public to environmental problems and to channel emotion engendered
into positive, intelligent action.
Publications: Magazine (quarterly); Newsletter
(monthly).

MAX McGRAW WILDLIFE FOUNDATION
P. O. Box 194, Dundee, IL 60118
(312) 741-8000
Foundation that conducts research, management, and
conservation education projects, and cooperates with
other conservation agencies and institutions in their

wildlife and fisheries activities.
Publications: Descriptive brochure; Wildlife Management Notes series.

NATARI WILDLIFE ASSOCIATION
Box 458, 15881 Rose Lane, Westminster, CA   92683
(714) 892-6661
    Fights pollution and helps protect, defend, and pre-
    serve all wildlife.
    Publication: Natari Gazette.

NATIONAL ASSOCIATION FOR ENVIRONMENTAL EDUCATION
P.O. Box 1295, Miami, FL   33143
(305) 666-3267
    Principal activities include the distribution of informa-
    tion about education programs on post-secondary
    levels; the promotion of such education programs;
    assisting educational institutions in developing these
    programs; fostering research and evaluation connec-
    tion with environmental education.
    Publication: N.A.E.E. Newsletter.

NATIONAL ASSOCIATION OF BIOLOGY TEACHERS
1420 N St. N.W., Washington, DC   20005
(202) 667-8268
    Publication: The American Biology Teacher.

NATIONAL ASSOCIATION OF CONSERVATION DISTRICTS
1025 Vermont Ave. N.W., Washington, DC   20005
(202) 347-5995
    Acts as the national instrument of its 3,000 local
    district and 52 state and territorial associations mem-
    bership. Works to conserve and develop land, water,
    forests, wildlife, and like natural resources.
    Publications: Tuesday Letter; America's Conserva-
    tion Districts; Environmental Action Guide; Guide
    to Conservation Careers; Environmental Film Cata-
    logue.

NATIONAL ASSOCIATION OF COUNTIES RESEARCH
1735 New York Ave. N.W., Washington, DC   20006
(202) 785-9577
    Works for the application of social science techniques
    to solving problems of local government. To this end
    publishes a series of action manuals on water and air
    pollution, solid waste management, outdoor recreation,
    soil erosion, and sediment control. A nonprofit,

public interest membership organization.
Publications: The American County; County News.

NATIONAL ASSOCIATION OF STATE OUTDOOR RECREATION
LIAISON OFFICERS
c/o Lawrence Stuart, President, Commissioner, Dept. of
Parks & Recreation, Statehouse, Augusta, ME 04301
(207) 289-3821
An advisory group which works with the Federal
Bureau of Outdoor Recreation for the purpose of
strengthening the nation's total out-of-doors recreation program. Represents state and local interests
in administration of the Land and Water Conservation
Fund Program.

NATIONAL AUDUBON SOCIETY
950 Third Ave., New York, NY 10022
(212) 832-3200
One of the oldest and largest conservation organizations in North America whose purposes are the promotion of wildlife and natural environment conservation and the education of man regarding his relationship with his natural environment and his proper
place within the ecological system. In coordination
with its 300 local chapters, the society works on a
variety of environmentally related issues such as the
protection of wildlife; air and water pollution control; land use planning and transportation and building practices aimed to curb waste of energy.
Publications: Audubon; Audubon Leader; American
Birds: Incorporating Audubon Field Notes.

NATIONAL CAMPERS AND HIKERS ASSOCIATION, INC.
7172 Transit Rd., Buffalo, NY 14221
(716) 634-5433

NATIONAL COALITION AGAINST POISONING OF WILDLIFE
P.O. Box 14156, San Francisco, CA 94114
(415) 863-2694
Nonprofit national affiliation of conservation activists
who are committed to preserving endangered wildlife
species and predatory animals and their habitats.

NATIONAL COUNCIL FOR GEOGRAPHIC EDUCATION
115 N. Marion St., Oak Park, IL 60301
(312) 383-5633
Membership organization dedicated to the promotion

and advancement of geographic and environmental edu-
cation in American public schools and colleges.
Publication: Journal of Geography. (List of other
publications available upon request; contact Harm J.
DeBlij, editor, University of Miami, Coral Gables,
FL 33124.)

NATIONAL COUNCIL OF STATE GARDEN CLUBS, INC.
4401 Magnolia Ave., St. Louis, MO 63110
(314) 776-7574
Coordinates its activities with those of the State Federation of Garden Clubs and similar organizations in
the United States and foreign countries to aid in the
protection and conservation of natural resources,
civic beauty and the improvement of roadsides and
parks, among other activities.
Publication: The National Gardener.

NATIONAL EDUCATION ASSOCIATION
1201 16th St. N.W., Washington, DC 20036
(202) 833-4000
Objective is to elevate the character of the teaching
profession, to advance its interests, and to promote
the cause of education in the United States.

NATIONAL FARMERS UNION
Box 2251, 12025 E. 45th Ave., Denver, CO 80201
(303) 371-1760
Avows its belief that soil, water, forest, and other
natural resources should be used and conserved in
such a way that they can be passed on undiminished
to future generations. Believes, also, that both
publicly and privately owned land and natural resources should be administered in the public's interest.
Publication: National Farmers Union Washington
Newsletter.

NATIONAL GEOGRAPHIC SOCIETY
1145 17th St. N.W., Washington, DC 20036
(202) 296-7500
Works to advance the interest of and the increase
and diffusion of geographic knowledge.
Publications: National Geographic; National Geographic School Bulletin; Books; Atlases; Maps;
Filmstrips.

NATIONAL PARKS AND CONSERVATION ASSOCIATION
1701 18th St. N.W., Washington, DC 20009
(202) 265-2717
  Private, nonprofit, public-service organization, primarily educational and scientific, whose interests and
  activities relate to the protection of national parks
  and monuments of America and conservation and restoration of the natural environment.
  Publication: National Parks and Conservation Magazine.

NATIONAL RECREATION AND PARK ASSOCIATION
1601 N. Kent St., Arlington, VA 22209
(703) 525-0606
  Nonprofit service, education, and research organization committed to improving park and recreation leadership, its programs, and its facilities. Attempts,
  also, to increase public understanding that leisure
  programs and the environment are vital to the national
  well-being.
  Publications: Parks & Recreation Magazine; Com-
  munique; Journal of Leisure Research; Therapeutic
  Recreation Journal; A Guide to Books on Parks,
  Recreation and Leisure; Washington Action Report.

NATIONAL RESEARCH COUNCIL, COMMISSION ON NATURAL
RESOURCES
2101 Constitution Ave., Washington, DC 20418
(202) 393-8100
  Initiates and reviews activities being carried on in
  the area of environmental quality and natural resource
  management; in response from decision-making or
  policy setting institutions and agencies, will arrange
  multidisciplinary advisory panels.

NATIONAL SPELEOLOGICAL SOCIETY, INC.
Cave Ave., Huntsville, AL 35810
(205) 852-1300
  Nonprofit membership organization formed for the
  purpose of exploration, study, and conservation of
  caves and caverns in the United States, related features, and the ecology of caves.
  Publications: NSS News; Bulletin.

NATIONAL WATER RESOURCES ASSOCIATION
897 National Press Bldg., Washington, DC 20004
(202) 347-2672

Dedicated to the development, conservation, and management of water resources of the 18 Reclamation States.
Publication: Water Life.

NATIONAL WATERFOWL COUNCIL
c/o William L. Holland, Chairman, Chief, Wildlife Section, Alabama Dept. of Conservation and Natural Resources, Montgomery, AL 36104
(205) 269-6704
Associated Flyway Councils: Atlantic Flyway, Mississippi Flyway, Central Flyway, and Pacific Flyway which cover all states in the Union, many of the Canadian provinces, Puerto Rico.

NATIONAL WATERSHED CONGRESS
Rm 1105, 1025 Vermont Ave. N.W., Washington, DC 20005
(202) 347-5995
Committed to the improvement of natural resources management and to the use on a watershed basis. At yearly meetings discusses and reviews watershed programs, problems, and progress.

NATIONAL WATERWAYS CONFERENCE, INC.
1130 17th St. N.W., Washington, DC 20036
(202) 638-0090
Dedicated to promoting a better understanding of the public value of water resource and transportation programs and their importance to the entire environment.
Publications: Newsletter; Criteria News.

NATIONAL WILDLIFE FEDERATION
1412 16th St. N.W., Washington, DC 20036
(202) 483-1550
Organized to create and encourage public awareness of the need for wise use and proper management of natural resources upon which the lives and welfare of men as well as plants and animals depend. Areas of interest include Air Pollution Control, Ecology, Fisheries, Forest Wildlife and Recreation, Forestry, Land Use, Public Lands, Soil Conservation, Water Pollution Control, Wildlife Conservation, and Community Planning.
Publications: International Wildlife; National Wildlife; Ranger Rick's Nature Magazine; Wildlife Conservation Stamps and Albums; Conservation News; Conservation Report; Conservation Directory;

Environmental Discovery Units; conservation pamphlets; catalog of nature-related merchandise. (Publications list and catalog available on request.)

NATIONAL WILDLIFE FEDERATION ENDOWMENT, INC.
1412 16th St. N.W., Washington, DC   20036
(703) 790-4321
     Established to finance conservation education and re-
     source management programs through the National
     Wildlife Federation. Only the income from gifts is
     used; the investment is held inviolate.

NATURAL RESOURCES COUNCIL OF AMERICA
Suite 911, 1025 Connecticut Ave. N.W., Washington, DC
20036
(202) 223-1536
     Society made up of major national and regional or-
     ganizations which seeks to advance sound management
     of natural resources for the interest of the general
     public by providing information on Congressional and
     Administration actions. Makes available to its mem-
     bers scientific data on conservation problems and
     gives them, also, a means of cooperation.

NATURAL RESOURCES DEFENSE COUNCIL, INC.
15 W. 44th St., New York, NY   10036
(212) 868-0150
1710 N St. N.W., Washington, DC   20036
(202) 783-5711
664 Hamilton Ave., Palo Alto, CA   94301
(415) 327-1080
     Set up to take necessary and appropriate legal action
     to preserve, protect, and defend natural resources,
     wildlife and environment against encroachment, mis-
     use, and destruction. Conducts research, collects,
     compiles, and publishes facts, information, and sta-
     tistics about natural resources, wildlife, and environ-
     mental questions. Conducts public education programs
     on environment, wildlife, and natural resources.
     Publications: Clean Air Manual; Citizens Manual on
     Clean Water.

NATURAL SCIENCE FOR YOUTH FOUNDATION
763 Silvermine Rd., New Canaan, CT   06840
(203) 966-5643
     Provides free counseling to community groups in
     planning and development of environmental and

natural science centers and museums specifically designed to meet needs and interests of children and
young people. Gives a training course in the management of small museums and nature centers. Annual
conference sponsored by this group promotes professional excellence in environmental and natural science
centers and museums.
Publications: Proceedings of Annual Conferences;
Directory of Natural Science Centers for Youth.

THE NATURE CONSERVANCY
Suite 800, 1800 N. Kent St. , Arlington, VA   22209
(703) 524-3151
Nonprofit membership corporation whose purpose is to
preserve natural areas for present and future generations.   Cooperates towards this end with colleges,
universities, and public and private conservation organizations to acquire lands for scientific and educational purposes as well as to help preserve the American natural heritage.
Publication: The Nature Conservancy News.

NEW ENGLAND ADVISORY BOARD FOR FISH AND GAME
PROBLEMS
25 Franklin St. , Concord, NH   03301
(603) no listing
Works for the creation and maintenance of close
coordination among New England sportsmen in an
attempt to promote better hunting and fishing by cooperation with conservation departments (state and
federal), in the hope of improving hunting, fishing,
and recreation by improving conservation.

NEW ENGLAND FORESTRY FOUNDATION, INC.
One Court St. , Boston, MA   02108
(617) 742-5586
Nonprofit organization established to provide education
in the practical, scientific management of private
woodlands throughout New England.

NEW ENGLAND NATURAL RESOURCES CENTER
506 Statler Office Bldg. , Boston, MA   02116
(617) 542-9370
Works to provide environmental liaison and counseling
services to private conservation organizations, governmental agencies, and business and industry throughout
New England.   Puts special emphasis on methods of

insuring the public's participation in sound environmental management programs.

NEW YORK-NEW JERSEY TRAIL CONFERENCE, INC.
G. P. O. 2250, New York, NY   10001
(212) no listing
    Nonprofit organization established in order to coordinate efforts of hiking and outdoor groups in New York and New Jersey to build and maintain trails and shelters, aid in the conservation of wild lands and wildlife, and protect areas of natural beauty and interest.
    Publication: Trail Walker.

THE NEW YORK ZOOLOGICAL SOCIETY
The Zoological Park, Bronx, NY   10460
(212) 933-1500
    Publications: Animal Kingdom;   Zoologica.

NORTH AMERICAN ASSOCIATION FOR THE PRESERVATION
OF PREDATORY ANIMALS
Box 161, Doyle, CA   96109
    Independent, nonprofit, nonpolitical voluntary organization established for the purpose of educating the public about the role of predators in the natural North American environment and of conducting behavioral research on predators.
    Publication: Monthly Newsletter.

NORTH AMERICAN ATLANTIC SALMON COUNCIL
P. O. Box 429, St. Andrews, NB, Canada
(506) 529-3293
    Attempts to advance Atlantic salmon conservation through coordinated efforts of its members organizations, to present a united approach to critical problems in Atlantic salmon management (national and international), to promote research and habitat improvement programs essential to the survival of salmon. Keeps member organizations and the public informed of all aspects of Atlantic salmon conservation.

NORTH AMERICAN WILDLIFE FOUNDATION
709 Wire Bldg. , Washington, DC   20005
(202) 347-1775
    Assists in the sponsoring of wildlife research through cooperation with like-minded organizations and institutions. Interest is in all phases of natural resource

conservation, restoration, and management.

NORTH AMERICA TRAIL COMPLEX (NOAMTRAC)
P. O. Box 3367, Tucson, AZ 85722
(602) no listing
  Established in order to research, design, map, and
  coordinate an interlocking network of foot trails in
  Canada, the United States, and Mexico; to support
  wilderness and natural area protection and preservation, and to build interest on the part of the general
  public in the importance of preserving the natural environment and limiting modern encroachments on the
  original quality of life.

NORTH CENTRAL AUDUBON COUNCIL
250 N. Court, Platteville, WI 53818
(608) 348-3491
  Established to provide an exchange of ideas and programs and to strengthen organizations and promote
  better use of our natural resources. Promotes conservation activities, particularly among the youth,
  and advances public understanding of ecology.
  Publication: The Trail (newsletter).

NORTHEAST CONSERVATION LAW ENFORCEMENT CHIEFS'
ASSOCIATION
c/o Walter C. Cabell, President, Chief Game Warden, Fish
& Game Department, 151 Main St. , Montpelier, VT 05602
(802) 828-3371

NORTHEASTERN BIRD-BANDING ASSOCIATION, INC.
c/o Dr. John H. Kennard, R. D. 5, Box 150, Manchester,
NH 03102
(603) 622-4152
  Promotes study of birds and their habits and disseminates information obtained.
  Publication: Bird-Banding.

NORTHERN ENVIRONMENTAL COUNCIL, INC.
P. O. Box 89, Ashland, WI 54806
(715) 682-5564
  Established to coordinate the activities and to distribute information to member organizations. Its
  purpose is to develop sound and constructive solutions or alternatives to economic or public threats
  to the natural environment in northern Michigan,
  Wisconsin, Minnesota, North Dakota, and South

Dakota by means of research, legislative action, education, publicity, educational seminars, and regional cooperation.

NORTHERN PLAINS RESOURCE COUNCIL
421 Stapleton Bldg., Billings, MT   59101
(406) 259-6114
Regional coalition of ranchers, farmers, and concerned citizens whose aim is to help the people of the Northern Plains make their wants known and their voices heard in decisions affecting the use of their mineral and water resources and their land and air.

NORTHWESTERN STUDENTS FOR A BETTER ENVIRONMENT (NSBE)
Rm 157, Cresap Lab, Northwestern University, Evanston, IL   60201
(312) 481-9627

OUTDOOR WRITERS ASSOCIATION OF AMERICA, INC.
4141 W. Brandley Rd., Milwaukee, WI   53209
(414) 354-9690
Established in an attempt to improve members in the art and media of the craft and to increase members' knowledge and understanding of the importance of conserving natural resources.
Publication: Outdoors Unlimited.

THE OZARK SOCIETY INCORPORATED
Box 38, Fayetteville, AR   72701
(501) no listing
Promotes knowledge and enjoyment of scenic and scientific resources of the Ozark-Ouchita mountain region. Helps protect those resources for present and future generations.
Publication: The Ozark Society Bulletin.

PLANNED PARENTHOOD-WORLD POPULATION
810 Seventh Ave., New York, NY   10019
(212) 541-7800
Federated nonprofit health agency of 190 affiliates that maintain medically supervised clinics that offer family planning services and information.

POPULATION COUNCIL
245 Park Ave., New York, NY   10017
(212) 687-8330

Supports research, training, and technical assistance
on population in the social and biomedical sciences.
Publications: Reports on Population/Family Planning;
Country Profiles; Current Publications in Population/
Family Planning; Studies in Family Planning.

POPULATION CRISIS COMMITTEE
1835 K St. N. W. , Washington, DC   20006
(202) 659-1833
Suite 922, 30 W. 54th St. , New York, NY   10019
(212) 582-2220
    Private, nonprofit organization that seeks to promote
    the public's understanding of the world population ac-
    tion and to galvanize it into action.
    Publications: Population Crisis; Victor-Bostrom
    Fund Reports.

POPULATION INSTITUTE
110 Maryland Ave. N. E. , Washington, DC
(202) 544-2202
    Seeks to halt population growth and to bring it into
    balance with natural resources to effect a quality
    environment. Among its activities, are holding con-
    ferences on ecological matters, distributing informa-
    tion to promote public understanding of population
    control and its relation to environmental concepts.

POPULATION REFERENCE BUREAU, INC.
1755 Massachusetts Ave. N. W. , Washington, DC   20036
(202) 232-2288
    Established to gather, interpret, publish, and dis-
    seminate information about population and related
    subject for the general public and formal education.
    Done on a nonprofit, scientific, and educational basis.
    Consults with likeminded groups in the United States
    and abroad; operates an information service, library,
    and international program whose particular emphasis
    is on Latin America.
    Publications: Population Bulletin; Population Profile;
    PRB Selection; Annual World Population Data Sheet;
    Population Education INTERCHANGE; Poblacion;
    Que Pasa.

PROJECT JONAH
1300 Sansome St. , San Francisco, CA   94111
(415) no listing
    Dedicated to the protection of the whale.

PUBLIC INTEREST RESEARCH GROUP
Rm 511, 2000 P St. N.W., Washington, DC 20036
(202) 833-9700
  Nonprofit public interest law firm that is engaged in
  research, investigation, and litigation on governmental
  and corporate responsibility, consumer affairs, and
  environmental and conservation problems. Director:
  Ralph Nader.

RACHEL CARSON TRUST FOR THE LIVING ENVIRONMENT,
INC.
8940 Jones Mill Rd., Washington, DC 20015
(301) 652-1877
  Established in order to develop, through research and
  education, awareness that the environment is being
  contaminated. Serves as a clearinghouse of information on the ecology of the environment (for scientists
  and laymen).

THE RESEARCH RANCH, INC.
Elgin, AZ 85611
(602) 455-5689
  Nonprofit foundation established to conduct ecological
  and environmental research and experimentation. The
  use of qualitative and computerized techniques for ecosystem evaluation is used in both zoological and botanical projects. Resulting information can be obtained
  by any public or private interest or institution.

RESOURCES FOR THE FUTURE, INC.
1755 Massachusetts Ave. N.W., Washington, DC 20036
(202) 462-4400
  Established for the purpose of advancing the development, conservation, and use of natural resources and
  improvement of environmental quality through research
  and educational programs. Results of studies are
  available to the public. Also organizes and supports
  seminars and conferences and offers fellowships for
  advanced studies.

ROCKY MOUNTAIN CENTER ON ENVIRONMENT
4260 E. Evans Ave., Denver, CO 80222
(303) 757-5439
  Private, nonprofit service center which works for
  environmental planning, communications, education,
  and research for minimizing the destructive forces
  of technology on scenic, scientific, historical,

wilderness, wildlife, open space and outdoor recreation resources of the Rocky Mountain 8-state region.
Publication: Romcoe Forum.

SAVE THE DUNES COUNCIL
c/o Sylvia Troy, President, 1512 Park Dr., Munster, IN
46321
(219) 838-5843
  Committed to establishing and developing the Indiana
  Dunes National Lakeshore for the purpose of protect-
  ing the ecological values of the dunes region, preserving Lake Michigan, and fighting air and water pollution.

SAVE-THE-REDWOODS LEAGUE
Rm 605, 114 Sansome St., San Francisco, CA 94104
(415) 362-2352

SAVE THE TALLGRASS PRAIRIE, INC.
P.O. Box 453, Emporia, DS 66801
(913) 722-4322
  Organized in order to restore and preserve the eco-
  system native to the now deteriorated Tallgrass
  Prairie that once covered 400,000 square miles.
  Seeks to establish a Tallgrass Prairie National Park
  of 60,000 acres in the Flint Hills of Kansas
  Publication: Save the Tallgrass Prairie News.

SCIENTISTS' INSTITUTE FOR PUBLIC INFORMATION
30 E. 68th St., New York, NY 10021
(212) 249-3200
  Seeks, informs, and enlists scientists of many disciplines for help in public information programs of
  social interest. Acts as the national coordinating
  group for local science information committees and
  works to stimulate and integrate their work with other
  committees and to promote their growth. Issues
  technical and scientific information for the layman on
  many environmental issues and publishes workbooks
  on these problems.
  Publications: Environment; SIPI Report.

SIERRA CLUB
1050 Mills Tower, San Francisco, CA 94104
(415) 981-8634
  Works for the protection and conservation of natural
  resources of the Sierra Nevada, the United States,

and the entire World. Undertakes and publishes the
results of scientific and educational studies concerning
all aspects of the environment and the natural ecosystems of the world and educates the world population to the need for preserving and restoring the
quality of its environment and natural ecosystems.
Publications: Sierra Club Bulletin; National News
Report.

SIERRA CLUB FOUNDATION
1050 Mills Tower, 220 Bush St., San Francisco, CA 94104
(415) 981-8637
Finances projects of groups that are concerned with
environmental problems. Groups eligible include
those engaged in educational, literary, and scientific
projects working on environmental problems across
the country.

SIERRA CLUB LEGAL DEFENSE FUND, INC.
311 California St., San Francisco 94104
(415) 398-1411
Nonprofit, tax-deductible corporation established to
support legal suits brought on behalf of citizens' organizations attempting to protect the environment.

SOCIETY FOR THE PRESERVATION OF BIRDS OF PREY
Box 891, Pacific Palisades, CA 90272
(213) no listing
Established for the purpose of educating the public to
the value of predatory birds, disseminating information and promoting communication among raptor en-
thusiasts, and attempting to prohibit the harvesting of
raptorial birds for falconry and research.
Publication: The Raptor Report.

SOCIETY FOR RANGE MANAGEMENT
2120 S. Birch St., Denver, CO 80222
(303) 756-3205
Established for the purpose of promoting the understanding of rangeland ecosystems and proper management and use for intangible values as well as concrete
products.
Publications: Journal of Range Management; Range-
man's News.

SOCIETY OF TYMPANUCHUS CUPIDO PINNATUS LTD.
611 E. Wisconsin Ave., P.O. Box 1156, Milwaukee, WI
53201

(414) 272-6200
>   Nonprofit organization established to preserve the
>   Prairie Chicken, among other ways, through acquisi-
>   tion of habitat.
>   Publication: Boom.

SOIL CONSERVATION SOCIETY OF AMERICA
7515 N. E. Ankeny Rd. , Ankeny, IA   50021
(515) 289-2331
>   Established to advance the science and art of good
>   land use through an annual meeting and publication of
>   educational booklets for children, teaching guides, and
>   other materials on the environment.
>   Publication: Journal of Soil and Water Conservation.

SOUTHERN FOREST INSTITUTE
Suite 280, One Corporate Sq. N. E. , Atlanta, GA   30329
(404) 633-5137
>   Seeks to encourage full development of forest lands
>   for multiple use.

SPORT FISHING INSTITUTE
Suite 801, 608 13th St. N. W. , Washington, DC   20005
(202) 737-0668
>   Seeks to improve sport fishing by means of fish con-
>   servation research, education, and service. Helps
>   to protect aquatic ecosystems by helping fish conser-
>   vationists in developing new and better fisheries re-
>   search and management programs to protect aquatic
>   environments and thus enhance fisheries resources.
>   Publication: SFI Bulletin.

STUDENT CONSERVATION ASSOCIATION, INC.
Olympic View Dr. , R. D. 1, Box 573A, Vashon, WA
(206) 567-4798
>   Nonprofit membership organization that conducts the
>   Student Conservation Program in cooperation with the
>   National Park Service and the Merck Forest Founda-
>   tion. Program consists of work and conservation edu-
>   cation for young people and enlists the voluntary ser-
>   vices of conservation-minded students from high
>   school through graduate levels to work and learn over
>   their summer vacations.

TAHOE REGIONAL PLANNING AGENCY
P. O. Box 8896, South Lake Tahoe, CA   94705
(916) 541-0246

Promotes the wise use and conservation of the waters
of Lake Tahoe and surrounding natural resources.
Publication: TRPA Newsletter.

THORNE ECOLOGICAL INSTITUTE
2305 Canyon Boulevard, Boulder, CO   80302
(303) 7325
> Public, tax-exempt corporation committed to augment-
> ing public understanding and utilization of the prin-
> ciples of ecology. Conducts ecology seminars, nat-
> ural science programs for young people, and offers
> ecological consulting services for industry and govern-
> ment.

TREES FOR TOMORROW, INC.
Box 216, Eagle River, WI   54521
(715) 479-4808

TROUT UNLIMITED
4260 E. Evans Ave. , Denver, CO   80222
(303) 757-7144
> Nonprofit, nonpolitical, conservation-minded member-
> ship organization established in order to preserve
> clear waters and perpetuate and improve fishing.
> Means of achieving goals sought through support and
> encouragement of laws, regulations, research pro-
> grams, and voluntary actions for wise management
> of water and trout populations, based on biological
> and synecological facts.
> Publication: Trout Magazine.

THE TRUMPETER SWAN SOCIETY
Box 32, Maple Plain, MN   55359
(612) 473-4693
> International scientific and educational organization to
> promote research into ecology and proper management
> of the trumpeter swan.   Works to restore trumpeter
> swan to its original breeding grounds.
> Publication: The Trumpeter Swan Society Newsletter.

THE TRUST FOR PUBLIC LAND
82 Second St. , San Francisco, CA   94105
(415) 495-4014
> Private, nonprofit land acquisition organization.
> Primary interest is urban open space and recrea-
> tional lands.

TRUSTEES FOR CONSERVATION
251 Kearny St., San Francisco, CA 94108
(415) 392-2838
235 Massachusetts Ave. N.E., Washington, DC 20002
(202) 547-1144
   Seeks support from private citizens and from the
   government to protect and preserve national monuments, parks, wildlife, and wilderness.

UNESCO (United Nations Educational Scientific and Cultural
Organization)
U.S. National Commission, Dept. of State, Washington, DC
20520
John E. Upston, Executive Secretary
(202) 632-2762
   National commission created for the purpose of fur-
   thering in the United States the objectives of UNESCO.

UNITED ECOLOGY ASSOCIATION
4835 N. Figueroa St., Los Angeles, CA 90042
(213) 254-6105
   Interested primarily in establishing cooperation and
   communication between environmental organizations,
   government, and the business community. Conducts
   applied research in balanced transportation, alternate
   energy sources, and solid waste recycling techniques.
   Publication: UEA Newsletter.

UNITED STATES TOURIST COUNCIL
Drawer 656, Venice, FL 33595
(813) no listing
   Association composed of conservation concerned citizens who travel or are involved in the travel business. Primary interest is in historic and scenic preservation, wilderness and roadside development, and
   ecology through sound planning and education.

UPPER MISSISSIPPI RIVER CONSERVATION COMMITTEE
Rock Island County Office Bldg., 1504 3rd Ave., Rock
Island, IL 61201
(309) 788-3991
   Dedicated to the promotion of preservation, development, and wise use of natural and recreational resources on the upper Mississippi River. Formulates
   policies, plans, and programs for the conduct of cooperative studies among member state conservation
   departments of Illinois, Iowa, Minnesota, Missouri,

and Wisconsin. Seeks to advance and apply knowledge
of the composition of wastewater and the design, construction, and operation of city and industrial wastewater collection and treatment systems. Publishes
periodicals and technical manuals, training materials.
Publications: UMRCC Newsletter; Annual Proceedings.

URBAN LAND INSTITUTE
1200 18th St. N.W., Washington, DC   20036
(202) 331-8500
Works to evaluate selected development projects pre-
pared with the benefit of research, planning, and management. Disseminates pertinent information on orderly and efficient land use policies and proposals.
Publication: Environmental Comment.

WATER POLLUTION CONTROL FEDERATION
3900 Wisconsin Ave. N.W., Washington, DC   20016
(202) 362-4100
Works to advance fundamental and practical knowledge
about the nature, collection, treatment, and disposal
of domestic and industrial waste water as well as the
design, construction, operation, and management of
waste water facilities.
Publications: Journal Water Pollution Control Federation; Highlights; Deeds and Data.

WATER RESOURCES ASSOCIATION OF THE DELAWARE
RIVER BASIN
21 S. 12th St., Philadelphia, PA   19107
(215) 563-8572
Nonprofit, unbiased federation of private citizens and
citizen organizations working for the orderly conservation, development, and fair use and reuse of water
and related land resources of the Delaware River
Basin.

WELDER WILDLIFE FOUNDATION
P.O. Box 1400, Sinton, TX   78387
(512) 364-2643
Works for conservation by means of research and education in wildlife and related fields through a small
staff and research fellowships to graduate students.

WESTERN FORESTRY AND CONSERVATION ASSOCIATION
1326 American Bank Bldg., Portland, OR   97205
(503) 226-4562

Seeks to promote forestry and the development of
forest conservation on all forest land in the western
United States and western Canada. Provides, also,
means for exchanging and disseminating forestry and
conservation information and seeks to foster cooperation between Federal, state, provincial, and private
forest agencies.

WESTERN REGIONAL ENVIRONMENTAL EDUCATION
COUNCIL
721 Capitol Mall, Sacramento, CA 95814
(916) 455-8010
Seeks to advance state and regional level formal and
nonformal programs cooperating with public and private agencies. Has a research and grant program.
Publication: Econotes.

WETLANDS FOR WILDLIFE, INC.
114 S. Main St., P. O. Box 147, Mayville, WI 53050
(414) 387-4878
Promotes and participates in the promotion, preservation, and acquisition of wetlands and wildlife habitat
throughout the United States that are then transferred
to federal, state, or county agencies to be maintained
and managed solely for public purpose.
Publication: Thirsty Times.

WHOOPING CRANE CONSERVATION ASSOCIATION, INC.
3000 Meadowlark Dr., Sierra Vista, AR 85635
(602) 458-0971
International scientific and educational organization
which works to prevent the extinction of the whooping
crane.
Publication: Grus Americana.

WILD ANIMAL PROPAGATION TRUST
American Association of Zoological Parks and Aquariums,
c/o Don G. Davis, President, Director, Cheyenne Mountain
Zoological Park, Colorado Springs, CO 80906
(303) 475-9555

THE WILDERNESS SOCIETY
1901 Pennsylvania Ave. N.W., Washington, DC 20006
(202) 293-2732
National conservation organization seeking to secure
the preservation of wilderness, execute an educational
program showing the value of wilderness and how it

is best utilized and preserved in the public interest.
Creates and encourages scientific studies of wilderness
and mobilizes cooperation in resisting its invasion.
Publications: The Living Wilderness; Wilderness
Report.

WILDERNESS WATCH
P.O. Box 3184, Green Bay, WI   54303
(414) 499-9131
Seeks to sustain use of America's wilderness lands
and waters through putting supreme priority on ecological considerations. Its decisions are made on
the advice of a scientific advisory staff of experts in
the behavioral and physical sciences.
Publication: Watch It.

WILDLIFE DISEASE ASSOCIATION
P.O. Box 886, Ames, IA   50010
(515) 597-2527
International nonprofit organization of scientists concerned for the advancement of knowledge of the effects
of diseases and the environmental factors affecting the
health and survival of free-living and captive wild
animals and on their relationships to man.
Publications: Journal of Wildlife Diseases; Wildlife
Disease-microfiche-serial.

WILDLIFE MANAGEMENT INSTITUTE
709 Wire Bldg., Washington, DC   20005
(202) 347-1774
National, nonprofit, private, membership organization
that is supported by industries, groups and individuals,
all interested in promoting better use of natural resources for the public benefit.
Publications: Outdoor News Bulletin; Transactions
North American Wildlife and Natural Resources Conference.

THE WILDLIFE SOCIETY
Suite S-176, 3900 Wisconsin Ave. N.W., Washington, DC
20016
(202) 363-2435
Association of professionals in biological or related
fields of wildlife conservation that seeks to develop
and promote sound stewardship of wildlife resources
and the environments upon which wildlife and men
both depend. Takes an active role in the prevention

of man-induced environmental degradation and seeks
to increase awareness and appreciation of wildlife
values.
Publications: Journal of Wildlife Management; Wildlife Society Bulletin; Wildlife Monographs.

WORLD WILDLIFE FUND
Suite 619, 910 17th St. N.W., Washington, DC 20006
(202) 296-6114
Private, tax-exempt organization which seeks to advance programs that will save the world's threatened
and endangered species of wildlife and wild areas.
Makes grants to existing agencies for work in making
surveys, habitat improvement and protection. Works
in cooperation with international office in Morges,
Switzerland that provides coordination of projects in
22 countries.

ZERO POPULATION GROWTH, INC.
4080 Fabian Way, Palo Alto, CA 94303
(415) 327-2000
Citizens' organization established in an attempt to
stabilize population in the United States by 1990
through voluntary means. Conducts educational and
media programs for students and the general public,
undertakes legal action to implement existing law and
legislative advocacy in Washington and state legisla-
tures.
Publications: National Reporter; Equilibrium.

Section VIII

ENVIRONMENTAL FILM DISTRIBUTORS

ABC Media Concepts
1330 Ave. of the Americas
New York, NY 10019

ACI Films, Inc.
35 W. 45th St.
New York, NY 10036

Aetna Life & Casualty
Audio Visual Services
151 Farmington Ave.
Hartford, CT 06115

American Educat. Films
331 N. Maple Dr.
Beverly Hills, CA 90210

American Iron and Steel
Institute
1000 16th St. N.W.
Washington, DC 20036

American Petroleum Institute
1801 K St. N.W.
Washington, DC 20006

Association-Sterling Films
866 Third Ave.
New York, NY 10022

Atlantic Richfield Co.
Public Relations Dept.
717 Fifth Ave.
New York, NY 10022

Benchmark Films, Inc.

145 Scarborough Rd.
Braircliff Manor, NY
10510

BFA Educat. Media
2211 Michigan Ave.
Santa Monica, CA 90404

Bitterroot Films, Inc.
Hammond Arcade Bldg.
Missoula, MT 59801

BP North America, Inc.
620 Fifth Ave.
New York, NY 10020

Byron Motion Pictures, Inc.
65 K St. N.E.
Washington, DC 20002

Carousel Films, Inc.
Suite 1503, 1501 Broadway
New York, NY 10036

Cntr. for Mass Communica-
tion of Columbia Univ. Press
562 W. 113th St.
New York, NY 10025

Centron Educat. Films
1821 W. 9th St.
Lawrence, KS 66044

Churchill Films
662 N. Robertson Blvd.
Los Angeles, CA 90069

Cinema Associate Prod., Inc.
Box 621
East Lansing, MI 48823

Colonial Williamsburg
Foundation, Drawer C
Williamsburg, VA 23185

Conservation Foundation
1717 Massachusetts Ave. N.W.
Washington, DC 20036

Contemporary/McGraw Hill
Films
1221 Ave. of the Americas
New York, NY 10020

Coronet Instruct. Materials
65 E. South Water St.
Chicago, IL 60601

Creative Film Society
14558 Valerio
Van Nuys, CA 91405

Deere & Co.
Audio-Visual Section
John Deere Rd.
Moline, IL 61265

Walt Disney Educat.
Materials Co.
500 S. Buena Vista
Burbank, CA 91505

Doubleday Multimedia
Box 11607
1371 Reynolds Ave.
Santa Ana, CA 92705

Encyclopaedia Britannica
Educat. Corp.
425 N. Michigan Ave.
Chicago, IL 60611

Enterprise Prod., Inc.
1019 Belmont Place East

Seattle, WA 98102

Environmental Educators,
Inc.
732 7th St. N.W.
Washington, DC 20006

Ethyl Corp.
Public Relations Dept.
330 S. 4th St.
Richmond, VA 23219

Farm Film Foundation
Suite 424, 1425 H St. N.W.
Washington, DC 20005

Federal Aviation Admin.
Film Library AC-44.5
P.O. Box 25082
Oklahoma City, OK 73125

The Film Company
212 W. Franklin Ave.
Minneapolis, MN 55404

Film Services
Tennessee Valley Authority
Knoxville, TN 37902

Films Incorporated
1144 Wilmette Ave.
Wilmette, IL 60091

Stuart Finley Inc.
3428 Mansfield Rd.
Falls Church, VA 22041

General Electric Educat.
Films
Corporations Park,
Bldg. 705
Scotia, NY 12302

General Services Admin.
National Archives and
Records Service
National Audiovisual Center

Washington, DC   20409

Group Against Smog and
Pollution
P.O. Box 2850
Pittsburgh, PA   15230

Grove Press Film Div.
53 E. 11th St.
New York, NY   10003

Handel Film Corp.
8730 Sunset Blvd.
West Hollywood, CA   90069

Alfred Higgins Prod.
9100 Sunset Blvd.
Los Angeles, CA   90069

Holt, Rinehart & Winston,
Inc.
Media Dept.
383 Madison Ave.
New York, NY   10017

Indiana Univ.
Audio-Visual Center
Bloomington, IN   47401

Stacey Keach Prod.
12240 Ventura Blvd.
Studio City, CA   91604

Jonathan Kress
Kerulos Films, Inc.
1020 Fifth Ave.
New York, NY   10028

Learning Corp. of America
711 Fifth Ave.
New York, NY   10022

Mass Media Associates
2116 N. Charles St.
Baltimore, MD   21218

Modern Talking Picture

Service, Inc.
1212 Ave. of the Americas
New York, NY   10036

Motion Picture Service
U. S. Dept of Commerce
National Oceanic &
Atmospheric Admin.
12231 Wilkins Ave.
Rockville, MD   20852

Motion Pictures
U. S. Dept of Interior
Bureau of Mines
4800 Forbes Ave.
Pittsburgh, PA   15213

Motor Vehicle Manufacturers
Assn., Inc.
320 New Center Bldg.
Detroit, MI   48202

Museum of Modern Art
Circulation Director
Dept. of Film
21 W. 53rd St.
New York, NY   10019

National Audubon Society
950 Third Ave.
New York, NY   10022

National Bank of Detroit
Public Relations Dept.
611 Woodward Ave.
Detroit, MI   48232

National Council of Churches
Broadcasting and Film
Commission
Rm 860, 475 Riverside Dr.
New York, NY   10027

National Film Board of
Canada
680 Fifth Ave.
New York, NY   10019

National Tuberculosis &
Respiratory Disease Assn.
1740 Broadway
New York, NY   10019

NBC Educat. Enterprises
30 Rockefeller Plaza
New York, NY   10020

North American Films, Inc.
4440 Ellenita
Tarzana, CA   91356

Northern Illinois Univ.
Film Library
Dekalb, IL   60115

Perennial Education, Inc.
1825 Willow Rd.
Northfield, IL   60093

Petroleum Equipment
Suppliers Assn.
1703 First National Bank
Bldg.
Houston, TX   77002

Piccadilly Films, Ltd.
715 Stadium Dr.
San Antonio, TX   78284

Pictura Films Dist. Corp.
43 W. 16th St.
New York, NY   10011

Planned Parenthood-
World Population
Film Library
267 W. 25th St.
New York, NY   10001

Portland Cement Assn.
Old Orchard Rd.
Skokie, IL   60076

Pyramid Films
2801 Colorado Ave.

Santa Monica, CA   90406

Radim Films, Inc.
17 W. 60th St.
New York, NY   10023

Rodale Press Inc.
Film Division
444 Turner St.
Allentown, PA   18102

Ruder and Finn, Inc.
110 E. 59th St.
New York, NY   10022

Shell Film Library
450 N. Meridian St.
Indianapolis, IN   46204

Stacey Keach Prod.   see
under   Keach

Sterling Educat. Films
(Walter Reade, Inc.)
241 E. 34th St.
New York, NY   10016

Summit Films, Inc.
538 E. Alameda Ave.
Denver, CO   80209

Texture Films Inc.
1600 Broadway
New York, NY   10019

Time-Life Films
43 W. 16th St.
New York, NY   10011

Trans-World Films, Inc.
332 S. Michigan Ave.
Chicago, IL   60604

Universal Education and
Visual Arts
221 Park Ave. S.
New York, NY   10003

Univ. of California
Extension Media Center
Berkeley, CA 94720

Univ. of Michigan
Television Center
310 Maynard St.
Ann Arbor, MI 48108

Univ. of Southern California
Div. of Cinema
University Park
Los Angeles, CA 90007

U.S. Atomic Energy
Commission
Film Library-TIC
P.O. Box 62
Oak Ridge, TN 37830

U.S. Dept of Agriculture
Office of Information
Motion Picture Service
Washington, DC 20250

U.S. Dept of the Interior
Bureau of Reclamation
P.O. Box 25007
Engineering Research Center
Denver, CO 80225

U.S. Dept of the Interior
Bureau of Sport Fisheries
and Wildlife
Washington, DC 20240

John Wiley & Sons, Inc.
605 Third Ave.
New York, NY 10016

Wrather Corp.
270 N. Canon Dr.
Beverly Hills, CA 90210

Xerox Films
Stamford, CT 06904

Appendix 1

CHRONOLOGY OF IMPORTANT U.S. ENVIRONMENTAL
LAWS, ORDINANCES, ETC.

1626   Plymouth Colony passes ordinance which regulated
            the cutting and sale of timber on colony lands.

1639   Deer hunting is prohibited for six months of the
            year in Newport, Rhode Island.

1681   William Penn issues a decree stipulating that one
            acre of land must be left forested for every five
            acres cleared.

1849   United States Department of Interior established.

1864   Yosemite Valley is reserved as a state park.

1872   Yellowstone National Park established.

1881   The Division of Forestry is created within the
            Department of Agriculture.

1885   New York and Ontario create the Niagara Reser-
            vation to protect the Falls.

            New York establishes the Adirondack Forest.

1891   Forest Reserve Act.   Permits President of the
            United States to establish forest reserves on the
            public domain.

1899   Rivers and Harbors Act.   Prohibited the dumping
            of pollution and debris into navigable waters or the
            construction of bridges, wharves, dams, etc. with-
            out federal permission.

1900   Lacey Act.   Interstate shipment of game killed in
            violation of state laws is made a federal offense.

1902   Reclamation Act. Allows the Secretary of the
            Interior to locate, construct, operate, and main-
            tain works for the storage, diversion, and develop-
            ment of waters for the reclamation of arid and
            semi-arid lands.

1906   Antiquities Act. Permits reservation of areas of
            scientific or historical interest on Federal lands
            as national monuments.

1908   Grand Canyon of the Colorado is established as a
            National Monument.

1911   Weeks Act. Permitted purchase of forested land
            at headwaters of navigable streams for inclusion
            in the national forest system; makes possible the
            establishment of national forests in the eastern
            United States.

1916   National Park Service Act. Established the Park
            Service.

1918   Migratory Bird Treaty Act. Implements treaty of
            1916 with Canada restricting the hunting of mi-
            gratory species.

1920   Mineral Leasing Act. Regulates mining on federal
            lands.

            Federal Water Power Act. Gives the Federal
            Power Commission authority to issue licenses for
            hydro-power development on public lands.

1924   Clarke-McNary Act. Extends federal ability to
            buy lands for inclusion in the National Forest
            System.

            Federal Oil Pollution Act. Prohibits oil pollution
            from ocean-going vessels (enforcement, however,
            proved difficult and ineffective).

1928   McSweeney-McNary Act authorizes a broad program
            of federal research in forestry.

1933   Civilian Conservation Corps is created.

            Franklin D. Roosevelt creates the Soil Erosion
            Service.

1934   Taylor Grazing Act. Provides for federal regula-
        tion of use of unreserved public domain.

1935   Soil Conservation Act. Extends federal influence
        in erosion control; establishes the Soil Conserva-
        tion Service in the Department of Interior.

1937   Pittman-Robertson Act. Federal funds are made
        available to states for wildlife protection and
        propagation.

1939   Forest Service "U" Regulations. Policy of wilder-
        ness preservation is extended within the National
        Forests.

1940   United States Fish and Wildlife Serve established.

1946   Atomic Energy Act. Establishes Atomic Energy
        Commission.

        U. S. Bureau of Land Management established.
        Consolidated the administration of the public
        domain.

1947   Insecticide, Fungicide, and Rodenticide Act
        (amended in 1964). Prohibits the marketing and
        transfer of any poison or device without proper
        registration and approval of the United States
        Public Health Service.

1948   Water Pollution Control Act. Establishes the
        authority of the federal government to have a role
        in controlling interstate water pollution. Its in-
        fluence, however, remained subordinate to that of
        the states.

1955   P. L. 84-159. Establishes grants to states and
        educational institutions to train personnel and con-
        duct research and control on air pollution.

1956   Water Pollution Control Acts Ammendments.
        Gives permanent water pollution control authority
        to the federal government, authorized court action
        to halt interstate water pollution, and provided for
        grants to construct waste water treatment pro-
        grams.

1960   Multiple Use Act. Defines more thoroughly and

precisely the purpose of the National Forests.

1961   P. L. 87-88. Provides increased grants for waste
        treatment plant construction, monies for research
        in water pollution control, and establishes seven
        field laboratories.

1963   Clean Air Act. Increases grants to states and
        institutions for research, and authorizes the fed-
        eral government to take action to abate interstate
        air pollution.

        The Bureau of Outdoor Recreation is established
        within the Department of the Interior. Its pur-
        pose: coordinate federal efforts in this sphere.

1964   Wilderness Act. Directs Secretary of the Interior
        to review every roadless area or island within the
        National Wildlife and Refuge System of 5000 acres
        or more and make recommendations to the Presi-
        dent to maintain these areas as wilderness in their
        natural and primitive state. Establishes the Na-
        tional Wilderness Preservation System.

        Land and Water Conservation Fund Act. Makes
        monies available for local, state, and federal ac-
        quisition and development of park lands and open
        spaces.

1965   Water Resources Planning Act. Provides for the
        development of the nation's water resources, es-
        tablishes a Water Resources Council and River
        Basin Commissions, and provides funds for state
        water planning programs.

        Water Quality Act. Establishes the Federal Water
        Pollution Control Administration within the Depart-
        ment of Health, Education and Welfare, sets water
        quality standards for federal and state regulation,
        streamlines enforcement procedures, and provides
        for project grants for research and development on
        combined sewers.

        Solid Waste Disposal Act. Provides: research and
        training grants for states to establish solid waste
        recycling and disposal plants; guidelines for system
        development; technical assistance to states, local
        governments, and interstate agencies for planning
        new systems; and funds to the same for the

demonstration, construction, and application of
solid waste systems.

Motor Vehicle Air Pollution Control Act.   Gives
Secretary of Health, Education, and Welfare the
authority to establish regulations controlling emissions from all new motor vehicles.

1966   Clean Water Restoration Act.   Transfers the
Federal Water Pollution Control Agency to Interior
and provides for increased grants to construct advanced waste water treatment facilities.

National Historic Preservation Act passes.

1967   Air Quality Act.   Gives power to each state to
set standards for primary and secondary ambient
air quality standards, provided they are approved
by the Secretary of Health, Education, and Welfare.   It further provides for the establishment of
air quality control regions, registration of fuel
additives, and a larger research program, vehicle
inspection, and grants power to HEW to seek a
court injunction against any air pollutor if an
emergency exists.

1968   Aircraft Noise Abatement Act.   Ammends the
Federal Aviation Act;   provides for standards of
measurement and control of aircraft noise and
sonic boom.

Wild and Scenic Rivers Act.   Requires joint studies
by the departments of Interior and Agriculture to
permanently preserve certain rivers in their natural state and conduct special studies on certain
named rivers before any construction or alteration
may be allowed on them.

1969   Endangered Species Conservation Act.   Instructs
the Bureau of Sport, Fisheries, and Wildlife to
compile data on near extinct wildlife, to plan and
to provide technical assistance, and to carry out
programs designed to protect and conserve fish
and wildlife.

National Environmental Policy Act.   Pledges the
Federal Government to "identify and develop
methods and procedures...which will insure that
presently unqualified environmental amenities and

values may be given appropriate consideration in decision making.... "

1970   Clean Air Amendments (an omnibus amendment to 1967 Clean Air Act). Authorizes national quality air control standards, with federal enforcement. It also makes specific demands on automobile manufacturers for better emission control devices; aircraft, air, and noise pollution controls also to be enforced.

Environmental Education Act. Funds various programs under the United States Office of Education. Included are: environmental education curriculum development, demonstration, evaluation, and dissemination; teacher training; elementary, secondary, and community education program initiation and maintenance; research grants; technical assistance; planning outdoor ecological study centers; and preparation of environmental and ecological materials suitable for use by the mass media. Environmental education is concerned with man's total relationship to his natural and manmade environment and includes the relation of population, pollution, resource management, conservation, transportation, technology, and urban and rural development.

Environmental Quality Improvement Act. Establishes the office of Environmental Quality to assist federal agencies to coordinate environmental programs and develop interrelated federal criteria.

National Materials Policy Act. Establishes a committee to study the supply, use, and recovery and disposal of natural resources by industry for the production of goods exclusive of food.

Resource Recovery Act (an amendment to the Solid Waste Disposal Act of 1965). Provides grants to the states, interstate agencies, and localities for the establishment of solid waste disposal facilities, provides funds for the training of personnel in this field, and sets regulations for solid waste recovery, collection, and disposal.

Water Quality Improvement Act. Establishes federal procedures relating to oil spills' pollution along the coastal areas and sets stiff penalties for willful pollutors. It provides, also, for more strict marine sanitation devices, training for waste treatment personnel, and for demonstration grants for water treatment in lakes and mine areas.

EPA (Environmental Protection Agency) established. Reorganization plan No. 3 of 1970.

1971   Pesticide Control Act.   Protects the public's health and welfare as well as the environment through improved pesticide control.

Water Quality Standards Act.   Calls for elimination of pollution discharge by 1985;   restoration of United States water resources;   achievement of water quality allowing fish propagation and swimming by 1981;   provision for grants for treatment plants;   and regulation of permits and licenses. (Presidential veto was overruled.)

1972   Technological Assessment Act.   Establishes an Office of Technology Assessment responsible to Congress.

Noise Control Act.   Charges the Environmental Protection Agency with responsibility for setting noise control standards, identifying major noise sources, and distributing information.

Oil Pollution Act Amendments.   Adds to the list of definitions of actions covered by the Oil Pollution Act of 1961;   provides for construction requirements of ships covered by the act;   provides penalties for violations.

Ocean Dumping Act.   Authorizes the Environmental Protection Agency to regulate ocean dumping; creates international monitoring program;   and establishes marine sanctuaries in U. S. coastal waters.

1973   Alaskan Pipeline.   Authorizes construction of the Alaskan Pipeline and prohibits court review on environmental grounds.

Highway and Mass Transit.   For the first time appropriates money ($19. 9 billion) from the Highway Trust Fund for construction of urban mass transit.

Auto Air Pollution Standards deadline extended by EPA to 1976, except in California where stringent

standards to take effect in 1975. Bill in Congress
(S2589) in mid-1974 would extend deadline until
1977.   Also pending in Congress is Bill S2680
which would relax other Clean Air Act requirements for coal burning.

1974   Environmental Warfare Treaty (Senate Resolution
71).   Currently (mid-1974) before the Senate.
This treaty seeks to prohibit any modification of
weather, climate, earthquakes, and the oceans for
military purposes.

S2062.   Bill pending before Congress (mid-1974)
which would ban the interstate shipment of non-
returnable bottles, require a deposit on all bottled
and canned beverages, and outlaw sale of cans
with detachable openers.

Extension of the Environmental Education Act.
Awaiting Presidential signature.

Appendix 2

GLOSSARY OF TERMS

ABIOTIC ENVIRONMENT   The environment which is non-
   living; of biological interest because of its inorganic
   nutrients, climatic factors, and topography.

ADDITIVE   Anything that is added to alter the original
   quality of a substance.

ALGAE   Chlorophyll-containing plants of the phylum
   Thallophyta that occur in salt or fresh water or on
   soil, rocks, trees, etc.   They proliferate in polluted
   water.

AMBIENT AIR QUALITY CRITERIA   The relationship between concentrations and durations of specific air con-
   taminents and their effects on living organisms and
   materials.

AQUIFER   Any water-bearing permeable geological formation
   (e. g. , rock, sand or gravel).

ASSIMILATION   The process by which plants receive nu-
   trition--absorption of foods and photosynthesis.

AUTECOLOGY   The branch of ecology that treats an individual organism in relation to environment.   Compare
   with SYNECOLOGY.

AUTOTROPH   see   PRIMARY PRODUCER

BASIC EQUILIBRIUM CONCEPT   The concept that everything within the universe is dependent on everything
   else.

BIOCHORES   Divisions of the biosphere.

BIOCLIMATIC   Of or pertaining to the effects of climate

on living organisms.

BIOCLIMATOLOGY   The study of climatic effects on the
    biological processes of plants and animals.

BIODEGRADABLE   Capable of being broken down naturally
    (usually by microorganisms) into innocuous stable com-
    pounds.

BIODYNAMICS   Branch of biology which treats the energy
    or activity of living organisms.

BIOECOLOGY   Study of interrelationships of plants and
    animals and their common environment.

BIOENERGETICS   The study of an ecosystem's energy flow.

BIOGEOGRAPHY   The geographical distribution of living
    things.

BIOMASS   The expression in weight of organisms per unit
    area of habitat or in volume or weight of organisms
    per unit volume of habitat.

BIOME   A large ecological area of basically similar vegeta-
    tion (which may include several different ecosystems).

BIONICS   The application of data about how biological sys-
    tems perform certain tasks to the solution of engineer-
    ing problems and to the design of computers and other
    electronic equipment.

BIOSPHERE   The thin, life-supporting layer of both the
    earth's crust--consisting of rivers, lakes, oceans, and
    soil--and the lower atmosphere.

BIOSYNTHESIS   The formation of chemical compounds by a
    living organism by means of synthesis or degradation.

BIOTA   The animal and plant life of a particular region or
    period.

BIOTIC POTENTIAL   The optimum capacity under optimum
    conditions that a population of animals or plants pos-
    sesses for increasing its numbers.

BIOTYPE   A group of organisms characterized by the

same hereditary features.

BOD (Biochemical Oxygen Demand)   The amount of oxygen needed by aerobic microorganisms to consume biodegradable organics (e. g. , sewage) in water.

CARBON DIOXIDE   A heavy, colorless, odorless gas CO_2, non-supportive of combustion, that is formed during animal respiration and the decay of plant and animal matter, and that is absorbed from the air by plants in photosynthesis.

CARBON MONOXIDE   A colorless, odorless, very poisonous gas CO produced by the incomplete combustion of fuels and emitted into the atmosphere by automobiles, planes, industrial plants, incinerators, and furnaces.

CARCINOGENIC   Cancer-producing.

CARNIVORE   Any mammal which eats the flesh of other animals; also, an insect-eating plant.

CATALYTIC CONVERTER   A sealed container which is inserted into the exhaust system of internal combustion engines to convert unburned hydrocarbons, carbon monoxide and oxides of nitrogen into water, carbon dioxide and nitrogen.

CHAIN OF LIFE   The system whereby lower forms of life are consumed by higher forms until the offal or body of the higher form is returned to the earth, its chemicals reintegrated into the system once again.

CHLORINATED HYDROCARBONS   Long-lived chemicals that kill a particular plant or insect but which damage other creatures in the ground, sea, and the air as well. DDT is an example.

CLIMATE   The composite or prevailing weather of a particular region.   The aggregate conditions of temperature, air pressure, humidity, precipitation, wind, sun, etc.

CLIMATIC CLIMAX   Either a relatively stable or the culminating stage of growth and development of organisms of a particular area as dictated by the climate of that area.

CLIMATIC AMELIORATION   Alteration of prevailing weather
    conditions.

CLIMATOLOGY   The science that deals with climates and
    climatic conditions.

CLIMAX   The stable, end-product of succession wherein
    plants and animals live in equilibrium with each other
    and with their environment (or, sometimes, a relatively
    stable stage through which populations pass on their
    way to the stable end-state).

COMMENSALISM   Association between two species in which
    one is benefited by the other and the other is not af-
    fected.

COMMUNITY   A collection of different kinds of individuals
    or populations living and interacting in a particular area.

CONSERVATION   Preservation from loss, harm, waste, or
    decay.

DECIBEL   A unit measuring the intensity of sound;   50 db
    is said to be moderate sound;   80 db is considered
    loud;   100 db and above, intolerable.

DEWATERING   Removing water from sludge by the pro-
    cesses of filtration, centrifugation, pressing, open-air
    drying, etc. , so that the end product is suitable for
    use as landfill or burning.

ECOLOGY   The branch of biology dealing with the relation-
    ship between organisms and their surrounding environ-
    ment.

ECOSPECIES   Roughly equivalent to a taxonomic species,
    consisting of one or more ecotypes which interbreed
    more freely with each other than with ecotypes of a
    related ecospecies.

ECOSPHERE   That part of the atmosphere where it is pos-
    sible to breathe without the aid of oxygen-supplying
    equipment.   It ranges from sea level to an altitude of
    approximately 13, 000 feet.

ECOSYSTEM   System that is formed by the interaction of
    a community of organisms with its abiotic environment.

ECOTONE   The area of transition from one biome to another; where the two merge. It has some characteristics of each as well as its own unique characteristics and species.

ECOTYPE   A community or strain of identical individuals which interbreed freely with other ecotypes within its ecospecies but which maintain an individual identity through environmental (e. g. , nutrient, climatic) factors.

EDAPHIC CLIMAX   An ecological climax (which see) resulting from peculiar soil factors, which persists within a given climatic climax (which see) but remains different from the rest of the climax.

EDAPHON   The organisms that live in the soil.

EFFLUENT   The outflows of waste from sewage plants or industry into water bodies such as lakes, rivers, the sea.

EFFLUVIUM   A flowing gaseous or liquid waste, especially an unpleasant one (pl. , effluvia, is most common form).

ENVIRONMENT   The aggregate of all surrounding things, influences, and conditions which affect the life of an organism, a population, or a community.

ENVIRONMENTAL RESISTANCE   The sum of restricting effects of prevalent environmental factors on a particular organism or population of organisms which tends to limit its numerical growth.

EUTROPHICATION   The choking of water bodies such as lakes, rivers, and streams with algae by depleting the waters of its natural oxygen content through large-scale biodegrading of wastes.

EVEN-AGE STANDS   Forest regions where all the trees are the same age because they were planted at the same time.

FAULT   A fracture in the earth's crust.

FERTILITY (Soil Fertility)   The tendency of a given area of soil to possess all ingredients necessary to support plant growth.

FLORA   All plants of a region or period.

FLY ASH   Fine particles of ash produced from the combustion of fuels.

FOOD CHAIN   A linear chain of organisms: each link in the chain feeds on the next. The primary producers are at the start of the chain, the carnivores at the end. See also CHAIN OF LIFE.

FOSSIL FUELS   Coal, petroleum, and natural gas.

GEOMORPHOLOGY   The study of land forms; their characteristics, origins, and development.

GRAZERS   Herbivores (primary consumers) that feed on plant species.

GREENHOUSE EFFECT   Hypothesis which states that the accumulation of carbon dioxide from the burning of fossil fuels acts like a greenhouse, allowing solar energy to radiate into the atmosphere but not back out, consequently raising the earth's temperature. The result over a period of time will be the melting of the icecaps and other environmental changes.

GROSS PRIMARY PRODUCTION   The amount of plant protoplasm which is formed per unit area per unit time.

HABITAT   The native environment of an animal or plant; its home; where it lives naturally.

HERBICIDE   A preparation for killing plants (generally weeds).

HERBIVORE   A primary consumer, plant-eater.

HETEROTROPHE   An organism that obtains its organic food from other organisms; these include all animals, some fungi, and most bacteria.

HOLOZOIC   Capable of feeding on insoluble as well as soluble food; not parasitic or saprophytic.

HUMUS   Partly decayed plant and animal matter in the soil; essential for both fertility and moisture supply.

HYDROCARBON   A class of compound that contains only
hydrogen and carbon.   Example: automobile exhausts.

HYDROSPHERE   Water that is on or surrounding the surface of the earth--i. e. , water vapor and bodies of
water such as the oceans, lakes, and seas.

INVERSION   A layer of cold air which is trapped beneath
a layer of warm air causing smog to be held close to
the ground and preventing its escape.

LANDFILL   A method of disposing of refuse on land whereby the refuse is compacted into the smallest practical
volume and confined to the smallest practical area.

LEACHING   Removing soluble compounds by means of down-
ward percolation of water through soil.

LICHEN   Compound composed of a fungus in symbiotic union
with an alga.   It is greenish, gray, yellow, brown, or
blackish, and forms on rocks, trees, etc.

LIFE CYCLE   The continuous sequence of alterations an
organism undergoes from a particular primary form
to the development of that same form once again.

LIMITING FACTOR   A factor of the abiotic environment
that limits optimum growth because it is in short
supply.

METABIOSIS   Modality of existence in which one organism
depends on another for the preparation of an environment in which it can survive.

MYCORRHIZA   A symbiotic relationship between a fungus
and the root of a higher plant.

NATURAL SELECTION   Process of nature whereby the
fittest of the plant or animal species survive and perpetuate those forms of life having the most favorable
characteristics for adapting to the specific environment.

NICHE   A site or habitat supplying all biotic and abiotic
life-controlling factors considered essential to the existence and development (or climax) of an organism.

NITROGEN CYCLE   The continuous sequence of changes by

which nitrogen in the air and soil is converted into substances that can be utilized by plants. After the plants decay, the substances return to their previous state. By denitrification, they are made into substances that the plants cannot use.

NITROGEN FIXATION   The synthesis of inorganic nitrogen compounds from atmospheric nitrogen by certain bacteria and algae.

NONRENEWABLE RESOURCES   Substances such as oil, gas, coal, copper, gold, and iron, etc. that once used cannot be replaced within our present geological age.

NUTRIENTS   The six essential ingredients for growth: carbohydrates, fats, proteins, water, salts, and vitamins. They also supply an organism with energy.

ORGANIC MATTER   Chemical compounds of carbon that are combined with other chemical elements (generally made during the life processes of plants and animals). They are, in most cases, combustible. They are also a source of food.

ORGANISM   An individual life form composed of mutually dependent parts maintaining the various life processes.

PALAEO-ECOLOGY   The study of past ecosystems.

PARASITE   An organism that relies for the completion of its life cycle on its connection with the tissues of another species. It harms the host species but generally does not kill it.

PHYLOGENY   The racial history or evolution of a kind of animal or plant.

PLAGIOCLIMAX   A subclimax maintained by the continuous activity of humans.

POLLUTION   Harmful substances deposited in the air, water, or soil that cause general filth, disease, and sometimes death.

POPULATION   A group of individuals of the same species living in a region.

POPULATION PRESSURE   The force a growing population
   exerts upon its environment.

PREDATOR   Any organism which preys on another.

PRESERVATION   The safeguarding and propagation of
   game, fish, forest, etc.

PRIMARY CONSUMER   An organism (herbivore) that feeds
   on primary producers (autotrophs).

PRIMARY PRODUCER (Autotroph)   An organism (e. g. , a
   plant) that synthesizes organic compounds from inorganic compounds.

PRIMATE   Any mammal of the order Primates, including
   man, the apes, monkeys, etc.

RECLAMATION   The restoring to cultivation or use of
   waste areas, deserts, exhausted farmlands, etc. ;
   also, the restoring to use of any waste material.

RECYCLING   The salvaging and reprocessing of used
   materials.

REFORESTATION   Replanting of trees or their seeds in
   denuded land.

SANITARY FILL   The dumping process in which garbage
   or refuse is covered with soil to control smell, rodents,
   etc. and speed the decay of organic substances.

SAPROPHYTE   An organism that is able to feed only on
   soluble organic matter from dead plants and animals.
   It includes some fungi, bacteria, and algae, but no
   animals.

SECONDARY CONSUMER (Carnivore)   An organism that
   feeds on a primary consumer, i. e. , a carnivore that
   feeds on animals that graze.

SECONDARY FIBER   Fibers reclaimed from waste products
   of paper, paperboard, cardboard, etc. and utilized as
   raw material for fabricating new products.

SERE: The series of ecological communities that succeed

each other in development toward a climax (which see).

SILVICULTURE   Forestry.

SLUDGE   Concentrated solids collected in treatment plants.

SMOG   The combination of fog and smoke or photochemical
haze produced by the action of the sun and air on automobile and industrial emissions.

SOIL CONSERVATION   Methods used to achieve maximum
utilization of the land and preservation of its resources
and quality through crop rotation, contour plowing, etc.

SOLID WASTE   Discarded items that have to be collected
and disposed of.   Although it does not include solid
matter discarded into the sewage systems or emitted
with smoke or gas, such matter if trapped or concentrated can then become solid waste.

SONIC BOOM   Loud noise caused when the shock wave from
the nose of an aircraft moving at supersonic speed hits
the ground.

SPECIES   A class having some common characteristics;
the major subdivision of biological classification.   Its
members are similar in appearance, are able to breed
among themselves, and are significantly less able to
breed with members of other species.

SUBCLIMAX   The penultimate stage of succession before
the climax (which see) that persists because of a
continuous factor preventing its final development to
the climax.

SYNECOLOGY   Branch of ecology that deals with the nature
of ecological communities in relation to environment.
Compare with AUTECOLOGY.

THERMAL POLLUTION   Usually, the influx of heated water
into a natural body of water, most often from a power
plant.   Waste heat can also be emitted by industry,
home appliances, machines, and other sources into the
air.

TOLERANCE LEVEL   The point of endurance beyond which
decline or death follows.

ZERO POPULATION GROWTH (ZPG)   The maintenance or
   holding of the numbers of a population at a fixed level;
   normally relates to human populations only.

Appendix 3

LATE ADDITIONS TO SECTION II

1006a ANDERSON, Susanne, (David Brower, ed.). Song of
       the Earth Spirit. New York: McGraw-Hill, 1973,
       $14.95, illus (L: JHS & up) (S: Lu/O).

1044a CARLETON, Milton. False Prophets of Pollution.
       Tampa, FL: Trend House, 1973, $3.95 (pap)
       (L: Adv HS & up) (S: C).

1073a DANTZIG, George and Saaty, Thomas. Compact
       City: A Plan for a Livable Urban Environment.
       San Francisco: Freeman, 1973, $9, $4.50 (pap)
       (L: Adv HS & up) (S: U).

1084a An Ecological Evaluation of Pound Ridge, N.Y., 1973.
       First of a 5-phase study conducted by Community
       Design Associates on Pound Ridge, New York.
       Funded by Pound Ridge United for Planning as
       initial step towards a town land use policy of de-
       velopment based on ecology. $6 (tax-deductible),
       avail from Pound Ridge United for Planning
       (PRUP), Pound Ridge, New York 10576.

1087a EHRLICH, Paul, Ehrlich, Anne, and Holdren, John.
       Human Ecology: Problems and Solutions. San
       Francisco: Freeman, 1973, $4.95 (L: Adv HS
       & up) (S: P).

1096a FALORP, Nelson. Cape May to Montauk. New
       York: Viking, 1973, $14.95 (L: Adv HS & up)
       (S: O).

1114a GOLDMAN, Charles, et al., eds. Environmental
       Quality and Water Development. Riverside, N.J.:
       Free Press (orders to Macmillan), 1973 (L: Adv
       HS & up) (S: Wp).

1184a KUMMERLY, Walter. The Forest. Washington, DC:
       Luce (orders to McKay), 1973, $25, illus (L: HS
       & up) (S: Ec/W).

1219a MANN, Roy. Rivers in the City. New York:
       Praeger, 1973, $20 (L: Adv HS & up) (S: Wp).

1296a RICHARDSON, Elmo. Dams, Parks and Politics.
       Lexington: University Press of Kentucky, 1973
       (L: Adv HS & up) (S: Cn/ Lu).

1304a ROTHSCHILD, Brian, ed. World Fisheries Policy:
       Multi-disciplinary Views. Seattle: University of
       Washington Press, 1973, $9.50 (L: Adv HS & up)
       (S: Wp).

1374a VETTER, Richard C. Oceanography: The Last
       Frontier. Scranton: Basic Books (Harper &
       Row), 1973, $10 (L: Adv HS & up) (S: Wp).

COAUTHOR INDEX (Numbers with * refer to Appendix 3)

GRADE LEVEL (READING LEVEL) INDEX
(Numbers with * refer to Appendix 3)

This is a general guide (with citations given in numerical order) to the reading comprehension and content level of books listed in sections I and II and in Appendix 3. The teacher or student, however, should not categorically rule out a book in the level immediately above or below his or her own particular grade or level of interest. We have often included the same books in several levels where either we, or the publisher, reviewers, or Books in Print cited levels that cut across our specific categories. We did this generally in the K-5 levels, listing the book in both K-3 and 4-6, or in the case of a JHS & up reference in 7-9 and HS & up. But this does not mean that an advanced sixth grader would not be able to read a 7-9 level book or that a senior in high school would not find a reference in HS & up or even 7-9 useful in particular instances. All books included in Section I have been given a level index. Books from Section II and Appendix 3 have been given a level only where the publisher or Books in Print indicated a level or where we were able to review the book.

Books recommended for grade levels K-3:

29	38	39	49	56	62
63	109	110	138	185	186
214	218	220	222	265	270
272	285	303	308	309	312
345	350	351	1001	1065a	1107
1129	1130	1131	1191	1221	1224
1263	1277	1289	1307	1391	

Books recommended for grade levels 4-6:

22	25	37	38	50	62
63	68	101	108	109	136

Books recommended for grade levels 4-6 (cont'd.):

138	139	151	153	154	160
167	168	169	182	184	186
200	214	215	217	218	222
230	239	240	241	256	264
270	284	285	286	287	309
312	313	314	332	335	345
350	351	352	354	355	356
359	364	365	398	1024	1062
1064	1065a	1083	1106	1107	1124
1126	1129	1130	1131	1154	1191
1221	1222	1226	1254	1274	1277
1286	1288	1289	1346	1348	1352
1362	1382	1391	1404	1407	

Books recommended for grade levels 7-9:

12	24	25	36	38	42
44	60	68	69	82	84
97	101	128	129	139	150
153	154	155	157	160	164
167	168	169	177	178	180
181	189	190	197	200	202
217	218	223	225	226	238
239	240	252	256	257	263
264	267	270	284	286	287
290	292	300	304	311	314
319	320	322	332	335	352
353	354	355	356	364	365
369	375	376	384	390	398
400	401	407	*1006a	1020	1024
1036	1037	1042	1048	1049	1050
1062	1064	1065	1080	1083	1098a
1106	1112	1140	1146	1154	1155
1168	1191	1211	1213	1222	1226
1244	1254	1286	1287	1304	1305
1346	1348	1349	1352	1355	1356

Books recommended for grade level HS and up:

3	4	7	8	9	11
13	15	16	17	18	19
20	30	31	35	36	38
41	42	44	46	47	48

53	55	57	59	60	61
64	65	66	67	68	69
72	73	74	75	76	77
79	80	82	83	84	85
86	87	88	90	92	96
98	102	103	104	105	106
108	110	113	114	115	116
117	118	119	120	121	122
123	124	128	129	130	132
140	143	144	146	147	148
149	150	155	157	158	162
163	164	173	175	177	178
180	183	187	188	190	192
196	197	200	201	203	204
206	211	212	219	223	224
225	226	231	232	234	236
237	242	243	244	245	246
248	250	252	253	258	260
262	263	267	268	269	270
271	273	274	275	276	280
282	283	289	292	295	296
297	298	299	300	302	304
305	306	307	310	311	316
319	320	321	325	326	329
333	334	340	341	342	344
346	353	354	355	356	361
366	367	368	372	374	375
376	377	378	384	386	392
396	398	399	400	401	402
403	405	406	408	1020	1021
1025	1036	1037	1042	1048	1049
1050	1065	1080	1081	1093	1098a
1112	1123	1140	1146	1155	1168
*1184a	1185	1198	1209	1211	1212
1213	1214	1222	1244	1287	1303
1304	1305	1349	1355	1399	

Books recommended for grade Level Adv HS and up:

1	6	14	21	23	26
27	32	34	43	45	51
52	54	68	71	78	81
89	93	94	99	100	111
125	126	127	131	133	137
141	142	159	161	165	166
170	171	174	176	193	194

Books recommended for grade level Adv HS and up (cont'd.):

360	362	363	370	379	381
382	383	385	387	388	389
393	394	395	397	404	1021
1025	*1044a	*1073a	*1084a	*1087a	*1096a
1098a	1105	*1114a	1140	1155	1173
1181	1211	1213	1214	*1219a	*1296a
1303	*1304a	1349	1355	*1374a	1383

Books recommended for college students, adults, and teachers:

5	33	56	68	70	71
95	112	134	135	145	152
195	210	247	251	288	291
293	301	324	337	347	358
371	373	380	391	1184b	1272

SUBJECT INDEX (Numbers with * refer to Appendix 3)

This section lists all books included in sections I and II and in Appendix 3, with the exception of one or two titles that defy categorization. Periodicals listed in Section III are not individually enumerated, as they all come under the general heading of education. We have indicated the main category covered in books listed in Section I (1-408) as well as important sub-topics. Only the principal categories are indicated for books in Section II (1001-1409) and Appendix 3 (1006a...1374a).

Anthologies (A)

7	8	13	23	27	43
53	64	76	79	81	89
90	91	93	117	119	124
132	135	170	171	192	198
199	212	226	228	236	237
245	271	295	318	323	328
349	370	382	1033	1036	1039
1040	1061	1066	1076	1097	1103
1104	1105	1110	1118	1144	1170
1178	1179	1184	1272	1275	1301
1314	1316	1324	1327a	1335	

Agriculture (Ag)   31   45   1212

Air Pollution (Ap)

12	21	28	62	109	122
131	146	156	172	194	200
204	215	223	225	256	267
303	308	323	350	356	366
1016	1020	1021	1129	1194	1197

Air Pollution (cont'd.)

1263	1277	1307	1330	1338	1349
1354	1369	1380	1386		

Art (At)   2   186   244

Biographies (B)

15	66	68	97	154	178
214	234	344	376	1009	1038
1065	1072	1098	1107	1126	1235
1238	1239	1257	1262	1278	1340
1345	1355	1360	1392	1399	1400

Careers (Cr)   297   1018   1080   1098a

Case Studies (Cs)

3	11	40	41	76	86
140	146	237	288	329	331
353	377	383	400	402	403
1199	1306	1405			

Conservation (Cn)

1	5	39	54	85	101
138	164	166	180	181	196
203	207	216	242	280	305
352	362	364	372	375	386
390	407	1004	1008	1011	1014
1034	1045	1067	1124	1128	1142
1145	1157	1168	1169	1176	1187
1266a	1270	1271	*1296a	1343	1355
1358	1363	1372	1373	1384	1387
1390	1398	1408			

Criticisms (C)

4	19	20	26	250	*1044a
1123	1409				

Dictionaries, Bibliographies, Indexes (DBI)

36	58	68	69	92	105
113	114	115	116	118	120
121	160	292	298	316	359
405	1046	1051	1060	1079	1082
1085	1092	1093	1093a	1094	1114
1185	1198	1215	1231	1247	1250
1252	1279	1282	1291	1309	1312
1337	1344	1379	1395	1403	

Ecology (Ec)

10	18	22	24	33	48
50	56	70	71	82	112
128	131	150	151	167	179
182	184	189	191	200	209
210	211	218	239	241	247
254	255	268	284	285	286
290	291	294	309	311	312
319	320	322	323	324	335
340	341	343	347	354	355
356	381	383	387	389	395
396	1001	1005	1010	1012	1013
1015	1024	1025	1026	1028	1029
1030	1031	1032	1042	1044	1053
1054	1058	1064	1066	1068	1074
1089	1090	1095	1102	1103	1106
1115	1122	1127	1132	1138	1154
1155	1157	1158	1172	1181	1183
1184	*1184a	1186	1187	1189	1193
1196	1208	1211	1216	1218	1224
1225	1254	1256	1259	1267	1276
1286	1288	1289	1292	1293	1294
1300	1302	1303	1314	1325	1334
1336	1346	1352	1357	1361	1368
1378	1382	1384	1385	1391	1407

Economics (E)

14	31	47	94	95	108
132	134	141	145	323	1033
1070	1074	1117	1153	1166	1178
1179	1313	1318	1333		

Education (Ed)

9	33	38	58	70	71
85	107	112	118	152	210
241	247	270	284	285	286
291	294	297	301	316	320
323	324	337	347	355	356
362	373	380	391	395	405
1002	1003	1022	1024	1025	1035
1051	1060	1061	1065a	1077	1084
1085	1091	1092	1094	1104	1109
1111	1139	1140	1159	1163	1184b
1186	1214	1228	1247	1248	1249
1251	1259	1273	1283	1285	1290
1296	1298	1302	1303	1334	1344
1357	1362	1365	Also included, all of Section III		

(numbers 2001-2123)

Endangered Species (Es)

88	186	217	230	238	246
248	258	264	275	276	296
357	369	400	1062	1063	1100
1121	1182	1191	1192	1213	1217
1297	1299	1329	1371		

Energy (Eg)

34	73	89	115	125	146
183	202	377	387	1090a	1113
1147	1260	1318	1404		

English (En)

9	27	187	188	308	309
346	384	1006	1303		

Ethics (Et)

6	13	93	159	161	323
1086	1088	1268	1284	1308	1317
1326	1401	1402			

Food Pollution (Fp)

| 21 | 162 | 200 | 253 | 272 | 1202 |

Forestry (F)

| 227 | 242 | 305 | 307 | 396 | 406 |
| 1073 | 1151 | 1161 | 1226 | | |

History (H)

15	16	39	66	69	72
96	97	111	123	129	130
147	148	159	166	169	174
178	180	181	187	201	207
214	227	231	234	242	245
246	251	254	255	258	259
277	280	281	282	293	295
305	306	321	327	336	344
352	353	358	360	361	363
364	372	375	376	385	386
390	402	1009	1038	1056	1065
1067	1072	1073	1107	1109	1126
1128	1160	1161	1162	1176	1219
1234	1235	1236	1237	1238	1239
1240	1241	1242	1243	1257	1262
1268	1306	1310	1323	1345	1356
1358	1370	1390	1392	1398	1399
1400	1406				

Home Action (Ha)

30	119	302	374	399	1043
1052	1111	1112	1174	1175	1273
1374					

International Studies (I)

23	51	52	78	87	96
141	142	143	168	195	266
289	315	370	371	397	398
404	1139	1153	1173	1179	1196

International Studies (cont'd.)

1276	1299	1339	1343	1368	1387
1388					

Land Use (Lu)

67	75	81	83	86	129
140	149	169	173	174	195
200	205	213	216	219	237
244	252	277	317	327	328
392	394	402	403	407	1023
1056	1069	*1084a	1130	1137	1160
1190	1201	1218	1262	1280	*1296a
1326	1328	1342	1364	1370	1376
1396	1397				

Law (L)

212	279	339	404	1118	1120
1144	1156	1209	1326	1331	1348
1351					

Noise Pollution (Np)

17	35	200	1254	1274	1350

Nuclear Power (N)   288   1071   1113

Oil (Ol)

34	46	61	77	102	103
173	202	262	310	331	1152
1245					

Overview (O)

1	7	25	26	30	32
51	52	60	72	78	80
81	84	87	98	100	104
108	124	126	135	136	139
143	155	161	165	170	171

Personal Narrative (Pn)

Pesticides (Pc)

Political Science (Ps)

Population (P)

53	89	106	107	108	133
190	200	293	251	313	378
1002	*1087a	1219	1245	1266	1311
1352					

Reader (R)

10	37	39	49	56	136
138	139	185	220	265	272
308	1001	1129	1130	1131	1133
1191	1224	1263	1307		

Strip Mining (S)   59   314   1341

Technology (T)

72	100	158	165	202	259
266	317	353	1097	1101	1315
1332	1369				

Urban Planning (U)

79	172	192	193	221	244
272	273	277	323	370	*1073a
*1084a	1116	1119	1190	1201	1229
1244	1305	1327	1328		

Waste (Wt)

21	144	153	177	206	257
261	300	345	351	1026	1057
1380					

Water Pollution (Wp)

12	21	29	55	63	77
102	103	110	127	156	157
168	203	222	223	260	263
264	265	267	274	308	310

323	350	356	365	366	1016
1017	1020	1021	1037	*1114a	1119
1131	1149	1152	1164	1188	1194
1195	1207	*1219a	1222	1223	1227
1232	1304	*1304a	1330	1347	1349
1354	1363	1372	*1374a	1380	1386

Wilderness (W)

15	41	42	43	44	84
123	129	150	208	226	228
233	281	307	352	376	1110
1150	*1184a	1310	1316	1356	1359
1360	1389	1393	1401	1402